REACHING OUT:

Sensitivity and Order in Recent

American Fiction by Women

by

ANNE Z. MICKELSON

The Scarecrow Press, Inc.

Metuchen, N.J. & London

1979

PS
379
.M45

Library of Congress Cataloging in Publication Data

Mickelson, Anne Z
   Reaching out.

   Includes bibliographical references and index.
   1. American fiction--20th century--History and
criticism. 2. American fiction--Women authors--History
and criticism. 3. Feminism in literature. I. Title.
PS379.M45   813'.5'409352   78-26164
ISBN 0-8108-1194-4

This book is for
my sister Alice

CONTENTS

ACKNOWLEDGMENTS

My special thanks go to Donald Phelps for his valuable criticism and to Rosemary Ritvo for her help with this book. I also wish to acknowledge the assistance of Daniel Bronson, D. H. Melhem, Lenore Rosenbluth and James Sileneck.

I am indebted to the MacDowell Colony for a Fellowship, Summer of 1978, which enabled me to do the necessary final thinking on the book.

NOTE ON THE TEXT

Notes in most cases refer to recent and available texts. Particular works of fiction by women writers are cited in this study. Each is preceded by the symbol used throughout for identifying quotations, and is followed by date of publication.

Joyce Carol Oates

Novels

T   them (Greenwich, Conn.: Fawcett Crest, 1970).

WSF   With Shuddering Fall (Greenwich, Conn.: Fawcett Crest, 1971).

W   Wonderland (Greenwich, Conn.: Fawcett Crest, 1973).

DWM   Do with me ... (New York: The Vanguard Press, 1973).

C   Childwold (New York: The Vanguard Press, 1976).

Short Stories

BNG   By the North Gate (Greenwich, Conn.: Fawcett Crest, 1971).

MI   Marriages and Infidelities (Greenwich, Conn.: Fawcett Crest, 1972).

USF   Upon the Sweeping Flood ... (Greenwich, Conn.: Fawcett Crest, 1972).

WL   The Wheel of Love ... (Greenwich, Conn.: Fawcett Crest, 1972).

G   The Goddess ... (New York: The Vanguard Press, 1974).

S   The Seduction ... (Santa Barbara: Black Sparrow Press, 1976).

Erica Jong

Novels

FF   Fear of Flying (New York: New American Library, 1974).

HT   How to save your own life (New York: Holt, Rinehart and Winston, 1977).

Lois Gould

Novels

SGF   Such Good Friends (New York: Random House, 1970).

NO   Necessary Objects (New York: Dell Publishing Co., 1973).

FA   Final Analysis (New York: Random House, 1974).

ASC   A Sea-Change (New York: Simon and Schuster, 1976).

Gail Godwin

Novels

P   The Perfectionists (New York: Harper & Row, 1970).

GP   Glass People (New York: Alfred A. Knopf, 1972).

OW   The Odd Woman (New York: Alfred A. Knopf, 1974).

Short Stories

DC   Dream Children (New York: Alfred A. Knopf, 1976).

Joan Didion

Novels

RR   Run River (New York: Astor-Honor, 1961).

PI   Play It As It Lays (New York: Bantam Books, 1972).

BCP   A Book of Common Prayer (New York: Simon and Schuster, 1977).

Essays

STB   Slouching Towards Bethlehem (New York: Dell Publishing Co., 1968).

Sarah E. Wright

Novel

TC   This Child's Gonna Live (New York: Delacorte Press, 1969).

Toni Morrison

Novels

BE   The Bluest Eye (New York: Holt, Rinehart and Winston, 1970).

S   Sula (New York: Alfred A. Knopf, 1974).

SS   Song of Solomon (New York: Alfred A. Knopf, 1977).

Alice Walker

Novel

M   Meridian (New York: Pocket Books, 1977).

Short Stories

ILT   In Love & Trouble ... (New York: Harcourt Brace Jovanovich, 1973).

Marge Piercy

Novel

SC   Small Changes (New York: Doubleday & Company, Inc., 1973).

Sara Davidson

Novel

LC   Loose Change: Three Women of the Sixties (New York: Doubleday & Co., 1977).

Marilyn French

Novel

WR   The Women's Room (New York: Summit Books, 1977).

Grace Paley

Short Stories

LD   The Little Disturbances of Man (New York: Doubleday & Co., 1959).

EC   Enormous Changes at the Last Minute (New York: Farrar Straus Giroux, 1974).

INTRODUCTION

As we enter into the last quarter of the twentieth century, it is appropriate to ask what has happened to the status of women in America since 1960, and more particularly since 1968, which saw the beginnings of the Women's Liberation Movement? Has that declaration of Women's Rights articulated at the First Women's Convention in a Wesleyan chapel, Seneca Falls, New York, July 19-20, 1848, and buried these many years, really been rescued? Has it been given new teeth and a broader strategy to insure its success? More important, did the Women's Liberation Movement in America usher in a new era of thinking about men and women, or does the dust of Victorianism still cling to many of our social attitudes? Once the psychologists and sociologists have made their tests, run their rats through the mazes, where do we turn for "ballast to their theorizing?"[1] asks Ellen Moers. To literature, of course, she answers, and adds that "literature is the only intellectual field to which women, over a long stretch of time, have made an indispensable contribution. "

I have turned to the fiction of recent American women writers to determine whether there is a new woman emerging in literature. If so, what is she like? Is she a Sue Bridehead (Thomas Hardy, Jude the Obscure), torn by the disparity between what she wants and what society permits her? Is she middle-class and educated? Poor and uneducated? Exceptional? Ordinary? Is she an angry woman, as feminist writers contend--angry because she is vulnerable and must wrestle with a diversity of attempts to reduce this vulnerability? Is she a woman in stasis? Or does she visualize herself as moving toward the center of a modern battlefield in which cultural changes are taking place at a rapid and dramatic rate? What are these changes? How extensive are they? Are women writers today dramatizing their heroines as reacting boldly to change, or do they picture them as timid, insecure, confused by a complexity of attitudes which they are unable to sort out successfully? Do they

1

show that some women are making choices which seem intellectually fashionable rather than in harmony with their emotional needs?

As a useful point of reference from which to measure the advance or regression of literature, we can begin with no better choice than Catharine Maria Sedgwick. From Sedgwick, who wanted to lessen the stigma placed on the term "old maid," and who endeavored to show that an unmarried woman could have a career (even if Sedgwick married off her young women in the end), to Ellen Glasgow's more successful rebellion against southern gentility, we find the same goal. American women writers have always attempted to explore woman's stumbling self-awareness through the framework of family and community. With the reappearance of Feminism in 1968, there is a strong sense of discovery of self on the part of women characters. But what this sense of discovery is based on presents a paradox.

Some believe in the statement made by one of Doris Lessing's heroes (The Golden Notebook), that the real revolution is woman against man. Others accept the masochistic realization voiced by Francine du Plessix Gray (Lovers and Tyrants), that women beg for love and tyranny, that women really want to be men. Still others seek to destroy what Andrea Dworkin terms the phallic identity in man and the masochistic faculty in women (Our Blood ...). Many call attention to the fact that a woman is not called feminine by a mere accident of nomenclature. Some women share a desire to be romanticized, which Anaïs Nin confesses to in one of her diaries, and which Gail Godwin's heroine seems to echo in The Odd Woman. And if we turn from literature to the movies and note the success of the film King Kong with women, then perhaps its producer, de Laurentiis, has a point when he says that women love Kong because he is willing to die for one of them. Interestingly enough, this is not far from the concept which James Joyce implies in his short story "The Dead." Lois Gould's novel A Sea-Change also elaborates on this idea, together with a bizarre twist when the heroine metamorphoses into a man and whispers to "his" lover: "He'd die to protect you."[2]

The diversity of attitudes eloquently illustrates that we have not fully grasped the thrust of the last two decades. We still must confront the issues raised by past and present writers of varied backgrounds. These issues are: love, sex, personal relationships, marriage, non-marriage, male/

female roles, work, the particular problems of the woman artist, etc. However, the recurrent preoccupations of women writers, and the burning questions in these books which revolve around the much debated issue of femininity, point to the need to give even more serious consideration to a redefinition of male and female roles in society.

Like Austen, the Brontës, Eliot, Woolf, Lessing, and a host of other British women writers, American women writers have always been concerned with the life of women. There are Sarah Orne Jewett's penetrating studies not only of provincial life, but of a woman physician; Kate Chopin's and Willa Cather's sexual women; Anne Douglas Sedgwick's probing into the animosity between mother and daughter; Mary Wilkins Freeman's compassionate treatment of the poor woman who accepts her ugly destiny with dignity; Gertrude Stein's portrayal of three women, notably "Melanctha, " and many, many others.

My aim, however, is not so much to demonstrate that women have always had a literature of their own, as Elaine Showalter so ably proves in her study of British women novelists (A Literature of Their Own ...), but to treat fictional portraits of women, with the following questions in mind. Do today's American women writers break with their male counterparts as to theme, scope, characterization, depiction of attitudes, objectivity, structure of language? Are the thought progressions of their heroines dissimilar from those of men? Is there the assumption that women define themselves through language and men through action? Is there a new sexual language? How much attention is paid to the thought processes of male characters? Do we find the same male and female stereotypes in the works of women writers as in the writings of men? Do we get a conceptual sense of "femininity, " "feminism, " "female?" Is there any truth to the remark that women writers produce brave but irrelevant books in order to prove that they can write like men?

I concentrate on the following writers whose work has been published largely in the last two decades: Joyce Carol Oates, Erica Jong, Lois Gould, Gail Godwin, Joan Didion, Alice Walker, Toni Morrison, Sarah E. Wright. In the concluding chapter, there are discussions of Marge Piercy, Sara Davidson, Marilyn French, and Grace Paley. There are a great many other excellent writers who deserve study. I have chosen the above, however, because while they frequently show the same thematic concerns, their approach to the

subject varies. My method of criticism and analysis is to
limit my discussions to those books that I consider important
to my purpose. For that reason, I do not examine every
book each author has written.

My main focus throughout is on the works of today's
women writers and the ways these women writers picture
contemporary women. I am concerned only occasionally with
a writer's personality, and then only when a nexus of ideas
appears constantly in the works and a consistent kind of female characterization emerges. My strong view is that current women writers are part of a historic process and their
works are about themselves as they exist in the fashioning
of their materials. What seems to unite them all is the
writers' criticism and rejection of the social system, and the
need for woman to be accepted as natural, decent humanity.

If we are to understand the variety, scope and
sometimes conflicting themes about today's fictional woman--
her body, sexuality, the conflict between artistic integrity
and the claims of family and duty; the struggle for egalitarianism, the effort to deal with personal relationships (man
and woman, woman and woman)--we must know not only the
background against which the contemporary writer of fiction
is working, but something of the many strands of past social history needed for comprehension of the female experience. With some measure of history behind us, it is useful to sift first through social data, to assess what substan-
tive changes (if any) have been made about our thinking on
women and their social status.

The present urgency to go back to the lean past to
find out about women has resulted in richly documented
studies. On the whole, they inform us eloquently of the
tangle of attitudes which have always surrounded social thinking about woman. She has been regarded as inferior, yet
somehow meant to be man's spiritual guide; half-divine in-
termediary between God and man, but looked upon as tempt-
ress/sinner, as well. She is passive, but inclined to mysterious activity during certain phases of the moon; intuitive,
but lacking the practical sense to select the correct deter-
gent for her washing machine; biologically weak, yet able
to lift heavy bags of groceries and husky children; incapable
of logic, but full of cunning arguments; sexually pure if
watched, uncontrollably sensual if not curbed; too feather-
brained to create a great work of art; psychologically subject to breakdown if faced with business or professional

competition; yet designed by nature to bear, nurture children, act as her husband's helpmate, help him fulfill his potential, and resign herself to her "limitations." The result is a polarization of roles, with woman's role as wife/mother defined as inferior and man's role as economic provider/domestic protector defined as superior. Once this pattern is set up, Bonnie Bullough points out, the "socialization process" helps to carry it forward. [3]

Of course, there were a few isolated voices which went to the other extreme, extolling woman's superiority and stressing man's inferiority. Eliza B. Gamble (The Evolution of Woman) contended: more men than women were color blind; men lacked physical endurance; they had structural defects; their abnormal sexual appetites led to early deterioration of the body. Another Eliza, Eliza Farnham (Woman and Her Era), argued: women were superior to men not because of their reason, but because of their intuition. This intuition enabled them to grasp ideas which man with his logic needed hours to assimilate. In addition, Farnham was convinced that women had more physical organs than men and that "organs are the representatives of power." [4] Furthermore, she said, women have structures which nourish life. She conceded that the male was sometimes larger than the female, but he was larger only in the "grosser" parts, such as the bones and sinews. Women had larger breasts, softer tissues, sweeter voices, and so on.

It is easy to understand why some women, goaded by the public's acceptance of them as inferior to men, would push arguments in the opposite direction. But, as Michael Korda[5] sensibly comments, biological arguments seldom prove anything. When women reason this way, they are simply chauvinists in reverse. Neither of the two Elizas, however, had much to fear or hope about influencing public opinion. Few accepted the view of women as superior, and generations of women accepted inequality without protest.

Why? asks Bonnie Bullough, and she answers her question with the suggestion that the probable reason is biological. In early times, she theorizes, physical strength was a determining factor in influencing women to be subordinate to men. Man's greater strength and size enabled him to fight off wild animals and human enemies. In return for man's protection, "woman offered obedience." [6]

Whether we accept the theory or not, it is obvious

that in an industrial society, physical strength and size are no longer important. Those who still cling to them as a basis for the discriminatory pattern against women ignore not only the society in which we live, but the fact that today's better knowledge of nutrition has resulted in taller, stronger women, and has controlled the biological tendency to anemia.

Numerous books have appeared on the subject. An inexpensive book such as Our Bodies, Ourselves ... [7] (issued by the Boston Women's Health Book Collective--and at the present moment [1978] on the best seller list) gives sensible and detailed information on the necessary nutrients for better health, especially during pregnancy. It describes exercises which will tone up and strengthen muscles at any time, and it also suggests learning self-defense arts such as Karate, in which a 120-pound woman can throw a 250-pound man. The book does not minimize the fact that there are anatomical as well as sexual differences between men and women. It stresses that physical differences can be compensated for by cultivation of skills, reflexes, endurance, and a belief in physical potential. I mention this book because of its sales success and its use in Women Studies programs, testifying to the increasing interest of women in their bodies.

Joining this discussion is the eloquent voice of Michael Korda (mentioned before), a sharp critic of the way women are treated in industry. He points out that the average business man is not much stronger than the average woman. A daily picking up of the telephone, he says, hardly gives the man an "edge" over any woman hauling groceries, children, laundry, etc. He disputes Norman Mailer's argument in The Prisoner of Sex that woman's biology disqualifies her from "man's" work such as flying a Boeing 747 or piloting a huge tanker into harbor. Mailer, he concludes, ignores the work women do every day, and behaves as if men had no biological weaknesses. [8]

In trying to make sense out of this subject, we can probably point to sports as an area in which women have distinguished themselves in the last decade. In addition to mastery on the tennis court, golf course, and other spheres, women have now entered the ranks of jockey racing and have become race track drivers. Howard Cosell, TV sports news commentator, praises Janet Guthrie as a "brave racing lady," the first woman to enter the Indianapolis 500 and gain distinction among the world's best thirty-three drivers. But he cannot resist adding that women must remember that their

"physiology" prohibits them from winning the long races.
They don't have the endurance, he claims!

If American women athletes don't have endurance,
says Dr. LeRoy Walker, United States track and field Olym-
pic coach, it is because American women athletes, unlike
their sisters in other countries, are not being given the
proper training. Weight lifting, he says, is recommended
for men, but not for women. In speaking of weight lifting,
swimming and track events, he says: "When you watch
Baerbel Eckert (East Germany) or Annegret Richter (West
Germany) in the two hundred meters ... you're watching
not the fastest but the most efficient runners. They have
endurance, they can keep up a fast pace, they don't run out
of steam. " He attributes the success of foreign women athletes to their conditioning through weight lifting, which aids
cardiovascular development and helps the heart to function
more efficiently. In short, he claims American women athletes are denied the training which would enable them to win.
"We have to completely retool our training programs"[9] for
women, says Dr. Walker.

Americans have found it both profitable and expedient
to maintain the idea of woman's body as inferior and unfit.
To drop the "fairer and weaker sex" distinction would mean
that women could no longer be considered as "vessels of
consumption and ornaments. " Hence, the idea that a woman's body must keep her from certain pursuits, up to this
time the domain of men, dies hard. Though a small percentage of women have been accepted at military academies,
there is a half-hearted attitude on the part of military authorities toward the whole idea of women in these places.
The same attitude is echoed by the Coast Guard Academy,
which has just begun to accept women. Nor have police
academies welcomed the fact of women working side by side
with fellow male officers. As for the FBI, there were no
women agents under J. Edgar Hoover, and his successors
are still cool to the idea. The Catholic Church, traditionally
biased against women, refuses to ordain women as priests.

Even the cult of the Virgin Mary is reductive of
women, claims Molly Haskell, because the son erases all
trace of the sin of copulation by recasting his mother "in
the image of the Virgin Mary. "[10] Mother is locked in her
chastity belt and imprisoned in the theological role of mother.
"The fusion of wife and mother into a character whose chief
attributes, even with regard to her husband, are maternal is

a reduction through sanctification, a delimiting of the woman's role by placing her on a pedestal."[11]

This belief in man's physical superiority and woman's biological inferiority, except as mother, gets a boost from another quarter. Irving Howe, the distinguished literary critic, in reviewing Kate Millett's Sexual Politics, sharply criticizes the writer for her "Middle-Class Mind"[12] and her writing, which he calls "a pastiche of scholarship" exhibiting "the rough and careless marks of what is called higher education"[13] and dwelling on a "nightmare vision of endless female subordination to and suffering at the hands of men."[14] Her major fault, however, seems to be that she refuses to accept the idea that biological and physiological differences between the sexes "may still crucially determine a sequence of secondary and social differences...."[15]

If we turn to fiction by contemporary male writers, and the way in which women's bodies are described, we are surrounded with smells and descriptions of anatomical deficiencies. In An American Dream, Mailer's Ruta has cold gasses coming from the womb, she smells of "rocks and grease and the sewer-damp of wet stones in poor European alleys."[16] Deborah exhales sweet rot and Cherry has ugly feet. Vonnegut's Valencia (Slaughterhouse-Five) is grotesquely fat, and his older women are grotesque in different ways. Bellow's heroes (Sammler, Herzog) invariably wrinkle their noses at women's female smells--all that "affluvia." Woman is a "sloppy cunt,"[17] says Dr. Gruner of his daughter. Charles Citrine (Humboldt's Gift) makes it even more explicit. His mistress, sitting crosslegged on the bed, "released the salt female odor, the bacterial background of deep love."[18]

I stress this continuing controversy about woman's biology because while many of the present women writers still appear to find love as the great value against the threat of meaninglessness, as did so many of the women writers of the past, they are devoting, as their predecessors did not, considerable space to the biological fact of the female body and sexuality. Some of it has the familiar ring found in the works of certain male writers: the body is a trap; the body is not a trap, but merely insulation against the cold of interstellar space. Yet we find something more than this in the works of women writers. There is curiosity, delight, fear, terror, self-hate, acceptance, exhilaration, suffering, fantasy, idealization, clash with reality, guilt feelings.

Oates's heroines, for example, tell us that they fear
men and sex. Their language, however, reveals an inner
voice which keeps shifting, is often without focus, and tries
to deflect us from their real problem. Many of the women
retreat into fantasy, slip from one role into another, and
lose sight of reality. On the other hand, Erica Jong's heroine, Isadora Wing (Fear of Flying; How to ...) revels un-
abashedly in eroticism and ultra-fashionable hedonism, but
remains convinced that she is impaled on guilt feelings.
Joan Didion's Maria Wyeth (Play It As It Lays) drifts numbly
through a world of pain and suffering, aware that her body,
like those of the women around her, is a physical commodity
to the men with whom she lives and works.

Lois Gould's women, in her first three books, seem
to view themselves as ugly and unattractive. They emerge
as living proof of the influence of the Judaic-Christian code
which formed the basis of the concept of woman's body as
mysterious and unclean. They diet, depilate, deodorize,
but are still helpless victims of a self-hatred which makes
them masochistically eager to please mothers, fathers, friends,
husbands, lovers, doctors, and just about everyone with whom
they come into contact. The author's latest novel, however,
A Sea-Change, shows woman's anger unleashed and woman
turning aggressive.

Gail Godwin's heroine in The Odd Woman marvels at
her stupidity about being reticent and ashamed of simple body
functions when spending a few days with her lover. Jill
Robinson's heroine (Bed/Time/Story) doses and props herself
up with drugs until love for a brilliant, gentle, but alcoholic
man challenges her to discover self. Other contemporary
women writers emphasize the body's importance and the re-
generative and redemptive power of sexual love. Few, however, voice the idea expressed by D. H. Lawrence's Tommy
Dukes (Lady Chatterley's Lover), that sex might be a sort
of physical conversation between men and women.

If the picture seems confused, we must remember
that the idea of woman having a right to her own body, and
of being a sexual person, is relatively new. The avoidance
of thought about woman's body, in the past, sometimes took
a ludicrous turn. Vern L. Bullough tells us that formerly
women were not encouraged to play certain instruments because these instruments called attention to the lady's body.
If she played the cello, she would have to spread her legs;
the violin made her twist her neck and upper torso; brass

instruments required visceral support for tonal quality, and
if she played the flute, she would have to purse her lips. [19]
It is significant that though women are no longer barred from
learning such instruments, the hiring of women for symphony
orchestras is still at a snail's pace.

If women are beginning to become better acquainted
with their bodies, the sexual woman, whether portrayed in
the fiction of writers like Mailer, Bellow, Roth, Brautigan
and others, or on TV or film, is often the embodiment of
male fantasy. For years, TV gave us Dean Martin's Ding-
A-Ling girls, and in the movies there is Sam Peckinpah, who
claims: "there are women and there's pussy." He demonstrates, however, in film after film that he really believes
"that all women, way down deep, are pussy."[20]

In fiction, we have Bellow's women--sex objects with
names like Renata (Humboldt's Gift) or Sono or Ramona, who
play out his hero's sexual fantasies by wearing a black gar-
ter belt and little else, or bathe him in hot, perfumed water
and refresh him with tea and other means (Herzog). The
younger writer, Brautigan, is no different. His women wear
flowers in their hair, have voluptuous bodies, cook marvelous
breakfasts, and are instantly ready for sexual love when the
hero returns from some place like the Watermelon Works or
iDeath.

When we go back to early American fiction, Hawthorne's, for example, we can note the display of much fear
of woman's sexuality. His heroes--Robin, Goodman Brown,
Wakefield, and Miles Coverdale--are alternately attracted
to and repulsed by women. They seem to want love, but
are afraid that it will damn them, since the sexual woman
represents sin.

Leslie Fiedler's Love and Death in the American
Novel assesses brilliantly (among other things) the way woman has been portrayed in American literature by male writers. He discusses Faulkner's misogynist attitude toward
women, which encompasses the view that women like to be
beaten. The anti-woman feeling found in Hemingway and
Fitzgerald, says Fiedler, attains its "fullest and shrillest
expression" in Faulkner. [21] Woman is devious, without
honor or morality, treacherous, unforgiving, uncharitable
even to her own sex, and uses her sexuality coldly and with
calculation. Only the woman past menopause is exempt from
his contempt. Faulkner, Fiedler points out, divides young

women into two classes: earthy, fertile daughters of peas-
ants, whose sexuality resembles that of animals in heat, and
slender daughters of the aristocracy, who are invariably
nymphomaniacs. Many of their names are allegorical (Dewy
Dell, Temple Drake). Where Dewy Dell suggests, of course,
the natural instinctive woman, Temple Drake, says Fiedler,
is unnatural: "woman become a sexual aggressor--more
drake than duck."[22] Fiedler is convinced that Faulkner's
portraits of women reflect prejudices so ingrained in the
American consciousness "that even hysterically rendered it
seems too familiar to be shocking."[23]

Fear of women and the idea of woman as destroyer
may help to explain the male backlash to woman's emerging
sexuality. Richard Brautigan's abrupt disposal of Margaret
by hanging (In Watermelon Sugar) and John Hawkes's representation of his Margaret's beating (The Lime Twig), in
which the truncheon makes a sound like a dead bird, may
not be the best of examples, but they do tell us something.
The movies inform us even more about male reaction to
woman's increasing assertiveness of her body and sexuality.
Films such as Clockwork Orange and Straw Dogs show wom-
en as prime targets of hatred and hostility. In addition,
suggests Molly Haskell, the decrease of movie roles for
women and the rise of "buddy films" like Easy Rider, Butch
Cassidy and the Sundance Kid, Midnight Cowboy, Dirty Harry,
in which men discover each other and give lyrical show to
their feelings, is but one manifestation of the reaction of
middle-class men, fearful of their eroding masculinity.

To digress a little more from literature, popular
music also gives expression to anti-woman feelings. A
male group which calls itself Queen has issued an album in
which one of its members sings a song entitled "I'm in Love
with My Car." The lyrics inform us: "Told my girl I just
had to forget her/ Rather buy me a new carburetor/ So she
made tracks saying this is the end now,/ Cars don't talk
back--they're just four-wheeled friends now." Queen is
simply exploiting a market which finds it profitable to voice
these sentiments.

Without question, the issue of woman's body as inferior to man's, as belonging to man, as having few or no
sexual needs, will remain part of the furniture of social
thinking for a long time. So will the idea of woman's intellectual limitations continue to be wreathed in clouds of
Victorianism. Though higher education is now available to

women and women are entering college teaching and other
fields formerly reserved for men, they find upon employment
that their salaries, chances of promotion and treatment in
general, when compared with those of men, give no cause
to ring out the bells.   Their work is often regarded as
something temporary, an interim between girlhood and the
more serious business of marriage and domesticity.   It is
interesting that Gail Godwin focuses on the college woman
professor in her novel The Odd Woman and touches on the
issue of job reappointment.   Her chief concentration, however, is on the emotional and fantasy life of her heroine,
who finds herself the mistress of a married man and enraged
by the role into which she falls.

The problems of the bright young college-educated
working woman are confronted by Lois Gould in Final Analysis (1974).   She shows a woman who is forced to face the
fact that she has been hired as a workhorse.   Her function
is to come up with shining ideas, but be content to earn less
than the men around her.   She finally admits that she must
reexamine her timidity and masochism in accepting the terms
of the job and the seedy conditions under which she has been
expected to work.

The black woman, whose problems have been even
more acute than those of the white woman, has not been
discussed up to this point because many black women leaders are convinced that the woman's movement is largely
composed of middle-class women whose concerns have not
proven relevant to the problems of the black woman.   "I
don't know that our priorities are the same," says Toni
Cade, "that our concerns and methods are the same, or
even similar enough so that we can afford to depend on this
new field of experts (white, female)."[24]

Probably, she is right.   If the white woman has been
considered inferior, the black woman is even lower in the
social scheme which is dominantly white and male.   She has
been sexually abused by the white man and often by the black
man.   She has been torn from her family and sold on the
open slave market.   She has worked in the white woman's
kitchen and taken care of the children in the household, while
her own home has had to be neglected.   She has frequently
been the scapegoat for the black man's humiliation at the
hands of Mr. Charlie, as many black women leaders point
out.

While it has awakened a sense of the need for self-worth, the Black Revolution has also caused bitterness among black women. Kay Lindsey points out that it is spearheaded by males. In "Poem" she writes: "But now that the revolution needs numbers/ Motherhood got a new position/ Five steps behind manhood. / And I thought sittin' in the back of the bus/ Went out with Martin Luther King. "[25] Frances Beale is caustic about the fact that black women are being told that for the black man to be strong, the woman has to be weak. Toni Cade explains that if a black woman is strong, she is called "a rough mamma, a strident bitch ... castrator. ... " Black male leaders want "to program Sapphire out of her 'evil' ways into a cover-up, shut-up, lay-back-and-be-cool obedience role. "[26] Abbey Lincoln is angry about the black man's diminution of the black woman by his preference for white women. He flaunts the white woman as an example of beauty, she says. "Our women are encouraged by our own men to strive to look and act as much like the white female image as possible.... At best, we are made to feel that we are poor imitations and excuses for white women. "[27]

Here, in the role of personal relationships between men and women and the necessary reevaluation of traditional roles, there is a great cultural crisis. This is true for both black and white women, and it appears in fiction and non-fiction. Black writers like Toni Morrison, Alice Walker and others, while dramatizing this crisis, are confident that the black woman is already on the road to a true definition of self. This is not so true of the literature of white women discussed here. Many white women are fearful that their increasing assertiveness will make them less attractive and less feminine. The success of Marabel Morgan's The Total Woman, as well as women's response to her classes, are proof of the insecurity of many women in the present climate of shifting values. Morgan's advice to women is simple: make your man feel like a king, be submissive, obey him even if he is wrong, wear lots of pink and indulge his fantasies. Much of the advice is full of piety, with many references to the Bible, and, as Joyce Maynard puts it, with "assignments and suggestions that could have come out of the memoirs of the Happy Hooker. "[28]

Even some current fiction shows that writers who consider themselves Feminists are not safe against the trap of this kind of thinking. The ending to Erica Jong's book How to save your own life could be a page out of The Total Woman, barring the language. But all the fiction by women writers discussed here documents at great length an intense,

inner search for individual role and identity. It often bristles with anger as women discover what Elizabeth Janeway[29]
argues: the world is still man's alone, with women left
to do what they can with male expectations. But together
with the anger, the awkward fumbling with identity, with
body, with the question of femininity, with woman's sexual
needs, the fiction traces an earnest effort to understand
women and the diverse social currents swirling about them.

The work of present writers of fiction, whether they
be white or black, has been influenced either by the Wom-
en's Movement or by the Black Revolution, or both. It incorporates many of the traditions of realism and naturalism
found in earlier works by women. At the same time, en-
larging on these traditions, the later writing introduces a
more emphatic strain of individual initiative and will. In
this it manifests an awareness of post-Freudian "ego psychology" usually associated with Erik Erikson as well as
with the views of Marx and Engels. This is especially true
of black women writers like Toni Morrison and Alice Walker.
In a time when interest in the female experience is growing
and men are beginning to listen to what women say, the
literature of both black and white women seems to be moving beyond alienation, despair, barrenness, solipsism, polarization of sexes, into weighing what Gerda Lerner says about
our culture. That is, that men and women have always had
different cultures and a different history of the past; and
that if the experience of the white man has been different
from that of the white woman, that of black men and women
has differed even more. [30] What is being brought out by
most writers is that basic attitudes must change, particularly
those of women toward themselves.

Where male writers are convinced that we are on the
brink of dissolution, or wrestling with what Tony Tanner
classifies as the fear of "non-identity," of "no-form,"[31] the
work of recent American women writers seems to be deeply
connected with three characteristic aspects of American
writing: the search for identity, the plea for egalitarianism,
and the revolutionary zeal to create new modes of expression.

CHAPTER 1

SEXUAL LOVE IN THE FICTION OF JOYCE CAROL OATES

"All art is autobiographical, " says Joyce Carol Oates
in her introduction to Scenes from American Life. She goes on
to explain: "It is the record of an artist's psychic experience, his attempt to explain something to himself: and in
the process of explaining it to himself, he explains it to
others. "[1] We do not know how much of Oates's books is
autobiographical. Interviews yield much information about
her theories on fiction, on the themes which she considers
crucial, and the writers who have influenced her. As Alfred Kazin, who traveled to Windsor, Ontario to interview
her, comments somewhat wryly: she "gamely responds to
every question put to her, but ... volunteers nothing--not
even a smile" (Harper's, 1971).

Of course, interviewers want interesting tidbits of
personal gossip, but it is unimportant whether or not an
author chooses to reveal little about herself/himself. What
is important is the thinking disclosed through the creative
process of art. "Never trust the artist. Trust the tale, "[2]
advises D. H. Lawrence, who seems to have been one of
Oates's tutors, even to a short story, "I Must Have You, "
patterned with some variations on his "The Horse Dealer's
Daughter. "

If we subscribe to Lawrence's theory (and I do),
Oates's impressive output of novels and short stories tells
us a great deal about her thinking on men and women,
especially women. At the same time, the works raise a
great many knotty questions which only Childwold, the latest
of her novels at this writing, helps to resolve somewhat. I
shall roam freely among most of the fiction, placing my distribution of emphasis on those short stories and novels which
have given rise to mixed feelings in my mind. My aim is

15

not so much to emphasize the writer's shortcomings, but more to trace my peregrinations through the fiction. By diagnosing language and characterization which provoke questions about her thinking on the female body and sexual love, I hope to explain my divided attitude toward her work.

No doubt, there is a proliferation of themes in Oates's works: the complexities of family relationships; sex as warfare; marriage as dead end for women; woman as man's invention--plus other themes such as: sexual perversion, illness, decay, death, hallucinatory adventures, a longing for order in disorder, etc. But rising above the orchestration of these themes is the insistent sound of women's voices. What do they say? Over and over again, we hear that women's bodies are clean, fragile, vulnerable, and always in danger of being hurt by men. In contrast to woman's cleanliness, fragility, and vulnerability, man's body is frequently odorous, dirty, and constantly threatening because of his size and strength. Man is a threat not only because of his size and strength, but because of his penis--a dangerous instrument capable of damaging a woman.

The word "damage" leaps up at us from the page over and over again. "I don't want to damage you," says Jack to Elena (DWM, p. 384 and p. 430). It is a word which reverberates in the minds of women and frequently occurs in their inward monologues. Here is Elena's reflection on her lover Jack: "You would shatter me if you came to me: if you forced yourself into me. And then there would be bits and parts, hunks of bleeding flesh, blood smeared on the bedspread and the walls ..." (DWM, p. 431) (author's italics).

Granted, there is considerable tension between Elena and Jack (as there always is between men and women in the author's works), but are we ready for such an explosion of fear when only a page before, Elena has reassured Jack that she loves him?

In other stories, images (real and fancied) of blood, torn tissue, reddened, irritated female flesh appear with almost monotonous frequency. Women feel soiled, bruised, infected after sexual intercourse--or even at the thought of it, as in "Bodies." Like the narrator of "Unmailed, Unwritten Letters" (WL), they can't wait to wash in order to rid themselves of the odor of man. Men frequently inquire of women: did I hurt you? (DWM, "The Lady with the Pet Dog," MI, etc.), or they reassure women that they will not hurt them, as we see both husband and lover doing with Elena (DWM). For some reason, the two men share a furtive compulsion to check her over after sexual intercourse to see if there has been any damage done to her body.

This 1973 fictional heroine tries to explain to the reader that man's violence against woman is due to the economic system and competitiveness. But neither the character nor the author is willing to make more of it. The explanation seems hurriedly tacked on to the bulk of the novel's 563 pages, which concentrate throughout on descriptions of Elena's repulsion for her husband's body, her fear of her lover's body, and the overwhelming fear of rape from any man, especially if the man is black.

Taken together at first, the novels and short stories with their gothic effects, gothic violence, and descriptions of sexual love in squalid rooms usually smelling of disinfectant or insecticide, dimly illuminated by windows hung with dirty, cracked blinds or shades which reach to sills covered with dead bugs, trouble us with questions. Does this mean that the women suffer from penis fear and androphobia? After all, the sexual act is almost always described as painful and the man as violent. Is Oates's fiction meant to lift a silence on women's fears, to counteract psychologists (mostly male) who tell us that the fear of physical damage is not as great in women as in men? Is women's penis fear meant to parallel men's fear of castration?

Then again, although the author deals with the problems of man's aging, there is no discussion of woman's aging, her body's changing. One wonders about the imbalance produced by focusing so exclusively on the fragility of the young woman's biological body, described by one of her characters as "a pretty vase ... delicate and costly ... " (WL, "Demons, " p. 216). What would a man do to such a body? the woman wonders. Elena answers the question for us to some extent by confiding that she considers her body "used as a vessel to accommodate him" (DWM, p. 444).

The idea of woman's body as a vase or a receptacle for husband or lover becomes an important metaphor because it encompasses the feelings of women as acted upon, as being simply a receptacle. It is the dominant metaphor in the fiction. It also brings up the related issue: does Oates share Norman Mailer's belief in the mystical powers of the male penis, the nature of which he never satisfactorily explains?

Neither does she explain--if, indeed, she does subscribe to the theory.

As we continue to read and study the many woefully passive women and their pathological fear of man, their repugnance to man's touch and his presence, we find ourselves asking: is Oates exaggerating? Women writers discussed in this book and elsewhere are concerned with men and sexual love, but they do not appear to share her approach to the subject. With the exception of Sylvia Plath's description of her heroine's painful deflowering, there is little of the sex descriptions found in Oates's fiction. The author's recurring images of men with soiled clothing, stained teeth, dirty boots, or men giving off the odor of stale cigarette smoke and unwashed flesh, force one to consider whether she is stereotyping men the way some male writers have stereotyped women: castrators, underminers, smelling of the zoo (Norman Mailer, An American Dream) or, as Philip Roth says, exhaling "some dank, odoriferous combination.... "3

Finally, we ask, since the fear of rape coils itself around the thinking of these women, just how does the author write about rape? What is behind those descriptions of sexual warfare which make of differences between men and women a blighting antinomy? The questions seem interchangeable.

Certainly, no one can deny that any insight into rape is timely and important. Recent studies such as Susan Brownmiller's have shown how traumatic the experience of rape can be to a woman. Men, too, can be raped and afterwards feel soiled and used, as James Dickey demonstrates in Deliverance. But there is ample evidence that women are victims of rape far more frequently than men. There are also considerable data showing that the period following rape, with its attendant feelings of shame, guilt, withdrawal, can be devastating for a woman. But is this what we discern in Oates's fiction? At first glance, the story "Assault" (G) seems to fall into this category.

A woman raped at fourteen returns to her childhood home after an absence of fifteen years because her father is reported missing. She has not seen him for a long time. There is a letter from him to his attorney with instructions that the house and property are to go to the daughter. Walking about the house, the woman recalls the period after the rape: the father's anger and shame, the mother's prophecy of the father: he will go crazy. During the night, she hears sounds and imagines that her father has returned. She calls out to him, but receives no answer. In the morning, she discovers evidence that a couple had entered the garden and made love on the ground. She thinks about sex, remembers the pain of the rapist's entry into her body, and reflects that sex is pain and assault.

Up to this point, the reader can accept this thinking on the basis of the woman's experience. But when she goes on to conclude that this is the same kind of pain her mother suffered, and her mother before her, and all those other women before her mother, there is an uneasy impression that Oates wants us to believe that sex is always a violation of woman's body. This is brought out in another story, "The Maniac." Using the elliptical style found so frequently in her works, the author has the wife tell us that she sees no difference between her husband's lovemaking and that of a stranger, or a maniac. The woman goes on to wish that she had a lover who did not have "a man's anguished thrusting hardness" (G, p. 123).

Previous stories contain this same kind of thinking, often with an added note of hysteria. A woman looks at a girl and thinks: "This is the girl some man, a husband, burrows into at night and would like to kill" (MI, p. 80, "29 Inventions"). Another woman is convinced that her woman's frail body is not strong enough for the exertions of sexual love: this "holding a man between my thighs ... sinking again and again beneath his body, those heavy shoulders with tufts of dark hair on them ... " (WL, p. 61, "Unmailed, Unwritten Letters"). She sees lovemaking as a frenzied dance in which the flesh of woman hurts and man pays no attention. Still another woman thinks of herself as a machine whose parts will soon wear out because of the stress and tear her husband puts on them. She is convinced that his parts will last forever.

Puzzling, too, is the picture of man as a form of Brobdingnagian species. Elena (DWM) shrinks in repulsion from her husband's body, which is described as having huge pores that secrete enormous quantities of sweat. Damp spots appear on the mattress, and Elena feels impelled to retreat to the other side of the bed. Maureen (T), an earlier heroine, tenses with fear and panic when she thinks of marriage and sleeping with Jim, a man who seems to be

a harmless school teacher. Then there is the ambivalent
woman who hates both husband and lover, especially the
lover. For her, the man is all tufts of hair growing out of
ears and elsewhere. He has huge swollen veins in his
throat. His breath is a "stale fury" (MI, p. 159, "Scenes
of Passion and Despair"). Above all, she hates his "sick-
ening" whiskers (p. 165). Women's dreams often reveal
their repulsion for men and sex. The heroine of "Bodies"
dreams of a couple making love among spiky weeds, and
near them is a large, frozen, dead rat.

The two themes: fear of rape, of damage, and woman's repulsion for man's body (and, perhaps her own) exist
in uneasy counterpoint and inevitably suggest the question of
homosexuality. Certainly, there are hints of homosexuality
in such remarks as those already mentioned, by the woman
who wishes she had a lover without a man's hard thrusting,
or the woman who is sickened by man's hairiness. They
sound like male homosexuals who express a distaste for the
feel of woman's skin--like marshmallow--or the smell of
women's genitals--rank.

Oates attempts to sidestep any hint of homosexuality
by insisting that the reason these women feel this way is
that sex is a solo performance for the man, with no regard
for the woman's feelings. This is why women like Elena
try to protect themselves by going absolutely still during
intercourse: "she felt no pain, no alarm; she felt nothing"
(DWM, p. 119). Elena behaves pretty much the same with
Jack for much of the book. This kind of immobility is
achieved during the sexual act by thinking of something else,
reminding us of Victoria's advice to her daughter: think of
England. Oates's heroines, like Elena and Maureen and
others, think of a washing machine, a favorite metaphor of
the author's in describing man as a sexual being. Maureen
reflects: "A man was like a machine: one of those machines
at the laundromat ... " (T, p. 194). Elena thinks along the
same lines, her mother having told her that a man is like an
automatic washer going through certain cycles. Elena soon
feels confident of her ability to predict the cycles in her two
men: Marvin and Jack.

There is no wholesome solution to the sexual problem,
and Oates appears to take the traditional attitude: man is
always the power figure and relationships between men and
women have a built-in power imbalance. It never occurs to
any woman to assert herself. Sex is always something done

to her by the man and she has little control over her body
other than by submitting and blocking out all thought.

The idea that woman in our culture has been regarded
as man's possession, to be used as he sees fit, is, of course,
true and has become familiar through the writings and utter-
ances of feminists. What becomes increasingly notable in
the fiction by Oates is the heightened sense of helplessness
and terror women seem to feel concerning their lack of control over their bodies, especially in the sex act. Loretta
(T) feels not only helpless, but betrayed by her body--a feeling that begins at age sixteen and lasts for a long time after-
ward. Elena is convinced that she has no control over her
body. Arlene, the mother in Childwold, dimly believes that
Nature and Society have conspired to enslave her. She
thinks of her bloody menstrual periods, which come with
painful regularity when she is not pregnant; of her terror
when she witnessed that first menstrual flow. She remembers the men who have regarded her as their exclusive possession, particularly her boyfriend Earl. Looking at her
young daughter Laney, she wants to tell her: "you don't
own your body" (C, p. 197).

Indeed, Oates demonstrates that Arlene never does
have control over her body. Her boyfriend Earl commands
her to wear high boots and tight pants that "make your ass
stick out" (p. 40). In one of his drunken rages, he beats
her so severely that she almost loses an eye. In the end,
alone and frightened after her beloved, authoritative father
dies, she turns to a married state trooper--another authority
figure. A special fact brought out about Arlene is that she
herself was conceived in sexual violence. Her father tells
us that he had to force his wife to have sex. He waded
"thigh-deep in his wife's hatred" (p. 100) to have Arlene
conceived. (More will be said about this later.)

It is significant that Arlene, her mother, and Loretta
are uneducated women from low economic circumstances.
Traditionally, such women have been conditioned to say little
in their own behalf concerning their sexual and other relations with men. In writing of the poor, Oates often exhibits insight into their ignorance and confusion. She also
seems to believe that all women are imprisoned in this
kind of thinking, especially beautiful women. Elena, for
example, sees her beauty and sexuality as a self-trap, an
agent for bondage, which is often true of the beautiful woman who is desired and bought by a wealthy man, as she is.

What is puzzling about Elena's thinking is that she believes
absolutely that any man can avail himself of her body because of his superior strength. Such theorizing, with its
attendant ambiguities, extends over into her relations with
wealthy husband, not-so-wealthy lawyer lover, and every
man she comes into contact with or sees on the street. She
lives in terror of physical violence throughout most of the
story's unfolding.

Elena's feelings of panic and fear take us back to
Wonderland, the novel which has the fullest development of
Oates's thinking on woman's terror of the body--her own and
man's. The novelist attempts to confront the fear by placing
it at the center of a world made up of doctors and the study
of the human body. The central figure is Jesse, whose entire family is wiped out when the father murders wife and
children. The plot is not complicated. Jesse is sheltered
for a while by relatives, and is then taken in by an ego-
maniac doctor. He escapes this environment and finally, by
superhuman struggles, succeeds in becoming a doctor himself. The background, however, despite a carefully detailed
study, is not deeply relevant to the central conflicts in the
book; these, like those in previous books and books following, have to do with the body and sexual love.

In an early scene, we see the boy Jesse glancing at
a drawing of a woman's body traced on a lavatory wall.
The picture shows woman as a house with all kinds of inviting entrances. Jesse thinks that he would like to enter
such a house and lose himself in it. Later, after Jesse is
married, he imagines a woman's body to be a corridor in
which doors open to the right and left, inviting exploration.
It goes without saying that his wife does not share his
pleasure and anticipation, though she visualizes herself in
similar terms. For Helene, her body has too many orifices
easily accessible to husband, doctor, or any prowler on the
street. She is terrified of walking down the street for fear
of something being done to her body: a man "might freely
enter ... and do such damage to it" (p. 268). There is no
point in saying that today's streets are certainly far from
safe and many women are frightened to walk them. But
there is something about Helene (and other women) that in-
tensifies a sense of déjà vu in Oates's work.

Helene is even more terrified of her husband's embrace than of a prowler's. She recalls and hates his "grinding" himself into her; slapping his body against hers (p. 278).

He is an assailant who has violated her, she thinks, reminding us of the language used by the woman in "The Maniac"
(G). Doctors are assailants, too, she is convinced. Their
sharp instruments enter a woman's body, and spread in her.
Doctors and instruments hurt. Surely, women who have had
rough handling from doctors will lend a sympathetic ear to
this latter thinking.

Still, what about Helene's fear of her husband's lovemaking? Is there any justification for this thinking? Some
discussion about her background hints at an explanation, but
it does not fully solve the problem in the book. It seems
that she was left motherless at twelve, and remained her
father's close companion until marriage. Neither parent gave
her any sex advice; nor did Helene, who received an M. A.
in biology, seek instruction on her own. Before marriage,
she thought of it as something necessary to complete a woman. However, sex with a man was ugly, brutish. The
author tells us that she had resisted the thought of sex as
she resisted thoughts of death. It was too ugly. Upon
meeting Jesse for the first time, she thinks: "too vigorous.
A threat" (p. 271). But she marries him anyway.

There is no magical transformation for Helene in
which love can be viewed without fear. Instead, the battle
between what Helene sees as feminine fragility and masculine brutality reaches its height with her pregnancy. She
wants to abort the child she is carrying. She thinks of in-
serting a sharp instrument within her, of pressing it the way
her husband's penis presses inside of her during sex. Then
she would get into a tub, leave it unplugged, and let fresh
water flow in: "everything would be clean" (p. 281). She
knows she would have pain, but rationalizes that she deserves
this pain. Why? Because she had let Jesse make love to
her; had lain in his arms, allowed him to do things to her.

In the first reading of Wonderland, we grasp that
we're getting into something much more than penis fear and
phobia against men; but the absence of interlocking characterization and apparent theme bars us from insight into Helene's
problem. It is granted that Helene's severe physical problems with pregnancy contribute to her emotional problems,
but her thinking that pain and punishment are the price for
having sex, that sex is something dirty and shameful, seems
to lie in something deeper than Helene or the author care to
reveal. We realize that there has been no psychic development of character with Helene, nor with any of the women

in the fiction. They remain frightened little girls like Elena
(the next novelistic heroine), who voices the conviction that
she deserves to die after having sex with Jack. We hear
the same thinking in Childwold and this time the heroine is
truly a little girl. She is fourteen and involved with a forty-
one-year-old man.

It should be stressed that one of the puzzling aspects
of Oates's fiction is her insistence that as much as women
fear men's bodies, men are not comfortable with their bodies
either. Kasch (C) asks Laney if he disgusts her; middle-
aged Marvin Howe wonders aloud to his wife if he is a monster or a freak (DWM). Young Jules feels filthy in contrast
to his lover Nadine's pristine cleanliness and shining hair.
He washes himself constantly, but still feels "filthy" right
after (T, p. 278). The word filthy is repeated so that Jules's
agitation over his body not be lost on the reader.

Taken by itself, this does not tell us much, but when
we observe Jules in his sexual role with Nadine, details assume a certain pattern. Generally kind to Grandmother,
Mother, Sister and other people about him, Jules turns almost homicidal when it comes to sex with Nadine. He wants
to hurt Nadine, see her bloodied. The thought excites him,
but we are advised that he really does not understand his
feelings of violence.

Going back and forth in Oates's fiction, we see that
men like Jules, Jesse, Jack come from a long line of heroes
of which her latest (at this date), Kasch (C), becomes a
paradigm. These are men who appear gentle, kind, and
good--except when it comes to sex. Then they turn into
some kind of monster. Jesse, for example, is a good
father, a competent doctor, and generally decent. Yet we
know that his wife considers him a brutal lover. However,
her descriptions of his lovemaking pale beside his own, when
he talks of a beautiful blonde named Reva. Prose which
verges on the turgid informs us that Jesse's desire for Reva
is "loaded with blood" (W, p. 328). He wants to drag her
into his car, drive down some hidden lane, pull her into a
cornfield and indulge in what can only be assumed are un-
speakable acts.

Jack Morrissey is no different. A Civil Rights lawyer, a humanitarian of sorts, and husband to an intelligent
woman who works side by side with him, he walks into a
library and immediately feels stirrings of desire for the

unattractive, middle-aged librarian. Why? Because the library is deserted and he immediately assumes that the librarian is terrified of him. Fear is an aphrodisiac to Oates's men: "this pleased him, excited him, the fact of his healthy, stubborn body and what it could do" (DWM, p. 229). Sex with Elena is described in the language already familiar to the reader: grinding, driving hardness.

In the latest novel, Childwold (1976), sex as animalistic violence seems to reach a peak. The following is a scene describing forty-one-year-old Kasch's first sex encounter with fourteen-year-old Laney. "That night I grappled with her and overcame her and snapped her fragile bones in my heated love, in my generous lust. I tore at her mouth with my own. I tore at her tiny breasts, her thighs. She did not resist--not much. I overcame her. I threw myself upon her from a great height and was transported, grappling guzzling whinnying groaning, excruciating pleasure, my brain turned to jelly ..." (p. 48). To justify his actions, he describes Laney as soiled and prematurely aged. Before the sexual act, she is an angel with shimmering, golden aureole of hair and freckled, lovely face. She is fresh, with small, hard breasts.

Sex with Laney is always brutal assault. Kasch burrows into her body, tears at her, while Laney struggles. He tells us that she puts up an excellent struggle, like that of a desperate animal, but he throws her down. She has no chance as he "scrambles" over her (p. 82).

When Laney and Kasch are not having sex, the relationship is that of a good, gentle father with his daughter. Laney, who bears a resemblance to Nabokov's Lolita, even to being given the romantic name of Evangeline, is talked to, advised by, and looked after by Kasch. He scolds her for drinking and smoking, gives her books to read, and takes her to picture galleries. He is as concerned as any good father would be over her relations with boys, and indignant when she permits them liberties: how can you let them touch you? he asks at their first meeting. Often he ruffles her hair in an affectionate, fatherly gesture. In a restaurant, he is concerned with her lack of appetite. Laney feels safe with him when he behaves this way, thinks him "beautiful" (p. 147) but pales at the thought. She wishes she could remain a child forever, and remembers how she starved herself to delay her menstrual periods. With Kasch in his father role, Laney never feels lonely, never has nightmares.

Childwold provides a key to the perplexing problem
of why so many of Oates's women express contempt, aversion, fear, disgust for man's body; why they view it as unclean, gross, monstrous; why they believe that they have to
be punished for having sex with a man. Plainly, the reason
appears to be sexual guilt for wanting to sleep with Father.
Laney, for example, has been looking for her father ever
since he died one New Year's Day in a five-car accident.
She hungers for some sort of sign that she had a father,
goes to the cemetery, and is desolate when she sees only a
marker with his name, date of birth, and date of death.
Dreaming of her father, constantly hostile to her mother,
she turns to Kasch, a forty-one-year-old man. He is as
lost as she is because of a destructive family relationship.
This is the basic theme of the book.

Sex with fathers, however, is taboo in our society,
incompatible with accepted social standards and behavior.
It follows then (say the psychologists) that sex must be ra-
tionalized as assault (as it almost always is described in
Oates's fiction). The sexual object must fulfill the condition
of being degraded, for sensual feelings to have free play.
Jung tells us that the unconscious is the repository of everything objectionable, infantile, even animal in ourselves--
everything we want to forget. It is no wonder that Laney's
guilt feelings manifest themselves early. She sees men
watching her and thinks that they are telling her to run:
"This thing can hurt you plenty" (p. 48) (author's italics).
She has guilt feelings about her mother, and this comes out
in dreams of Kasch's mouth, her mother with a bleeding
face, a white tombstone, etc.

The fundamental theme, then, in Oates's fiction is
the Oedipal Conflict. Though she writes of mothers and
sons, especially in the group of stories The Seduction ...,
her focus throughout is on the father/daughter relationship.
Childwold has not one but two sets of father/daughter relationships; for Laney's mother, Arlene, is shown as feeling
closer to her father than to any other man in her life. During her marriage, she visits him constantly. After the
death of her husband, she takes her family and goes to live
with him. She looks after him, defers to him, obeys him,
thinks him handsome, and is tremendously proud of his re-
covery from a massive heart attack. In turn, she is his
"kitten, " "his pretty one" (p. 100). After the breakup with
her boyfriend Earl, there is a scene in which Arlene sits
with her father drinking brandy and feeling safe, cozy, and

protected--the reverse of her feeling with Earl. After the
father's death, she is lonely and bewildered and remains so
to the end of the book.

Oates makes a point that the special quality of this
father/daughter relationship is due to the fact that the father
wanted Arlene born and had to brave his wife's hatred to
have her conceived. The idea that fathers want daughters
and mothers do not may be true in some cases, but it hardly
explains the unrelenting gallery of hostile mothers populating
Oates's fiction. The answer may be in the author's awareness of Freudian theory that a daughter feels guilt over her
sexual feelings for Father. Seeing Mother as hostile, she
connects her with punishment, and thus experiences the fear
of damage and mutilation discussed at the beginning of this
chapter. She fears that Mother will discover Daughter's
love for Father and attempt to win Father back.

This is precisely what is dramatized in Childwold.
Arlene confronts Laney about Kasch, and in an interesting
denouement goes to Kasch's apartment, seduces him, and
takes "Father" away from Laney. Now that there is no incest threat, the language of love is romantic. There is no
mention of Kasch's filthy socks or dead bugs on the window
sill, as there is when he is with Laney. There is only the
murmur of voices, Kasch's and Arlene's, pledging undying
love--that they will never leave each other.

A mother taking the father away from the daughter is
prefigured in "The Daughter" (G). In this story, a fourteen-
year-old wants to live with her beloved stepfather, and not
with the mother, who has left the man and is divorcing him.
She runs away to his house; the mother comes after her,
spends the night with the man, and in the morning trium-
phantly bears the stricken girl away with the man's approval.
In this same collection of short stories, published before
Childwold, and dealing with what one reviewer calls the
"dark side of women," a wife takes in a young girl and befriends her. The girl becomes pregnant by the husband.
He ends up driving his car into a fence and killing himself.
Obviously, the wages of sin. ...

What the reader may have already deduced from this
discussion is that Oates's fiction is filled with the presence
of Fathers--blood and surrogate. Fathers stalk through the
pages of her books from beginning to end. They are Old
Testament figures, or tall, stern farmers with powerful

throats and huge hands, or massive, silent men who work
in factories, or men once powerful and strong but now
shrunken and eaten away by cancer, or mad men who kidnap
daughters, or kill daughters, or men who read papers at
medical conventions and whose daughters commit anti-social
acts in order to get their attention. Fathers are everywhere
in the fiction. Daughters constantly yearn for approval from
Father. It is in the smile of approval in Father's eyes that
they feel caressed and dandled.

This theme appears early in the writer's career.
Karen, the first of Oates's many novelistic heroines, sees
herself as Daddy's "littlest girl" (WSF, p. 15) and is happiest when she sits with her hand curled in his. When she
meets Shar, a cross between Heathcliff and Evel Knievel,
and goes away with him, it is only because he has struck
her father and the father has commanded her to kill him.
This she does by telling Shar, the night before his big race,
that he makes her sick. She has had a dream that her
father is young again. Shar, who has been more puzzled
by her cold behavior than the reader has, goes out and dutifully gets himself killed by crashing his stock car. Karen
goes back to Father, and the last scene shows Karen sitting
next to him in church. This is not one of the author's
better novels, and neither Shar nor Karen can be taken very
seriously as characters. But the novel is significant as the
jumping-off point for Oates's brooding on the father/daughter
relationship.

Karen is followed by scores of other girls with fathers,
such as Nina ("The Heavy Sorrow of the Body, " WL), who is
so devastated by her father's death that she wants to turn
into her father and does so by giving up her lover, living in
the father's cabin, and wearing his old clothes. There is
the waif in the excellent story "Stray Children, " (MI), who seeks
out her father (who is ignorant of her existence), demands
money of him, and then tells him to leave. We see that
money is her only security and pledge that she has a father.
And there is Elena, who is kidnapped as a child by her mad
father, kept prisoner for sixty-one days, and almost dies
from neglect before she is rescued by the authorities. Here
she is reconstructing the episode to her lover: "I remember
being wrapped in a blanket ... he was trying to protect me."
She goes on to explain that it wasn't her father's fault that
she got sick, and tells Jack that she loved her father, loves
him still (DWM, pp. 379-80).

Inevitably, there are many young girls with surrogate

fathers, older men with whom these girls have desperate and unsuccessful relationships. When they blunder into marriage for some kind of imagined security, they find themselves unable to respond sexually. The climate of marriage in Marriages and Infidelities is usually like the one described in "The Metamorphosis," in which a man and woman lie side by side with a distance of inches between them.

The odor of incest hangs over Oates's works. Her women are invariably pretty little blonde girls blocked from developing because of father fixation. They are confused by their sexual feelings and by their tendency to turn to older men. The view of man as massive, with too much flesh to him--expressed by Maureen, Elena, and others--is a child's view. Hence, we have the repeated descriptions of men with big hands on which grow tufts of hair, of men with stained teeth, etc. The stress on woman's cleanliness and man's dirt is not androphobia, but is linked to the concept of sex as dirty because of incestuous feelings.

It becomes clearer why there are so many stories in which the setting is a hospital room, the man is very ill, very clean, and the heroine is very much at ease ("Dying," USF; "Loving/Losing/Loving a Man," MI, etc.). Obviously a sick man, or better yet a dying man, is no sexual threat. Without some auctorial referent to the crucial relationship which makes the woman act in a certain way, it is difficult to understand a story like "Dying," in which the woman acts and sounds like a ghoul. We get no help from the author.

The story concerns itself with a woman who visits a sick man she keeps calling "friend." We see her noting with satisfaction the color of his blue-white chest when the blanket falls away and exposes it and the man's weight loss. She is "pleased" with the way the bones have begun to protrude through the fragile flesh, and is glad that there is a recording of the weight loss on the calendar by the man's bed. We learn that this is a "landmark" (USF, p. 179) for her and it stimulates her into a show of coquetry. But when the man feels encouraged to plead with her to get into his bed, she turns indignant and nasty. As soon as he returns to his former passivity, "even the foul air in the room seemed to weaken" (p. 184).

"Loving/Losing/Loving ..." (MI) is equally ambiguous, with a woman who suppresses a desire to crawl into her sick lover's bed, even though she views it as a sisterly gesture.

Obviously, a woman cannot be too careful about the threat of incest, but we never know that this is the theme. There is confusion in the character's mind and frequently in ours.

There is no question that the Oedipus Complex has a tremendous fascination for writers. Writers as different as Lawrence, Dostoevsky, O'Neill, and Lessing have provided us with interesting insights into the problem. The work of Joyce Carol Oates, if I understand it correctly, deals primarily with the same issue. She is one of the first American women authors to write of women arrested in what psychoanalytic theory calls the pre-genital state. If a woman is blocked in emotional development at the pre-genital state, she expresses her feelings around her father and cannot love other men. She may become frigid, not bear children, or, if she has children, she may have the unconscious fear that the child is the father's, and want to do away with it (see the mother in "The Children," MI, "I Was in Love," WL). She will also suffer fears of mutilation resulting from apprehension of the mother's anger and punishment.

The novels and short fiction for the most part revolve around women damaged for life, unable to move from a childhood love to a mature love. Like Thomas Hardy's men, they want to stop the biological clock and remain children forever. But it must be added that despite a multiplicity of literary styles: epistolary, diary, journal, notes for a theme, stream-of-consciousness, interior monologue, etc., the work is too often weakened by a repetitiousness of language and character. The same language and characterization, surrounding her young women as frigid, sexually fearful, seeing man as power figure and the enemy, do not evoke new feelings or exercise old ones. We are not led away from these standardized characters into new levels of reality.

There is no question that the women feel intensely, and to place feeling above seeing may be good imaginative writing. Too often, the response to existence pushes the character into nightmare, and over the edge into breakdown and death. Women suffer, of course, and have suffered physical pain and psychological pain. But in these stories, the author follows the nineteenth-century novel, in which woman's only form of protest is self-destruction or breakdown. The breakdown for Oates is never self-healing, as we find so frequently in Lessing. There simply is no catharsis for the feelings of despair and hopelessness; no effort to do something about the baffled confusion; no salvation.

Nor is the family, which Oates examines constantly, a source of comfort. For Jules (T), family is plates stacked together, and for Elena (DWM) it is dirty clothes in a laundry basket. The women suffer from deep depression, fed by conflict generated by sexual guilt. We are asked in story after story to accept that woman's area of self-understanding is limited, often nonexistent.

For this reason, many of the works, notably the short stories, fail to engross or engage our sympathies, or teach us something new. They become case histories of a specific neurosis (which only a visit to the analyst's couch may help to solve), instead of a seminal force for change. We become as eager to escape the story as the narrator is to escape the man/love marriage. Another reason for this is that the women (and men) are not fully-sketched characters. They exist in snatches of dialogue, inner monologues, and as part of fragmentated scenes. This in itself is not bad if some clues are provided for the reader. Too often, however, we fail to grasp the crucial relationship which has caused the woman's sickness. We are plunged into a scene or an action that bewilders us and tells us nothing. We realize that we are meeting a sexually sick woman, but we have no means with which to probe and understand the psychic disturbance. The exact telling detail and adept presentation is missing. The woman too often exists as a peg on which to hang a concept, for example, sexual warfare.

What happens, then, is that a story may move through a series of emotional tones culminating in the character's hysteria, or breakdown, or death wish, or death itself. Yet, we fail to share in the woman's emotions, not only because we have heard it before, but because at the flood of feeling one detects a certain dryness. The woman remains for us a forced character clothed in the accouterments of realism.

Part of the problem lies in what I conjecture as the author working out her own fears and obsessions through the medium of fiction. Observations here on the possible psychology of the author are based on the repetitive themes and characterizations in her works. As discussed, there is a pattern of fathers and daughters. One cannot help noticing, moreover, the author's presence in the physical description of a certain young woman character who is fragile-looking and delicate (so like the author herself). This woman is unable to throw off her sexual fears. She remains a child imprisoned in a woman's body--a child searching for Father.

It is highly significant that <u>Childwold</u> closes with the cry of
fourteen-year-old Laney weeping for "Father." She has
come back to the old house in which she believes Kasch is
hiding. Catching a glimpse of him as bearded, gaunt, sickly-
pale (hence, safe to love), she pleads: "It's Laney ... Do
you remember ... ? Kasch? Is it really you ... ? After
so long? Waiting ... My Love?" (pp. 294-95). She pleads
for a sign.

Of course it is risky and perhaps irrelevant to advance the hypothesis that in Laney's heartbroken wail, we
detect the author's own inability to throw off the drag of
father love. It is even more risky to make anything out of
statements by the author about the possibility of drug addic-
tion (because drugs tame the emotions), or that she writes to
relieve her mind of things that haunt it. Nevertheless, I
continue to believe that the writer is haunted by Father.
Her first novel, <u>With Shuddering Fall</u>, ends with Karen reunited with her father, and the latest, <u>Childwold</u>, ends with
Laney's crying to be reunited. Even Arlene is given a temporary father figure in Wally, the state trooper.

To be haunted by one's father or mother may be all
to the good for literary purposes. Lawrence was haunted
by his mother and the result was the fine, if uneven, <u>Sons</u>
<u>and Lovers</u>, followed by an impressive body of work, some
of it good, some of it bad, but most of it dealing with new
aspects of human relationships. The artist, Lawrence believed, "must invent and discover a new world within the
known world." Unfortunately, for the most part, there is
no new world in Oates's fiction, no invention. Because she
enslaves her imagination to her personal devils, her fictional world remains static.

We have a steady procession of young women convinced
of the greater durability of man's physical equipment. They
are women who express self-division and separateness from
men, and who are convinced that they have no choice in love
and marriage. Woman is chosen and accepts her destiny.
Marriage changes nothing for woman, and the Oates woman
reveals no willingness to deal with the problem. At times,
there erupts what appears to be editorial concern and protest against the way women have been programmed into becoming what men want them to be, in statements such as:
woman is man's invention, yet remains a mystery to man.
In other words, man doesn't know what he wants (the reversal
of Freud's "What does woman want?"). But these are buried
under the heavy lava of emphasis on the Oedipal Complex.

We observe that when the writer is not dealing with the frightened young woman character and the language of sexual fear, but with working class women like the later Loretta, Grandma Wendall (T), Arlene (C), or even with Ardis and Rachel (DWM) who aspire to be men, the characters come alive. These women talk; they bombard us with words; they never stop talking in the effort to articulate the unrealized meanings of their lives. Loretta talks about work, the price of food, the troubles in the neighborhood--and men. She expresses anger, wants to be somebody, doesn't want to be used by her fat husband whenever he wants to climb up on top of her, as she puts it. Ardis schemes to break into something big and rich, and, like Mrs. Durbeyfield with Tess (Tess ...), does not hesitate to use her daughter's beauty as a stepping-stone to a more affluent life--in her case, a money settlement by her rich son-in-law. Grandma Wendall is a tough, old woman who rules her sons and daughters-in-law and commands grudging respect from all. Arlene tries to find her identity through numerous pregnancies. Like Lawrence's Anna Brangwen, she is happiest when pregnant.

It should be mentioned that though these women talk of men and at men, they do not talk to men. There is no communication and no assumption that the air could be cleared sometimes if the man and woman sat down and talked things over. Perhaps there is a definite correlation between silence and economics. Working men are portrayed as inarticulate and withdrawn. As they slide down the economic scale (like Howard and Furlong) (T), they become more and more silent. Failure not only bows the shoulders and shuffles the feet, but silences the tongue.

Though women like Loretta talk, they never really understand self or transcend the limits of self. Hampered by poverty and ignorance, they turn to dreams as compensation for an unbearable life. They try to escape reality by seeing themselves as characters in movies, TV, magazines, or as disembodied people in mirrors. Dreams become their reality: "Christ!" says Loretta, "I'm sick of all this. I want to be like people in that movie. I want to know what I am doing" (p. 108). In the effort to know what they are doing, the women constantly change makeup, color of hair, clothes, and, as in the case of Ardis, resort to plastic surgery when the money is there. Victims of the media which instruct them that only in self-improvement lies success, trapped in a physical and social shell, they have a feeling of helplessness which results in blurring of fantasy and reality. Finally, the fantasy world is no comfort. "What good did it do?" sobs Loretta at the end when she watches her son Jules on TV affirm his faith in violence. "Jesus Christ, this is a waste" (T, p. 474) (author's italics).

This is good writing. Though them is not pulled together as tightly as Childwold nor as ambitious as Do With Me ..., and though the characters are not fully realized, particularly the women, the book is an excellent re-creation of a working class family--their baffled confusions, their attempts to deal with the circumstances surrounding them. I consider it to be the best of Oates's works. What fails to make it a work of art is the absence of that fusion--suffering, cruelty, compassion, love for humanity, a declaration of faith in woman (and man). Woman, in this novel, as elsewhere, is what Elena implies when she looks at the sick elms: diseased but still standing. This is a bleak picture which fails to take into account the great world out there, bubbling, fermenting with change. Women, directly or indirectly, are caught up in this change. Oates needs to make a leap of the imagination to comprehend these changes and break out of the theme with which she has been working. Her talent cries out for it.

CHAPTER 2

ERICA JONG: FLYING OR GROUNDED?

In striking contrast to the fears of the body expressed
in the fiction of Joyce Carol Oates, both novels by Erica
Jong--Fear of Flying and How to save your own life--end
with a kind of symbolic ritual baptism in celebration of the
female body. In the first novel, Fear of Flying, the heroine,
Isadora Wing, returns to her patient but dull husband after
an unsuccessful attempt to find in Adrian Goodlove the perfect combination of friend and lover. Stripping off her
clothes, she climbs into the claw-footed bathtub, immerses
herself in water up to her neck and contemplates her body.
"A nice body, " she tells us. "Mine. I decided to keep it"
(FF, p. 311). It's a comforting picture which leaves the
reader with a sense of well-being. At the end of the second
novel, How to save your own life, Isadora, now husbandless
but firmly clasped in the arms of her young lover, Josh,
finally experiences orgasm with him. Paradoxically, she
has up to this point been automatically responsive to her
husband's mechanical embrace, but unable to achieve orgasm
with Josh's more spontaneous and inspired lovemaking. In
Joycean fashion, Isadora commemorates the momentous occasion by passing water.

True, this act is involuntary and not conscious as
when Leopold Bloom and Stephen Dedalus make water together
in front of Bloom's house at the end of Ulysses. Isadora is
embarrassed, demonstrating that her flaunted lack of inhibi-
tion has not yet successfully embraced the debatable Joycean
idea that the indecorous, the vulgar, the commonplace reveal
the higher things. She has to be assured by her lover that
he loves everything about her: her "shit, " her "pee, "
"farts, " her "tight snatch, " etc. (HT, p. 285). The scene
resembles the one between Connie Chatterley and Oliver
Mellors in D. H. Lawrence's Lady Chatterley's Lover (Jong,

35

like Oates, has read her Lawrence) in which Mellors tells
Connie that he is glad that she shits and pisses: "I don't
want a woman as couldna shit nor piss."[1] More will be
said about Jong's language and style in the discussion of
How to save your own life.

Although Jong concentrates on woman's body, its hungers, its drives, more centrally the novels are the story of
a dying marriage and a woman's odyssey to love. Both books
pose the questions: what is it to be a woman? where lies
salvation? In Fear of Flying, the sense of crisis is communicated by a quaking, picaresque Isadora who finally leaves
her uncommunicative, joyless, psychiatrist husband for a
Laingian psychologist, Adrian Goodlove. Adrian offers her
the promise of sensual love (by squeezing her ass) and the
promise of a life which he calls twentieth-century existen-
tialism. This, he explains, means making no plans for the
future, seizing the day, and feeling no guilt. As it turns
out, neither promise has substance. Adrian is sensual in
public where consummation is impossible, and impotent in
private. He makes all the rules for the relationship while
pretending there are none, and he does have plans of his
own, which include going back to his wife and children and
leaving Isadora. In one of the many good one-liner observations in the book, Isadora concludes that her fling with
Adrian has been desperation masquerading as freedom.

Neither husband nor lover provides Isadora with a
sense of her own identity or gives her any security. Ultimately, she has to, as all women must, try and fashion her
own sense of destiny. In the course of her quest, we get
good insights into how difficult this is for women in our society. Thomas Hardy observed of women in English Victorian society, "doing means marrying."[2] Things haven't
changed much since Hardy's day, according to Jong. The
cruel jests aimed at unmarried women, found so frequently
in fiction and comic strips, are still with us. Isadora fears
being the butt of ridicule, or a "pariah" (FF, p. 10), since
a woman alone "is a reproach to the American way of life"
(FF, p. 11). Accustomed to being dependent first on father,
then on husband, she is timid about losing dependency on
some man. She dreads being alone. So she marries, and
finds out that her loneliness is compounded.

In the late nineteenth-century novel and throughout
twentieth-century novels, marriage is often the death of love.
We are told in Fear of Flying that Isadora's first husband,

Brian, is a good friend and lover until marriage. Then he
turns into a man so completely devoted to work that he eventually breaks down. It must be said that it is difficult to
be sympathetic to Isadora's early plaint about Brian's lack
of virility, because of work pressures. After all, he is the
one who works hard while she has time to pursue her studies
and putter around the small apartment. But her confusion
and unhappiness, stemming from Brian's growing madness
until he is committed, are understandable. So is the story
of her second marriage to a dour Chinese psychiatrist whose
own life is one vast analysis, as Isadora puts it. She discovers that he punishes her with long silences which precipi-
tate her into still greater isolation. Obstinately, despite the
fact that Bennett, the husband, is no companion and insists
on her dependence on him and his independence of her, Isadora clings to the idea that even a bad marriage is better
than none. She demonstrates that although western woman's
feet were never bound like the Chinese woman's, making the
latter dependent on man for food, shelter, clothing, etc. ,
her woman's mind has been crippled into accepting so-called
inherent limitations. The author makes it clear that family,
school, society have conditioned Isadora in her thinking.
She is, for a while, a woman who conforms to the rigid and
restraining role imposed on her, and defers to her husband's
view of reality.

But despite the brain-washing, Isadora's mind persists
in nagging her with questions: How can an intelligent woman
fuse the physical and intellectual parts of her being into one
healthy whole? How to achieve integration, exhorts Isadora?
How to resolve the conflict between the creative woman and
the wife? How to be feminine? What is being feminine?
Is it more feminine to be a wife and mother than to be a
writer?

It can be argued that some of the drama surrounding
the heroine's dilemma is rubbed off by the presence of abun-
dance: plenty of time to write, and enough money to pay
analysts' fees or walk into Bloomingdale's and buy an expensive pair of shoes when she is feeling low. Certainly, there
is a marked difference between Isadora and the working-
class mother who is a wage earner/housewife/mother, or
the artist woman who tries to paint, sculpt or write while
wrestling with laundry, bills, cooking, cleaning the toilet,
and checking the temperature of a sick child. There is no
evidence that Isadora performs any of the chores of domesticity outside of whipping up an airy soufflé now and then.

But this is irrelevant. As Virginia Woolf points out grate-
fully: it was the money an Aunt left her which allowed her
the freedom to write. The issue which the author poses is:
how can woman find self-fulfillment in some creative work
without accompanying feelings of guilt?--a universal problem
which is just now receiving attention.

The other problem which plagues Isadora is one which
more often revolves around men, and is generally found in
male writing: marriage claustrophobia, the itch to escape
marriage, the desire for the mate you can't have. John Updike's stories of marriage frequently deal with this theme;
for example, "Museums and Women." Isadora, in her own
words, itches for men, and particularly for some man who
would be friend, lover, everything. In short, like Fellini's
hero in $8\frac{1}{2}$, she fantasizes about her ideal, composite mate.
In the meantime, she looks with delighted longing at men;
tells us how much she loves their smells, their shapes,
their genitals, and is collectively in love with all men, except her husband. If there is none of the repugnance for
the male body found in Oates's fiction, there is, however, a
hint of female chauvinism. Isadora may revel in fantasies
about the male body's perfections even when there are none,
as in the case of the unappetizing would-be music conductor
Charlie, but she confides that while men's bodies are beautiful, their minds are befuddled.

In between, there are comments, as in Portnoy's
Complaint, on the problems of being Jewish and having a
Jewish mother, but without the self-righteousness which mars
Roth's book. Isadora's mother is an intelligent, talented
woman, frustrated in her aspirations to be a painter, and
anxious for her daughter to fulfill her dreams for her. It's
not an uncommon wish in disappointed women, as Lawrence
demonstrates with Mrs. Morel (Sons and Lovers) and Hardy
with Mrs. Yeobright (The Return of the Native). Both these
last-mentioned women seek self-esteem. In their particular
cases, it is through their sons. Isadora's mother is not a
tragic figure in the sense that Mrs. Yeobright and Mrs.
Morel are. The author's observations and sentiments about
family and mother are tempered with banter and humor.

Isak Dinesen once remarked that what the modern
novel needs is humor, and Fear of Flying has that much
needed ingredient. There is the funny bit about Isadora's
fear on the plane: if the plane should fall how would she
face God after stamping her religion Unitarian. The satire

on analysts going to the Vienna convention, accompanied by scowling children and wives padding around in space shoes, is one of the best passages in the book. This high-spirited satire is not diminished by her kind words on the value of analysis. For Isadora, analysis enabled her to get some neuroses out of the way, thus permitting her to write. There is also playful wit in Isadora's sexual fantasies, for example the "zipless fuck," about which so much has been written. The departure with Adrian is truly a comedy of errors, as she describes it.

Her eye for social observation is shrewd. The scatological digression on French, German, and other nations' toilets is as incisive as Colette's observations on primitive toilet facilities provided for actresses while on tour. Good, too, are her descriptions of Beirut: veiled ladies riding in the back of a Chevrolet or a Mercedes Benz; shepherds who smoke cigarettes and carry transistors while tending flocks. There is, however, more than a hint of ethnic prejudice in her descriptions of the red-capillaried faces of German women, with their heavy bodies made still more heavy by costumes of loden cloth. But this is balanced by her honest appraisal of the former Nazi official who gives her a job (during her stay in Germany), and her self-questioning: how would she have behaved during the Hitler era?

Fear of Flying shuttles backward and forward for 311 pages, giving us a woman in Isadora Wing who is part little girl, part female rogue, part troubled artist/wife/daughter and, more specifically, a woman who gets all kinds of advice from family and the men in her life. The family wants her "to settle down" and Bennett warns her that if she leaves him, she will mess up her life. Adrian counsels her that if she is going to have something interesting to write about, she must have experience--with him. It's very much like the advice given the ladies of the Russian court by Rasputin: if you want redemption, you must sin with me. All things considered, Adrian's advice proves to be correct. Isadora fares better than the Russian ladies. If there is no salvation with him, the Adrian experience at least provides Isadora with piquant and serious material for a book (as we learn in How to ...), proving the wisdom of that statement by Anaïs Nin: make literature out of misery. Isadora returns to her husband after the Adrian fiasco, convinced that no matter what her reception by Bennett will be, she will survive. "Surviving meant being born over and over. It wasn't easy, and it was always painful. But there wasn't any other choice except death" (FF, p. 311).

These are brave words which promise that the woman
we meet in Fear of Flying and who tells us: she never
wants to age; wants to give birth to herself; wants a blazing
sensual love and a blazing career; wants freedom and secur-
ity--that this woman will find some solution to conflicting desires.   To put it another way, Isadora Wing appears like
some modern Persephone, who will continue to move out of
the gloom of her marriage into the sunshine of a better relationship, and mature as woman and artist.

How to save your own life, sequel to Fear of Flying,
begins with "I left my husband on Thanksgiving Day" (p. 3).
A few pages later, Isadora confides that she had saved the
thought of leaving her husband "like a sweet before bedtime,
like a piece of bubble gum put on the childhood bedpost ... "
(HT, p. 7).   Some 300 pages later, the reader learns that
the heroine is now leaving apartment and husband.   The plot
is stuck, like that bubble gum on the bedpost, with repetitions
of what we have already learned in Fear of Flying.   Briefly,
Bennett is dull, lacks joy and makes love mechanically, yet
Isadora is afraid to leave him, clinging to the myth of husband as protector and Daddy figure.   She is convinced that
compromise is a way of life.   The further they drift apart,
the more frenetic is their lovemaking.   The only new ingredient of plot is Isadora's discovery of her husband's infidelity,
and her jealousy and anger that he has played the role of
saint while casting her in the role of villain.   However, the
reader has long foreseen that Isadora, like Hemingway's
Nick Adams, has concluded that "it's not fun anymore."   Unlike the Hemingway hero, she is unable to make an "end to
something."   Maybe that's the point of the novel--the difference between the way men and women go about dissolving a
relationship.   Where men are active, women are passive.

Granted this, there is nothing in the characterization
of the bouncing, skipping, giggling, gutsy-thinking Isadora
that makes her a classic example of the intelligent but passive woman, without the self-assurance to take responsibility
for her own life.   She knows how to seek help from friends,
analysts, lovers, and how to compensate for any failure of
feminine nerve with a range of consolations that include masturbation, sniffing cocaine, smoking joints, making love with
a woman, drinking six gin and tonics plus wine at one sitting,
participating in a sex orgy, reading mail in the nude, and
taking pot shots at critics who write nasty reviews about
her work.   She's about as helpless as Moll Flanders.

Nor is her jealousy of Penny, with whom Bennett has

had a love affair, entirely credible since she, herself, looks upon infidelity as a diversion in an unhappy marriage. Some effort is made to enlist the reader's sympathy by noting that Penny read Isadora's short stories with Bennett during post coitus, but this is not too convincing. Ultimately, Isadora is redeemed for us by her honesty. She gives a belated palm to Penny for the courage to have an affair with Bennett, leave the husband who saddled her with six pregnancies, get a degree, and start a new life for herself. However, Isadora's early references to Penny as goyish, dumb, possessing "washed-out shiksa eyes" (HT, p. 45) are ethnic slurs which settle like a thin layer of sludge in otherwise humorous appraisals of people. Along with certain other disclosures of malice, they detract from the picture of Isadora as a warm, Jewish girl filled with gregarious good humor, animated by kind instincts, and in love with most people and the whole universe, despite her jealousy and other problems.

The central emphasis in the novel keeps shifting to Bennett, and there are no attempts to lighten the dark strokes with which his characterization is sketched. Although Jong's men are not the unsavory characters Oates portrays so often, Bennett comes close to being the villain in this domestic drama. Isadora rationalizes that he slept with Penny in order to get back at her for her writing, while at the same time he played the role of the forgiving husband. The accusation is legitimate, for even at the end, when a childish Isadora seeks sexual revenge against Bennett by embellishing on the number of lovers she has had, he keeps intoning piously that he is prepared to forgive her. The most valuable thing to come out of this exchange, for the heroine and the reader, is Isadora's realization that during the entire marriage she has been made to feel grateful to Bennett for letting her write. Not once has she asked herself if it were all right for Bennett to practice his vocation of psychology. After all, that was his job. Her writing, he made her see, was a self-indulgence, toward which he was prepared to be generous. Unfortunately, the problem of writer versus woman and the guilt feelings that the conflict engenders is not satisfactorily resolved in this novel, as we see in the relationship with Isadora's next love, Josh.

Not so evident here is the humor present in the first novel, Fear of Flying, which keeps the details of the disintegrating marriage from falling into self-pity, and makes of Isadora a kind of Thackerayan heroine whose "one eye brims with pity while the other watches the family spoons" (for Isadora, her writing). There is one amusing description of a skiing accident, a broken leg, and a ride to the hospital in which a drugged Isadora tries to urinate into a wadded kleenex and then tosses it out of the car window, while a morose Bennett frowns over his spoiled vacation. Typically, however, where an Oates heroine traces the downward curve of her marriage by the number of miscarriages she has had, Isadora (like a Hemingway hero) sees it in terms of accidents and physical scars. And just as rain is always a presentiment of trouble in Hemingway's stories, so we read that Bennett arrives at the ski lodge bearing with him the rain.

While continuing to unravel a marriage already reduced to a limp, tangled skein, the novel retains in crumpled form many of the themes, from creativity and femininity to the hunger for love, with which the author worked in the first novel. It also contains telling observations on the drawbacks of fame; Hollywood, which is filled with divorced men with hair transplants; bachelors who give Jacuzzi parties; the loving camaraderie between intelligent, talented women; the way other women, in the scramble for success, imitate the worst of men's vices; the pressures by husband and society for a woman to use her husband's name. About the latter, Isadora is not only chagrined but feels cheated and betrayed at giving her husband--neither a reader (except for his psychology books) nor a writer--immortality by placing his name on her books.

This is a legitimate complaint. Names are important to men, as Shakespeare points out in Othello: "Who steals my purse steals trash; 'tis something, nothing;/ ... But he that filches from me my good name/ Robs me of that which not enriches him, / And makes me poor indeed. " Of course Shakespeare is speaking of slander, but writers have always been concerned that their name "will not perish in the dust, " as Southey writes. Why should women writers, or any woman, be deprived of her name, Isadora asks? Why indeed? In the case of Isadora, she is honest enough to confess that the fault lies not so much with society as with herself. She is so hungry for Bennett's approval that she gives him her work--and makes him famous.

If the heroine is chilled by her foolishness and her husband's lack of affection and care, particularly when she needs him, she is warmed by her many friendships with women. Where there are no developing and deepening relationships between women in Oates's fiction, Jong's second book emphasizes the value of women friends. The short description of the episode with Jeannie (a thinly-veiled portrait of Anne Sexton?) contains warmth and tenderness. It is Jeannie, a poet, who, at times, lives desperately on Valium and Stolichnaya vodka ("anything to oil the unconscious," HT, p. 166) who gives Isadora the push to break with husband: "Live or die ... but for god's sake don't poison yourself with indecision" (HT, p. 173). There is also lusty, 5'9" Gretchen, who points out that Bennett has treated Isadora badly until fame made her for him the goose which laid the golden egg. In reply to Isadora's wonderment that her jealousy of Penny has improved their sex life, Gretchen replies: "jealousy makes the prick grow harder. And the cunt wetter" (HT, p. 61). A tough woman!

Hope, another friend, twenty-two years older than Isadora, advises her to get rid of Jewish guilt, and helps her with the publishing of her poems. Then there is Holly, a plant lover, who offers her studio, herbal tea, and sympathy. Not least among this cast of women characters is Rosanna Howard, who provides a chauffeured Rolls Royce, champagne, caviar, and her musk-scented body. Isadora, her head filled with images of Missy and Colette, Violet and Vita, Gertrude and Alice, and her blood fired by expensive wines, reels off to bed with Rosanna. She discovers that her rakish joy in breaking a taboo, and her view of her act as a punitive measure against her mother ("I felt I had gone down on my mother," HT, p. 149), do not compensate for her aversion to vaginal taste and smell. She invokes the indulgence of "Gentle Reader" and Lesbians everywhere for her distaste: "I tried, I put my best tongue forward ..." (HT, p. 153).

There are male friendships, too, but these are predominantly sexual, except for the one with eighty-seven-year-old Kurt (Henry Miller?), who is generally accompanied by his male nurse or two former Japanese wives. Isadora talks and makes love with two men, both conveniently named Jeffrey. These Belle du Jour diversions take place in the afternoon and Isadora is able to explain her absences to Bennett as "shopping at Bloomingdale's." Later, when she does take a token walk through the store, she notes the way some women buy, and rationalizes that the compulsive woman buyer is trying to compensate for a lack of love. It is not a very relevant or sage observation, since she herself does not look upon these afternoons of sexual love as fulfill-

ing. Yet, obviously they give her an ego boost. Sauntering
down the avenue, she is no fearful Oates heroine shrinking
from the stares of men. On the contrary, she invites looks
and boldly stares back with the smug assurance of sexual
magnetism, and that men detect the aroma of the afternoon's
lovemaking on her.

Any successful novel, as we have been told repeatedly,
must deal with love in one form or another. Love must be
the pervasive thread which binds the whole together in some
form of tapestry. Isadora's Hollywood trip not only serves
the purpose of tracing her increasing disillusionment with
the unscrupulous woman producer Britt and her unhappy realization that no writer can control the quality of the movie
made out of her/his work; it also brings love into her life--
Josh. There is no question that describing Josh with his
furry, warm, likeable face always gives Isadora pleasure.
Despite the age difference of six years, which troubles Isadora only briefly, she decides to take her friend Jeannie's
advice, be a fool, and give herself up to her passion for
Josh.

The language of love here, as elsewhere in the author's
writing, contains a sexual vocabulary in which "cunt," "cock"
and "fuck" predominate, although there is also an ample
sprinkling of "shit," "piss," "crap," "getting knocked up,"
etc. Language has always been the concern of American
writers, from Hawthorne and Melville to Hemingway and to
contemporary writers like Gould, Brautigan, Godwin, and
Burroughs. They have attempted to find a language through
which to convey the essential experience of love and of
American life, while leaving the impress of personality on
language. Jong chooses to write in what she feels is an
earthy style. How to save your own life reveals that she
is troubled by whether she has succeeded in finding the right
words and voice. Through Isadora she asks: how should
one write about sex? She admits that she is "plagued by
the confusion between natural earthiness and licentiousness,
the mistaking of openness and lack of pretense for a desire
to titillate and shock" (p. 169).

Certainly, since women have been taught for centuries
that they are not sexual beings and that only "bad" women
like sex, we need frankness on the subject. But how to
write about it?

This is not a new dilemma. It faced D. H. Lawrence

in Lady Chatterley's Lover at a time when sex was a for-
bidden subject both for men and women and censorship fet-
tered all writers from treating it in an intelligent way.
Lawrence, however, was determined to break through Victorian prudery. There is no doubt that he was using this
last novel as a final way of ridding himself of sexual reser-
vations resulting from the influence of early Chapel religion
and a clinging to Oedipal love for his mother, which had
haunted him all his life.

His purpose in Lady Chatterley's Lover was to structure a hero who would be earthy and, at the same time,
well-read and filled with social concern. The man, Mellors,
was to meet a titled lady suffering from emotional attrition;
he would make her aware of the necessary value of the body's
physical life. To accomplish this, Lawrence decided to have
Mellors employ a special language of Midlands dialect and
four-letter words during sexual scenes. At other times,
Mellors would expound in perfect English on the horrors of
industrialization and its effect on men and women. The
shift from an educated man to one who speaks a slurring dialect interposed with "fuck," "cunt," "shit," etc. is unsuccessful. Connie's sister sums it up succinctly: "he was no simple working man, not he: he was acting! acting!"[3]

We get the same impression of Jong's language, in
which Isadora at one point is making literary references to
John Keats and the next moment is sprinkling around the
familiar cunts and cocks. We are to understand that education has not robbed Isadora of her essential earthiness and
that she can use the language of warm, simple common
woman or man, who accepts sex and the body as a natural
part of life--unlike educated people who extol the mind, deny
sex its rightful place in life, and are shocked by forthright
language.

One serious argument against this line of reasoning
is that representing the common man or woman in this way
propagates a sentimental myth. Civilization long ago caught
up with the simple human being who, at some time or other,
expressed the physical part of his or her nature in natural,
instinctive, and graceful ways. When today's dock worker,
or mechanic, or farmer, or gas station attendant uses the
language of "fuck," "cock," "cunt," it is as expletives or
insults, regardless of their original sexual meaning. No
writer to date has succeeded in semantically restoring the
words. For those who grew up in poor areas, or lower

middle-class neighborhoods, and heard this language every day from dull, uninteresting men and boys in their daily comments on sports, women, or the weather, it lost its shock value around the fifth grade.

I am not making the absurd claim that women don't talk this way now. I am saying that many women have utilized this means of expression as an assertion of their independence and freedom from former reticence about sex. Also, to many women writers from comfortable, middle-class homes, it may seem like a fresh, exciting, and original approach to sexual love.

But is it? As with all patterns of language, the writer after a while is imprisoned within a rigid enclosure of words in which, as in How to ..., love is reduced to cunt and cock. We don't have a man and woman experiencing a warmly human relationship in which ultimately there is a sense of rebirth and a feeling of unity with the living universe (as that post-sexual love dialogue between Isadora and Josh would have us believe). There is only an impression of disembodied genitalia in which dripping cunt meets hard cock.

Witness the following descriptions: "She wanted this one, this copper-colored lover, this pink cock ... " (HT, p. 280). "Only his cock inside of her could give her peace" (p. 281). "His cock was bulging under the copper buttons of his jeans ... " (p. 282). There is a lot of copper around here and we are constantly reminded that if Josh's member is bulging, Isadora's is dripping. Together with the description of the ocean thundering outside the love chamber and the water sloshing in the water bed from the exertions of the two lovers, the reader is drenched with verbal and scenic descriptions.

A more serious criticism is that what we're really looking at is genitalia parodying physical and emotional experience. If the writer is trying to tell us that for the man, his male reality is his hard, erect penis, and that for the woman, the female reality is the wetness and slipperiness of her vagina, the reader has difficulty in accepting this. In Jong's emphasis on "cock, " and on "cunt" as "a dark hole, " we are only too conscious of the language of pornography in which women are not women but "hot slits, " "gaping holes, " and "fuck tubes. "

The writer attempts to cope with the sexual scenes

in various ways: she avoids the greyness of clinical language; she shifts narrative voice from first to third; she gives realistic details of Isadora's various positions during intercourse. In respect to the latter, though the reader is awed by Isadora's athletic agility, the overall impression of all this rapture is of a scene straight out of Playboy or a Mickey Spillane novel. We have a virile, masterful Josh demanding: do you want my sperm? And Isadora, clad in a filmy, black nightgown slit up the front and with pink ribbons which push up her breasts, confiding to the reader: "She needed him. She needed this man" (p. 284). Instead of a woman finding her own self-worth, language and scene crystallize in the kind of male fantasy found in girlie magazines.

In using this kind of sexual vocabulary, there is a sense of the writer beggared for expression and falling back on a vocabulary of male street usage. Woman needs a sexual vocabulary of her own--not one borrowed from men's street language. Such language is always self-limiting, because it is more geared to voicing frustrations than fulfillment (God is "a shout in the street," says Stephen Dedalus). 4 Language needs to be precise, original. It should give a sense of independent, first-hand experience as response to the encounter. It should avoid filtering the experience through terms associated with male attitudes which are demeaning to women. By adopting the male language of sexuality, Jong is also fooling herself that she is preempting man's power. All she is preempting is the pose of sexual prowess.

I said at the beginning that both works by Jong end with some sort of water ritual, which is to be interpreted as a celebration of the female body. In Fear of Flying, Isadora's warm, appreciative, anatomical description of her body lying in scented, soapy water helps to do just that. The water bed in How to ..., on which Isadora's love odyssey comes to a climax, is an ersatz symbol of baptism and a new life, not unlike the black nightgown that Isadora is wearing--"proof" of her womanhood. As for the question of salvation, Isadora sums it up in one phrase: "He had the cock" (p. 279). Freud would love it, especially since earlier Isadora has voiced the idea that women must have power.

The world of Fear of Flying and its sequel How to ... offers us a heroine who appears to be far more intrepid and confident than any of Oates's women. Yet, ultimately, we see that Jong's Isadora Wing is as helpless as the most timid of Oates's women characters--in the common avowal that man has the power. True, Isadora's discovery comes out of sexual need and not fear, but her conclusion is basically the same as the one affirmed in book after book by Oates. Woman is helpless. Man is powerful.

CHAPTER 3

LOIS GOULD: THE MUSICAL CHAIRS OF POWER

In 1970, Lois Gould published her first novel, Such
Good Friends, which, to a certain extent, shows some provocative similarities to Ralph Ellison's Invisible Man, while
being rooted in what Gould feels is essentially the feminine
experience. Like the narrator in Ellison's book, Julie Messinger, in search of some kind of identity, learns early in
life that power is what keeps society going. For Julie, the
representatives of social power are men to whom woman is
essentially "a thing" (p. 145). Their faithful advocates are
mothers and teachers, who impress upon women docility,
acceptance, submission, and rigid conformity. Like Ellison's
invisible hero, Julie also learns that she is as likely to be
betrayed by friends as by enemies.

Here the similarity ends. Ellison's invisible man
struggles and finally rejects both the alternative which protean Rinehart offers--to be all things to all people--and his
grandfather's advice: "Agree 'em to death and destruction."[1]
Instead, he chooses temporary hibernation as his answer to
fixed patterns and variable mobility. Underground, he
achieves a kind of affirmation with life. The world is both
"vile and sublimely wonderful."[2] He concludes that he must
emerge, shake off the old skin, and enter a world which is
"one of infinite possibilities. What a phrase--still it's a
good phrase and a good view of life, and a man shouldn't
accept any other; that much I've learned underground."[3]

Lois Gould's narrator, on the other hand, reflects
bitterness, hatred, and what she judges as the world's self-
limiting and self-justifying scope. Her world is the world
of Beat analyses--bad, bad, bad, and any effort only makes
it worse. Yet the heroine, like the people around her, is
unable to break out of sealed patterns of thinking and appears
fixed in stasis at the end.

Obviously, Gould's artistic problem is not the black man in white America, but white woman in white man's society. Both writers, however, Ellison and Gould, are dealing with minorities, their subordination by society, and how subordination shapes identity. Both novels cry out for an individual's minimal recognition as a human being. Both dramatize the dehumanization process which turns the minority figure into an abstraction for society. For Ellison, the black becomes dehumanized by ranting racists or sanctimonious do-gooders. For Gould, woman is an abstraction, subject to dehumanization as a result of brutal chauvinism or romantic mythmaking. Where Ellison leaves the reader with some hope, Gould does not, and the difference lies in the fact that sex and marriage constitute the main plot in Such Good Friends and not in Invisible Man. There is one sexual incident in Ellison's novel, but the subject of marriage is absent. The struggles of Ellison's hero are with color, jobs, and other things connected with his socio-economic condition. Julie's problem is that she is a woman, and for Lois Gould the treatment of women calls for no celebration of life--at the present moment.

The tension within Julie, an intelligent woman, stems from the ideal of sexual equality and the reality of sexual subordination. As convinced as Ellison's invisible man that she has never been in charge of her own destiny, she still falls back into the conventional trap of marriage as a goal after the death of her unfaithful husband. Like Jong's fictional heroine, Isadora Wing (equally disillusioned with marriage), Julie's way of giving pattern to the chaos within and without is to find another man to love and to serve. She achieves no stature in the end, only the tired realization that she no longer hates her husband: "Ah, Richard, I'm sorry we didn't get to grow up together" (p. 283). She also consoles herself half-heartedly that her reason for remarriage is that the children need a father. In essence, the reader knows it is not the children who need a father so much as Julie who needs marriage as a prosthetic appliance.

The insistence we find in the writings of such different authors as Hemingway and Nabokov, that life is what you make it and you must shape your own reality, is precisely what Lois Gould deliberately omits in her novel. Taking the underlying theme in current American fiction, that in this world the problem of identity is tremendously acute, she enlarges upon it to emphasize that it is doubly difficult for woman to shape her own life. The author leans heavily on

the staples of recent American fiction by women writers,
which has given us more than a hint of what is damaging to
the growth of woman's self-awareness and self-worth. These
include: the perfectionist parent (usually a mother) who
wants "a good little girl, " a perfect daughter; the process
of dating, which involves blind dates who never call again;
the proms and social events which often brand woman as a
wall flower; the experimental sex which leaves her bewildered
and humiliated--and marriage.

In Such Good Friends, marriage gives nihilism a new
definition--no love.   The process of chipping the ego begun
by mother: "your mouth looks sick. Like a beatnik" (p.
43); continued by teachers: "Julie Wallman, step forward"
(p. 55), when she moves during picture taking; by boys: "I
asked you because two other girls I asked said no" (p. 80),
finally reaches its sharpest pitch with a husband who rejects
her sexually: "It's a bitch ... but I guess you've emascu-
lated me somehow" (p. 16).   When she makes timid sexual
advances, he explains that it makes him uncomfortable: "It
turns me off, you know?" (p. 17).   Julie's reaction is to
blame herself: "Ugly.   Oh God, I must be so ugly" (p. 17).
Even after she spends hours putting on nail polish, tweezing
her eyebrows, shaving legs, and doing isometrics, she looks
at her body and thinks: "Look at those buttocks, curdling
like milk, no wonder he can't stand me" (p. 73).   Finally
discovering that her husband has been unfaithful to her during most of their married life, has kept a log in erotic code
of orgasms and oral sex, and that his latest mistress is a
"friend" of theirs, she yields to anger; however, mixed with
the anger is the usual self-blame.

To prove why women stripped of any recognition as
persons are easy prey for men and for Madison Avenue huck-
sters, the author has Julie comment on a product named
"Fantlashtic. " This product promises women that it will
"Up Your Batting Average" (p. 49).   Fantlashtic consists of
false lashes implanted with glue on the eyelids and takes
four hours to apply. Despite the FTC's warning about gran-
ulated eyelids, says Julie, 5000 New York women hasten to
put down $375 for the process.

Granted we have become only too acquainted with this
kind of social comment, granted that the minute cataloging
of the wife's misery (her turning on the shower to drown the
sound of her tears, etc.) threatens at times to turn the novel
into soap opera, as Paul Zimmerman charges (Newsweek,

June 1, 1970). What saves the book from melodrama, however, is the author's careful detailing of Julie's actions and thoughts, which reveals how firmly they are grounded in self-hatred, anger, bitterness, need for expiation, sexual insecurity, and a masochism so strong that she becomes a symbol of a certain Gestalt perspective: that for the masochist it is better to be wanted as a victim than not to be wanted at all.

Another factor which lifts the narrative out of the ordinary and blends the important threads of story is Gould's setting. The hospital in which Julie spends most of her time allows the reader to respond imaginatively to certain grotesqueries and awful features of modern life. The verbal and psychological interplay between narrator and people surrounding Julie turn the hospital into a microcosm of society. The drama of the story then proceeds to derive from the fact that Julie is a victim who is often called upon for self-degrading cooperation in her own undoing--and, to our horror and hers, masochistically cooperates.

The hospital itself is a place in which the innocuous overnight belongings of Julie's husband, Richard, consisting of a bottle of Kaopectate and two boxes of Mallomars, are safely and carefully locked away. No attempt is made, however, to determine his reaction to the anesthetic which he is given for removal of a mole. The result is liver damage and coma. From there on, the hospital's actions and language toward Julie and her comatose husband revive the important theme in Camus' The Stranger--you are not noticed until behavior departs from "normal." Once Richard Messinger goes into coma, he becomes "interesting." His inert body is hooked up to machines which flush his kidneys and change his blood to a chorus of doctors clucking their approval. They congratulate themselves and each other on the "success" of the patient's response to plastic tubes and machinery. Their own role is to lean over and shout "Mr. Messinger" into his unhearing ears.

As for Julie, she is for the most part ignored or told what Mark Twain calls "lies, damned lies, and statistics." On the few occasions when she yields to spurts of anger or questions a doctor's carefully-spaced ambiguities, she is given a disapproving look. It takes very little of this to bring Julie to heel and have her chide herself for behaving like a "hysterical," "pre-menopausal" (p. 36) female.

The portrait of Julie which emerges is a terrifying

one. Locked in the flytrap of masochism, Julie says "yes" to everything: to endless cups of coffee thrust upon her, which induce nausea; to her mother's instructions that she dress with more chic; to doctors who thrust papers before her to sign; to Cal, whom she doesn't want to see again after she realizes that he has produced his own interpretation of his sexual impotency; to Miranda, her husband's latest mistress, who suggests the music for the husband's funeral. Above all, she says "yes" to Dr. Timmy Spector, "family friend."

It is in the relationship with Dr. Spector that we see the extent of her self-destructiveness and degrading cooperation in her own victimization. She allows Spector to appoint himself to the case and to call in various specialists--all the time aware that he is privately interested in sharpening his own professional reputation. Yet she continues to agree with him that her husband's condition is stabilizing, despite all evidence to the contrary, and assures Spector that he is doing a remarkable job. Occasionally, she asks questions which he brushes aside as irrelevant, hysterical, or hostile, and she apologizes.

In what can only be taken as the climactic scene between Spector and Julie, the author skillfully discloses to us her full knowledge of her narrator's weaknesses and self-hatred. After one of Julie's apologies, Spector squeezes her hand in forgiveness and asks her to accompany him to his apartment. She finds that his wife is away, accepts a drink that she doesn't want, and learns additional details of her husband's infidelities from Spector who, himself, has been habitually unfaithful to his wife. The two men have kept score of their sexual conquests and Spector proudly admits that he taught Richard all he knew.

The grotesque sequel to this scene presents an emotional counterpart to the Stalin trials of the thirties, in which prisoners, imbued with the doctrine of self-criticism, were brain-washed to welcome punishment as for their own good. Shivering with nerves, Julie offers no resistance when Spector pulls her to him and then begins to push her head down. She drops to her knees and attempts to unzip his fly: "show the nice doctor you appreciate his hurting you ..." (p. 191), "down on your knees" (p. 193). Remembering her husband's grudging praise of her expertise in oral sex, she frantically tries to unzip Spector's stuck zipper.

The scene is awful and sad, reminding one of Nabokov's Invitation to a Beheading in which the victim is expected to participate in his own self-degrading. In Invitation ... (Nabokov's answer to Stalin), Nabokov's hero Cin-
cinnatus refuses to act out the perversion of waltzing with
the warden. Not Julie. Spector gets superlative oral sex
and Julie, in her own words, commemorates the occasion
by removing a crinkly hair from her mouth and placing it
carefully in her pocketbook. As Joel Lieber says, it is an
awful, believable book (Saturday Review, June 13, 1970).

What braces the plot and makes Julie an awful, believable character is the style, which ranges over gallows
humor, satire, illuminating metaphors, self-parody, imaginary role-playing, and food imagery. The food imagery is
especially relevant because it not only reveals character, but
embodies emotion itself. The restaurant scene in which
Julie mechanically chews on shreds of lettuce as Cal Jaffe
tells her that Richard has been having an affair with Miranda
(Cal's roommate) has the crunch of pain in it. Her inward
state of being is eloquently revealed as she watches Cal poke
out the eye of his egg and bleed the yolk slowly on his plate.

Julie's increasing reactions to food in the cafeteria
and elsewhere convey her mounting revulsion for her "ugly
body," her hatred of her husband, and her feeling of sexual
humiliation. Frankfurters appear phallic-looking and intes-
tinal. Soda pop is poisonous in color. Particularly is her
sense of sexual humiliation expressed in her repulsion for
food that looks gelatinous: oozing pies, jello cut in perfect
cubes. It recalls Richard's preference for oral sex and his
flat refusal to reciprocate: "I don't like to do that" (p. 75).

The book is laced with a blend of humor consisting of
wisecracks, understatement, quips, ironical observations,
undercutting, and slang--all a means of conveying the narrator's attempts to deal with her emotions. Consider the following, when Julie hears Dr. Spector's lame explanation
that it just might have been the anesthetic which caused her
husband's coma. "Well, that's just great," replies Julie.
"Here's this big hospital with turrets and elevators and ...
soda machines, but somebody forgot to put in fresh anesthetic? No, the drug company did it. They had a nifty half-
price sale on slightly irregulars ... everybody loves a bargain" (p. 37). Told that the nurses were praying for autopsy
evidence that Richard's death was justified by cancer and
that they cried when informed that he was totally clean and

would have lived a normal life, Julie reacts characteristically. "Got a clean bill of health on my late husband ... Clean bill ... came to a little more than we figured on, but certainly ... probably ... worth it in the long ... run" (p. 265).

As her defenses threaten to buckle under the pressures connected with her husband's illness and the disclosures of his infidelities, Julie forces herself to visualize the situation as a play. Box office sales alternately flag and rally depending on the performances given by herself, doctors, and friends. With Dr. Mahler, she is grieving wife, hands clasped tremblingly to chin; with blood donors she is a woman undecided whether to waft them a celebrity kiss, or give a dignified wave of the hand in the manner of Elizabeth II. To preserve the illusion that the nightmare in which she is living is only a play, she constantly reminds herself: curtain time, lights dimming. She whispers reassurances to herself: "there you go, you big brave girl you ... fix your face for the nice people" (pp. 64-65). Sometimes she refers to herself in the third person: "Yessir, that little girl is all right" (p. 185) or urges herself to show "a little warm resentment" (p. 146).

Metaphors are expressive of her role as wife and mother. Where Bellow's Augie March philosophizes about America and likens it to a shapeless orange bursting with the juices of vitality, Lois Gould's heroine thinks in homely and domestic metaphors. Standing by her husband's bed and trying to sort out in her mind his motives for blaming her for his "impotence," she gives up: "all my ill-sorted reactions thudding and colliding soggily in my head like heavy blankets in the washing machine" (p. 150).

At first glance, the weakest part of the book appears to be the satire on the Jewish social scene in which Julie moves. No one is allowed any redeeming humanity. A visitor to the hospital is a "sickbed voyeur" (p. 66); relatives come out of duty; blood donors contribute their blood because they get a sense of well-being cheaply: "God, what other gift takes so little time, thought and effort and yields such an immediate, huge reward?" (p. 53). Over and over again, there is a heavy stress on the vulgarity, materialism, and over-preoccupation with social decorum of well-to-do American Jews. The wives of Richard's former Jewish fraternity brothers from Brown University wear red harlequin glasses and plant plastic orchids around the rims of their sunken bathtubs. A friend has a gold-plated garbage can. Jewish husbands provide their wives with decent minks before the age of forty. The very correct rabbi who eulogizes Richard at the funeral mispronounces his name as "Messingill" (similar to the name of a commercial douche).

The accumulation of evidence does not deflect us from recognizing that Julie's surrender to bitterness is so complete that she cannot accept or even consider the fact that the spurious and the noble may sometimes exist side by side. To do so would be to transcend self and the isolation in which her emotions root her. Now and then a human Julie threatens to break through. Thinking about the people who have come to the hospital, she muses that most of them showed up because they had to, but maybe, she adds, "they felt something like love" (p. 67). The idea is pushed away because of doubts. Only Laurie, who covers everything in sight with Contac paper and lives on coke, is her friend. She understands why, after Richard dies, Julie lets Spector, Miranda, and Cal take her home and stay with her: they belong, Julie tells her.

Lois Gould's Julie Messinger, like Ralph Ellison's black invisible man, lives in a world of betrayal and humiliation. Both writers translate the abstractions of personal and social relationships into human actuality. Like invisible man's color, history, and character, Julie's gender, past, and character are given to her to be struggled with at every turn. Thrust into a world in which humiliation and betrayal constantly trip her up, Julie responds with the same mixture of drug taking, confusion, hate, despair that the black man does. In a psychological sense, she, too, goes underground at the end, but without the hope that she will emerge. We leave her still sorting out her personal agony: "What it is, I guess, is that I don't really miss him; I miss something that must have been us. Because we were something, in spite of each other, weren't we?" (p. 283) (author's italics). Still afraid of emotion piercing through the Dexamyl with which she has armed herself, she turns flippant: "Anyway, anyway, we have--how does the phrase go?--we have parted amicably" (p. 283).

There is no tentative whisper of a new heroine here. For that we have to go to A Sea-Change, the author's latest novel. The solution to the shedding of old skin takes the unconventional turn into magic.

Lois Gould's A Sea-Change (1976) attempts to break
with her first work, Such Good Friends, and the subsequent
novels, Necessary Objects (1973) and Final Analysis (1974).
More specifically, the author's literary aim in this novel is
to make it thematically and, to a lesser degree, stylistically
different. While there is still the use of interior monologue
and role playing as in the first novel ("Let's run through it
once more, Jessie," says the heroine to herself) (p. 17),
there is none of the dark humor squeezed out of the sense-
less condition in which self-hating Julie Messinger finds herself. Nor does this book echo Julie's attempts to ward off
despair's debilitating power with wry comments and wisecracks on masculine and feminine roles. Instead, Jessie
Waterman, heroine of A Sea-Change, confronts the paradoxes
of her position as a woman, rejects her womanhood, and
elects to be a certain kind of "man"--organized, mechanical,
a sexual bully and predator of women. Where in Such Good
Friends there is detailed accuracy and subjective recording
of Julie's lonely struggle with the hostile forces of society,
A Sea-Change has an abstract plot teetering on a collection
of shaky symbols and metaphors.

In a New York Times article (September 19, 1976)
about books which she found interesting reading, Lois Gould
praises Amazon One by M. F. Beal as a book dealing with
"heroism and violence in women" and which discovers "the
fatal connection--with love." Possibly, this book might have
been an influence on the writing of her latest novel. Certainly, A Sea-Change is concerned with violence, sexual
bullying, and the power struggle between men and women.
But there is little heroism here, and only survival on a primal level in which men and women are stunted human beings,
and only the strongest elicits obedience and respect. In A
Sea-Change, we enter not so much the world of Amazon One
as the inverted world of Genet's Miracle of the Rose, in
which the passive and masochistic become the aggressor and
attacker. Genet's novel dramatizes the conversion of a
timid, passive "female" homosexual into an aggressive as-
saulter of Bulkaen, a weakling tattooed all over, even to his
eyelids. Gould's novel deals with a beautiful model, Jessie
Waterman, who for the space of her union with a much-
married man, years her senior, accepts humiliation and
abasement as the fabric of marriage. Then, by some fanciful means, she turns into a "man" and becomes authoritative,
bullying, domineering, and cruel at times. From this point
on, we are led into a world where human relationships are
devoid of any tenderness and only strength and power count.

As in Genet's book, the author seems to believe that
the weak are loved only for their ignominy. Jessie's husband refers to her "affectionately" as "crazy cunt" (p. 14)
and warns her that though she is his latest and best wife,
this does not necessarily mean that she will be his last.
Jessie's answer, we learn, is to smile and smile radiantly
as if he had just paid her a dazzling compliment. She is
aware that his sexual approach to her (and to other women,
including her best friend Kate) always contains a hint of violence followed by a blend of sexual tenderness which keeps
her alternately terrified and uncertain. But she accepts this
as the basis of "love" and does not permit herself the comfort of mystical consolation, as sometimes happens with
women in similar circumstances.

Eventually, the isolating experience takes its toll.
Jessie begins to lapse into silence. In silence, she performs
her wifely duties. But it is in the greater silence following
what appears to be rape one night, at the hands of a character only referred to as B. G. , that she begins to examine
the thinking that has dominated her life as a woman up to
this time. The result is anger, acknowledged hatred of men,
and the perverse desire to be B. G. --a black rapist who vio-
lates women and forces them to experience his power through
unconventional sex. Apparently, the author is convinced that
if you can't beat them (men), you should join them. The
basis for the reasoning is a belief that women have a certain weakness. They are aroused sexually by brutality; they
thrill to brutality. We are told that a bond of intimacy is
established between attacker and victim which makes for submission and slavishness on the part of the attacked woman.

No one will deny that some women fantasize about
rape and subjugation, and we need to comprehend this as a
key to woman's liberation and self-understanding. But the
book offers no insight into the problem, nor into how the
self can be released. Characters are maneuvered into the
position of puppet voices and speak in generalities, as we
shall see. In totality, the novel presents a cramped view
which forces us into a moral realm that holds no hope for
the future.

Genet's work is created out of his own life, one of
crime and homosexuality. The world of pimps, big shots,
and chickens, which he exalts as something beautiful, represents his freeing himself of society's moral concepts and
values. Lois Gould's novel seems to be fantasy--how does

it feel to be a man--a powerful, sexually-bullying man? To be more specific, it follows the fictional type of metaphysical fantasy with overtones of the man/woman struggle. Avoiding a fictional realism in which the concept of shifting identity constantly dissolves and is reconditioned, the author leans heavily on metaphor and symbol. The central character, Jessie, is first a weak and slavish woman, then an aggressive masculine figure, then a black rapist named B. G.

The transformation begins with B. G. 's assault on Jessie with pistol instead of penis, and culminates in Jessie's violation (at her own request) by coast guardsman Leo Bailey. Jessie's purpose in inviting the act is to kill any female weakness still lurking inside her. Metaphorically, Bailey's "kill ... in there" (p. 121) "destroys" Jessie's womb and her slavish self. Narrative technique paces the transformation by focusing first on Jessie's thought of B. G. , then juxtaposing Jessie's thinking with B. G. 's in the same paragraph, and finally showing Jessie totally embracing B. G. 's viewpoint: It's better to be a man than a woman. It's better yet to be a threatening man. Narration and fanciful plot often threaten to swamp the reader in confusion, but they do serve as a frail peg on which the author hangs some generalizations on the nature of women and men.

Some of these statements about women and men have been encountered before and are not without validity. The idea that women want to experience a man's brutality at some time or another, and be violated, is voiced by two such different writers as Anaïs Nin in her diary (1934-39) and William Faulkner in Sanctuary. Nin writes of experiencing a sensual tremor of fear at the sight of a brutal-looking man: "To be violated is perhaps a need in woman, a secret erotic need. I have to shake myself from the invasion of these violent images, awaken."[4] Faulkner's nubile, socially-prominent Temple Drake is described as looking inviolate and cool, but her eyes convey a discrete message to men. At the very moment of her rape, her scream contains not only protest but exultation.

The Faulknerian locker room idea that women ask for it and invite rape seems to find a concurring voice in A Sea-Change. It is the dark side of women as both writers see it. As a matter of fact, Gould's major rape scene is modeled on the one in Faulkner's Sanctuary. In Faulkner's book, Temple Drake's violation is through the mechanical means of Popeye's corn cob. Jessie's is accomplished with a steel gun. Popeye gets his sexual excitement not with the corncob, but later by watching Temple and Red (the thug and stud) make sexual love. In Gould's novel, there is an implied impression (or maybe it is Jessie's fantasy) that Jessie's husband Roy surprises B. G. with Jessie and is commanded to repeat B. G. 's sexual act on Jessie while B. G. watches.

It is an unlovely episode, but brutality, the writer maintains repeatedly, is what turns women on. Jessie responds to the cold steel with hard, raised nipples. Later, in another kind of scene, this time with a masculinized Jessie and a feminine, yielding Kate (her lover), we read that Kate reacts with erect nipples to Jessie's cuffing. Early in the book, the author steps in with a comment on women and their physical response to the sexual bullying of men like Roy Waterman, Jessie's husband: "There was still a yielding part of them--somewhere behind the knees, between the thighs, or deep inside the womb--that drew them to Roy Waterman in spite of themselves.... And even as they despised him ... their eyes blazed, that other part, wherever it was, still answered, Yes--oh, yes" (p. 30). Nipples? Knees? Thighs? Womb? Whatever? Author and reader are at a loss as to what part of woman's anatomy betrays (though evidence is weighted against the nipples).

One is tempted to speculate that if some women are sexually aroused by cruelty and brutality, perhaps economics may have something to do with it. Anaïs Nin, who admits to sensual tremors at the sight of a brutal-looking man, was often low on funds, but indigence was not a serious problem. Faulkner's Temple Drake and Gould's women are upper-middle-class women who do not suffer from a lack of money. The desire of these women to avoid boredom may be the spur to experience violence. Certainly, the economically-deprived women of Tillie Olsen's fiction, for whom the world's brutality is no abstraction, seldom eroticize or express longing for brutal men.

However, this is a limited comparison and unfair to writers like Nin, Gould, and others. For to them, as well as to many other writers, sex is often the testing ground for self. Perhaps this is why Lois Gould's Jessie, almost metamorphosed into B. G. , yet sensing some female weakness still hidden in her, swears to force it out "once and for all. Weaken and destroy. B. G. would understand" (p. 104). And what is it that B. G. understands? For men, there is no line

between intercourse and rape.   (We return to the world of
Joyce Carol Oates.)

In a scene whose intensity of feeling, with its expec-
tant mood of Jessie's final transformation into B. G. , is
played out with the coast guardsman Leo Bailey, Jessie
learns what she has always suspected.   Intercourse for the
male ("Thrust, drive, penetrate, shoot" p. 28) is always a
victory and rape is the ultimate thrill.   Leo Bailey, who
comes to the cottage to warn Jessie, Kate, and the children
of Hurricane Minerva's coming, is persuaded to stay.   After
much wine and prodding by Jessie, Leo admits to a youthful
gang rape of a defenseless girl: "it was exciting ... " but
"a man has to take his women alone, like anything else" (p.
115).   A page later, we read that the man is always in control during the sex act even if no rape is involved.   "I get
all the power back, and then some ... I won--" (p. 117).

How does it feel to be a sexual winner?   Jessie learns
during "hate fucking" when she comes to Leo's bed and whispers: give it to me "hard, and cold, and very fast" (p. 120).
Needless to say, Leo, while puzzled by the request, responds with alacrity.   His animalistic nature is conveyed
through such language as "howled" and "tearing. "   At the
moment of climax, there is an explosion of blood and semen
and the "hate fucking" becomes for Leo "the greatest ...
Only one other thing in the world ... would feel like this.
Killing. " (p. 121).

It is an anxious attempt to underscore Jessie's final
decision to become B. G. , for when she does she experiences
a great sense of release.   Gone are her early speculations
on how to survive as a woman by discovering appropriate
female weapons in this war of the sexes--some kind of sucking device.   The only thing that matters in this universe, as
far as Jessie is concerned, is power--and power is male--
and real power is B. G. --a male with a gun.

Whether or not there really is a B. G. or whether he
is a fantasy of the kind in which previous Gould heroines
indulge is irrelevant.   Throughout the novel, Jessie's imagination, anger, speculations constantly coalesce around the
shadowy figure of B. G.   Following the episode with Leo
Bailey and her determination to become B. G. , we are permitted fuller details of what happened the night B. G. entered
Jessie's bedroom and silently padded toward her bed.   The
question of time is handled competently.   There is no lumpy

flashback to this incident, which has so profoundly affected
Jessie's decision. Instead, prior to the climax just discussed, the writer moves from snatches of the past into the
present, giving us just enough detail to make us wonder what
had actually transpired. Following the scene with Bailey and
Jessie's metamorphosis into B. G., past and present are
allowed to meet and commingle:

> Look at that, the way [the gun] just nosed right in.
> Adapting. B. G. laughed. Bang.... After your
> husband has a turn. Fair enough; fair play. Roy
> could have used his own gun. No, man, she likes
> mine, B. G. had insisted. Look, man, look at that.
> They all like mine. Stop Roy, she had screamed.
> There was a sharp sudden sound, a bursting inside,
> something running red and black. B. G. had
> laughed. Jessie exploding red-black, red-black
> running down. Stop Roy ... And Roy would not
> stop ... (p. 122).

There is little omniscient control and interpretation
in this passage. Characters are allowed to speak in their
own voice and the cacophony of voices is filtered through
Jessie's consciousness. This is good writing, but it falters
when the author attempts to bring in nature and science as
metaphors for the male/female struggle. As angry Hurricane Minerva roars through the town lifting church steeples,
cutting swathes through flooded roadbeds and splitting the
beach club, "rapist" scientists attempt to break her down.
They send "their ejaculate in bomb casings" right into her
warm "cunt of the storm" (p. 66).

Still another version of the male/female struggle is
acted out by Jessie's precocious eight-year-old daughter,
with male dolls without penises and dolls of famous women--
Elizabeth I, Charlotte Corday, Catherine the Great, and Hat-
shepsut. Robin knows an awesome amount of history, such
as the fact that the Egyptian queen donned a beard in order
to gain her subjects' obedience and respect.

Under ideological pressures of this sort, language has
to surrender much of its ability to describe reality as well
as its logic. If Minerva is so powerful that she can with-
stand the gang rape of scientists and wreck everything in
sight until she decides to veer voluntarily off her course,
then why does Jessie feel it necessary to become a man?
Then, too, Jessie's final resolve to be B. G., leave Andrea

Island with the two children, Diane and Robin, for some re-
mote place where "he" can hunt, fish, and enjoy the favors
of the local belles is hardly different from the male/female
relationships described in the author's previous novels.
Furthermore, there are the children. Teenager Diane patterns herself after masculinized Jessie, and it should be remembered that at the height of the storm when Diane and
Robin are on the beach, Diane abandons her young half-sister and streaks off to save herself. It's Darwinian survival,
as far as she is concerned. As for the relationship between Jessie and Kate (when Kate finally rejoins her lover),
the keynote is set by a docile Kate upon her arrival at the
island when she learns that Jessie is not there: "I'll wait."

Without question, A Sea-Change demonstrates the author's doubts as to whether woman can become a mature
sexual being who refuses to yield to self-debasing acts and
insists on equality in the sexual relationship. Previous
novels, Such Good Friends and Final Analysis, dramatize
heroines who are scarcely distinguishable one from another.
They are women who are timid, indecisive, sexually insecure, masochistic, self-hating, given to masturbation,
fantasizing, self-parody, and a gallows humor which seldom
hides the pain behind the slang and wisecracks. Even the
rich Lowen sisters of Necessary Objects (1973), the writer's
second novel and the least interesting of her books, fall into
one or several of the categories listed above. They live
truncated lives and their neuroses are a commentary not
only on the materialism which dominates their culture, but
on the fact that affluent middle-class women who are dependent in one way or another on husband or father may
have lady-like status but no real autonomy.

The Lowen women spend their lives acquiring jewels
and husbands, redoing rooms, and manipulating their children's lives--only to continue an existence prescribed by
custom and tradition. They have no real power. Ultimately,
even Alison, who seems the strongest and most powerful of
the four sisters, is shown as a pawn of the homosexual Pem-
broke who finally takes charge of the store and her. As in
the first novel, Such Good Friends, the writer's women see
themselves as whole people only in connection with a man--
even if he is homosexual.

This is most forcibly brought out in Final Analysis,
which again presents the self-hating, masochistic heroine
("So that's what I really love most: hating me. The man

who helps me do it is the only lover I understand"--p. 37)
(author's italics). At one point, she hires a seaplane to
visit her lover, and he is reluctant to greet her when she
disembarks; it would disturb his tennis game. The book,
written largely in epistolary style, consisting of letters to
her lover (who is also her former analyst), bogs us down
for seventy-odd pages in material already made familiar to
us in previous books. It picks up, however, when we are
introduced to the world of business and the way men demean
women as workhorses and sex objects.

Toward the end there is an earnest effort to convince
the reader that love can eventually bloom between two psychologically crippled people. A man who has, for the most
part, treated a woman shabbily will be made to appreciate
the gift of love offered him, and become supportive of the
woman's efforts to realize herself creatively. However, in
this case the man's epiphany is aided by his own mistreat-
ment and conning done by a male "friend," whom he trusts
to the extent of investing thousands of dollars in a business
which never exists. In the democracy of suffering (his and
hers), love inevitably becomes a redemptive force. The
heroine is able to free herself from work bondage and experience a burst of creativity which results in an almost fin-
ished book.

It is a pat solution which seems a little hurriedly
tacked on. Furthermore, in the heroine's frantic scurrying
to get the cottage in order in preparation for the lover's
visit, and the cataloging of her psychological anxieties, there
is too much of the presence of the woman's previous guilt-
ridden self to make the new "she" (as she is referred to
throughout) convincing. Then, too, there is that final scene
in the book in which the heroine offers verbal as well as
physical comfort in the way of food, back rub, bathing, etc.,
until the man is happily asleep. Then, like a good housewife, her chores all done, she retires to the window to
write: "He was smiling in his sleep when she began to
write" (FA, p. 194). While we salute her humanity in offer-
ing comfort to her lover when he needs it, our minds are
also tweaked by memories of all those women who get to
their own work only after they have administered to the
house and to their mates.

The opening pages of A Sea-Change begin on a note
of hope--an angry woman. This angry woman, tied by B. G.
with strips of nylon which tighten with her every move, re-

flects that her present bonds are only the outer manifestation
of the bonds which have kept her imprisoned throughout her
life to this point. She has been filled with fears: of cars,
driving, Tampax, employers, husband, all men, and now B.
G. She broods on her indecisiveness, which makes meal-
ordering in a restaurant such a strain that her husband finally, contemptuously, takes it over for her. She reviews
the masochism which makes her continue her career of mod-
eling even though she hates it, so that she can hand over
her fees to the husband who in turn can coddle his ego by
sneering, "a model, after all" (p. 21). She counts the number of times she has wiped surfaces, dusted furniture,
washed dishes, prepared meals, and taken out garbage--al-
ways to a chorus of Roy's criticism of her competence, and
always at the expense of allowing no time for herself.

As we already know, Jessie is not permitted to stay
entangled in vacillations and indecision, but to embark on a
course of action. This process commences with her taking
Kate as lover. Through exercise and other means, she
loses her softness, grows angular and lean. Somewhere
she finds a tool belt and takes to wearing it slung low on
her hips, which helps to give her walk a masculine stride.
Even her voice deepens, takes on a commanding, harsh,
even brutal tone to Kate. Kate, in turn, becomes slavish
and submissive. To reenforce herself psychologically, Jessie sketches fantastic animals, male and female, and writes
in a corner of the sketch: "Active exercise of control is
necessary to establish and maintain social order" (p. 77)
(author's italics). Between the words "of" and "control" she
adds "male." After the episode with Bailey, she draws a
line through her signature "Jessie" and puts B. G.

Any hope that this novel will offer some new solution
to the man/woman struggle is soon quickly dissipated. In
the end, Jessie, now B. G. Kilroy (Kill Roy), elects flight
to some unknown island. In a sense, she follows in the
footsteps of countless American heroes who have sought to
find the self by withdrawing from the world which has hurt
them. But Jessie is not Hemingway's psychologically and
physically scarred Nick Adams, who retreats to the woods
in order to find dignity and peace of mind. Above all, she
is not Margaret Atwood's nameless heroine (Surfacing, 1972),
looking for some communion with nature as a last resort from
a world which is a spiritual wasteland for her. Together
with children and Kate, Jessie establishes the same order
of dominant and dominated in which she has always lived.

Both Jessie and Kate appear to be locked into habits and patterns of living which twist and atrophy the essential self, never
saying as does Margaret Atwood's heroine at the end: "This
above all, to refuse to be a victim ... I have to recant,
give up the old belief that I am powerless.... "[5] Kate, like
the "chickens" in Genet's Miracle of the Rose, passively
accepts the role of "necessary object" to Jessie.

There is a kinship with Genet in this latest novel by
Lois Gould in addition to the fact that the drama has another
ancestry--the relationship between man and woman. To be
fair, the writer does not celebrate her fictional universe in
the way Genet romanticizes the harsh, homosexual microcosm of the prison world as paradise. But she does follow
his lead in glorifying love between two people of the same
sex, in which one is a weakling and the other the big shot,
to use Genet's words.

From the beginning, even before Jessie turns into
B. G. , Jessie and Kate are aware of each other's bodies.
The language of love between them becomes wreathed in romantic imagery. For Kate, the taste of Jessie is "essences
of chypre and musk and oak moss until it [is] all blended
into a single rare perfume" (p. 59). At another time, she
sees Jessie as a beautiful woman who loves strawberries,
the color violet, the taste of vanilla. Jessie is glorified
even when she hits Kate. The author describes the marks
left on Kate's face as glowing "like scattered rose petals"
against the pale skin (p. 96).

Interestingly enough, before Jessie's metamorphosis
into "man" and B. G. , she considers Kate a parasite. But
she is not incensed by Kate sleeping with Roy, her husband.
Apparently, it is not Roy she wants but Kate. Sharing Roy
with Kate is one way of having Kate. For when Roy is out
of the picture (business trip), the scene becomes idyllic.
The two women (and children) laugh, joke, and smile at one
another. The deepening relationship between the two women
is conveyed both literally and figuratively. As the howling
wind swings doors open, the women's faces unfold in bright-
ness. We are told quite frankly that Jessie wants to experience loving a woman, and being loved by a woman (p.
68). She realizes her desire, as already described, and
though the path of true love does not at first run smoothly,
Kate rejoins Jessie/B. G. Kilroy on Reef Island, on New
Year's Day.

Lois Gould's moral universe is an uncompromising,

rigid one.   No categorical phrases allow for glimpses into
a world in which men and women or woman and woman can
achieve a proper balance between self-assertiveness and
those qualities of love, sympathy, honor, and integrity which
require a giving of oneself.   It's all a matter of power and
who holds it.

CHAPTER 4

GAIL GODWIN: ORDER AND ACCOMMODATION

Gail Godwin, on first reading, seems to stand apart from contemporary women writers. She appears immune to experiments with style and the contemporary raw language of sexuality. Her works are plotted symmetrically in the manner of George Eliot, whom she admires, and at a time when many women writers are primarily concerned with woman's emerging sexuality as well as with her active participation in the outside world, Godwin maintains that the demands of the inner woman are much more complex than this. Inner life, says her heroine, Jane Clifford (The Odd Woman, 1974), is as important as outer life. But it is obvious that the author considers the inner life even more important. Her first two novels, The Perfectionists (1970) and Glass People (1972), are clever, well-executed works about women who attempt to grapple with the domestic life and with sexual partnership. More specifically, the heroine of Glass People is confronted with what she comes to regard as the awful responsibility of freedom.

How to achieve freedom while in union with another person, and impose one's own order on life so as to find self-fulfillment, is the theme which runs through Godwin's works and becomes the major theme of exploration in her third novel, The Odd Woman, which will be the focus of this chapter. Where some other women writers maintain a pessimism about the man/woman relationship, Godwin has her heroine doggedly affirm that man and woman can be a unit; man and woman need each other. Yet it is worth noting that the heroine is alone in the end. The open ending, however, indicates that the author is still the writer of freedom, marriage, love, children, and the relationship between generations. Her subsequent work, Dream Children (1976), continues these themes with variations.

68

The optimism concerning men and women voiced by Jane Clifford of The Odd Woman is not present in the first two novels, nor is it markedly obvious in Dream Children, the collection of short stories following the novel. Though the idea that woman's destiny lies in a personal, meaningful relationship with man is stressed, there is a close affinity in the early novels and some of the short stories in Dream Children with Lois Gould's thinking that communication is a lost art in marriage and that wives have no identity for their husbands. Dane (a name which ironically connotes a fearless character), the heroine of The Perfectionists, quickly realizes that her hope of marriage to self-styled genius John Empson as a union of mind, spirit, and heart is doomed. The novel ends with Dane unable to say "yes" or "no" to her husband: "Either answer made her lose" (p. 204). Ultimately, she vents her frustrations on John's three-year-old illegitimate son (who never speaks), by beating him when he points to a glass of water instead of asking for it. Our last picture of Dane is of her mouthing the word "bastard" as she watches her husband scramble over some rocks in the distance.

In the second novel, Glass People, Francesca Bolt is the prized possession (like Elena in Joyce Carol Oates's Do With Me ...) of an ambitious, powerful district attorney. Francesca sleeps a great deal and on alternate days plucks her legs. She makes one "bolt" for freedom only to discover that this freedom represents a wrench from husband and "protection" which she cannot handle. Like her surname which has a double meaning, Francesca's action only fixes her more rigidly in the role where her husband places her. The ambivalences structured about her moral-psychological outlook, however, are too numerous to make her a distinct personality. We are left in the end with the same feelings of numbness and blankness which the heroine herself has exhibited throughout much of the story. The author's own impatience with Francesca is indicated in the irony surrounding Francesca's picking up a magazine and reading about the new woman who is "beautiful because she is bold in affirming her existence as a free being" (GP, p. 170) (author's italics).

The message of the book is that woman is frightened by freedom, wants man's protection, and that man doesn't want a flesh and blood woman, but a madonna. "She is like a vision" (GP, p. 196), says the saleslady helping Francesca into the new, expensive gown titled "The Madonna" from the

St. Axel collection. We read that the husband's eyes fill
with tears of adoration as he looks at his wife who is carrying another man's child. He has assured Francesca that it
makes no difference to him: "we will raise him" (GP, p.
202). It's a witty ingenious ending, but both novels emphasize women giving up the struggle to achieve some autonomy
and control over their lives in order to attain the peace and
sterility of total accommodation to their husbands' lives.

The story "Interstices" (DC) has a more sinister
message. A woman artist who allows herself to be frozen
in the domestic role suffers a breakdown. Hospitalized and
then returned home as cured, she is "refrozen" in her role
of wife/mother. Images of freezing, thawing, breaking down
and madness are conveyed through the minute detailing of
food thawing and spoiling in the refrigerator, the door of
which has been left ajar. The symbol of wife as a sweet
icy sherbet which the husband consumes almost daily comes
through in descriptions of lime, rasberry and orange sher-
bets melting onto cuts of thawing meat. (The husband has
stocked the freezer with huge quantities of sherbet.) The
idea that refreezing of food is often dangerous or even unthinkable is given a wider meaning in connection with a
wife's "refreezing." We learn that the wife plans to have
a party--to cook all the spoiled food and serve it to family
and guests. She herself will feed it to the baby.

For the most part, the author's fiction emphasizes
that the metamorphosis from clinging, dependent woman into
an individual who attempts to bring some control into her
life is a process filled with contradictions. Order and control, she implies, are part of an evolutionary procedure, in
which woman often finds herself caught in the middle of the
old sexual roles. This is most vividly brought out in the
latest novel (to date), The Odd Woman. For Jane Clifford,
through whose consciousness the story unfolds, order and
control, and organization are vital words. Reading and re-
reading George Gissing's The Odd Woman, a story of a poor,
uneducated, unmarried woman; researching George Eliot's
life, which seems to Jane a model of order; and observing
the lives of grandmother, mother, half-sister, colleagues,
and friends, Jane attempts to formulate a comprehensive
statement from all this and use it to impose order on her
own life.

The difficulty of overcoming the obstacles to woman's
control over her own life, and achieving self-determinism,

is dramatized as due to both human nature and very often, social conditions surrounding the individual. Though Jane is not one of Gissing's uneducated, illiterate women, she finds herself fragmented in relation to self, body, society, and other people in general--all this despite a concerted effort to chart a definite course of action. Several things point to her attempt to arrive at some kind of system, now that she is in her early thirties. Her life thus far has consisted of achieving a Ph. D. and teaching nineteenth-century British literature. As the story opens, we find her evaluating not only these accomplishments but her relationship as mistress to an almost fifty-year-old and married professor of art whom she has seen fourteen times in two years. What appears to militate against Jane more than anything else is her emotional vulnerability and, to a small degree, a nagging worry that over the centuries women have given up certain things to men and this has tipped the balance in favor of men. What those things are, she doesn't know.

Unlike Jessie Waterman of Lois Gould's A Sea-Change, who interprets order and control as the assumption of a masculinized identity, Jane has no intention of discarding her womanhood, nor does she strive to achieve power in the love relationship. She wants a union with a man very much like the one D. H. Lawrence has Birkin articulate in Women in Love. This is a relationship in which permanency is stressed, yet each is permitted to fulfill himself/herself in whatever way necessary. Decency, self-respect, loyalty balance one another, and the idea of separateness with union can be expressed in the phrase: separate yet whole. In other words, each one is free to build his/her own life without leaning on the other, yet each draws from the other the nourishment to do one's best work.

Jane does not think of Birkin and Ursula (if she did, she would realize that it is Birkin who sets the guidelines for the relationship with Ursula, with Ursula's willing consent), but of George Eliot and George Henry Lewes. Her research into the life of George Eliot, born Mary Ann Evans, has convinced her that the two did their best work together and enjoyed twenty-five years of outrageous happiness, as she tells her mother. Her mother's ironic retort is that if a woman wants twenty-five years of outrageous happiness, she had better learn to make accommodations in order "to keep the peace" (p. 180). This is what the mother has had to do. Hence, as modern woman attempting to wrestle with the concepts of order and control, Jane is at the same time

plagued by the word "accommodation" as she turns from her
idyllic literary models (Eliot and Lewes) to the lives of
grandmother Edith, mother Kitty, younger half-sister Emily,
and friends Gerda and Sonia--all of whom, with perhaps the
exception of the more enigmatic Sonia, seem to be making
compromises in one way or another. The reader perceives
that the reasoning, probing, questioning Jane, who attempts
to surround herself with the accouterments of order, lives
in the same state of troublesome anxiety, has the same preoccupations and fears, that we find in the heroines of Godwin's contemporaries. For example, the heroine of Francine
du Plessix Gray's novel Lovers and Tyrants speaks of the
way her husband's idea of order has obstructed her personal
freedom: "God how miserable he looks when a meal or a
fuck isn't on time, that's what an orderly life is about...."[1]

Reading Godwin's books, we discover the prose edged
with fear. The fear and the dread come from the same related sources: the anguish of being unloved and the dread of
increasing isolation which disintegrates identity. Jane
agrees with George Gissing and Ellen Glasgow that women
can do without marriage, but not without love. Living alone,
Jane tells her friend Sonia that it has certain advantages:
no one to please except oneself; you are one self, one
schedule. But Godwin's account clearly projects fear of
the penalty which isolation carries: the self splits into "tor-
mentor and victim." There is the terror of losing identity
and disintegrating (OW, p. 62).

This theme is even more brilliantly brought out in
the short story "Some Side Effects of Time Travel" (DC).
The thirty-one-year-old woman named Gretchen has tried
marriage, Scientology, ESP, Search and Discovery, and is
now a graduate student of English whose idols are a sixty-
one-year-old professor of Old English and Borges. When
Borges gives a colloquium at her school, she goes out and
buys a yellow jersey at Woolworth's because she has read
that yellow is the only color which Borges can see. Borges
keeps her pen after signing Dreamtigers for her and she
is thrilled that he will carry a part of her back into his
timeless world. Listening to her professor translate "The
Wanderer" as "he who is solitarily situated," she answers
inwardly, "yes" (p. 35). Gretchen identifies with the lost
world of the scop and believes that the Middle Ages will
come back, but with a difference. People will form a co-
hesion, but will be allowed to keep their egos. Confused
by a world of Burger Chefs, freeze-dried coffee which she

drinks sitting under posters of Che Guevara and Paul Mc-
Cartney, she often awakes not knowing what, where, or who
she is. To help herself, she carries voluminous notes with
her, and writes additional notes by the dozen. "Why can't
I just live?" (p. 59), she asks herself at one point. In the
end, she joins a clapping crowd watching a black girl dance
the Bugaloo, while the nearby pile driver supplies the beat.

Here again is something which women writers like
Gail Godwin share with male writers: the fear of entropy,
of not being. Where in writers like Updike there is the
fear of death as well as the sense of something lost which
gave meaning to the past, Godwin is not overly concerned
with death. She is close to Updike, however, in a nostal-
gia for the past.

For Updike, the former emphasis on religion, marriage, family, and pride in one's handicrafts gave life meaning. There is often a definite impression of the richness
of the past and the sterility of the present. In his bad novel
Couples (bad because of its blurred focus concerning sex and
lust), there is the implied concept that the only insulation
for modern man against the fear of nothingness and ultimate
death is in sexual union. In his other and better novels we
learn that if man cannot find his way to God, he must take
substitute routes. Godwin, too, looks back to the past in
the story cited above and in the novel The Odd Woman, but
with a difference. The past represents security. For Jane
Clifford, the past is often symbolized by her grandmother
Edith (she refuses to think of her grandmother as a symbol,
but a symbol she is).

Edith's life held no questions: you married a man so
that he would take care of you; you did not marry after his
death. You scented your sheets with lavender; you wore
white gloves and bought a new hat at Easter time. You
called upon a department store owner to tell him you were
coming in to buy some clothes, and he would be there to
assist you with your purchases. You did not socialize with
"common" people like the Wurtburgs who came from Detroit
and became your landlords; you gave your granddaughter a
European trip as a graduation gift. In short, you were a
scented, pampered woman--but one living within the rules
of your ordered society. You decided one day that you had
lived long enough, planned your own funeral, and finally
with God's help gave up the ghost. That was control. In
death, Jane sees her grandmother as "elegant," no fears

marring her face. In death, thinks Jane, Edith had rid herself finally of "troublesome womanhood" (OW, p. 139).

This last statement is puzzling, since at no time does the reader have any example of Edith being confused by her womanhood, or of the correct protocol which governs being a woman. Of course, she is disappointed in her daughter's marriages--the first to a charming but indigent man, and the second to a man who is a good provider but "common." She is also troubled, at times, by her granddaughter's unmarried state, but comfortably accepts the fact that perhaps this bookish granddaughter is better off unmarried. Though Jane is not entirely at ease with all of her grandmother's ideas, she loves her and admires her. This is why she often confuses principle with idealism and decorum with order. The two women are very much alike in their attachment to objects, and in their distrust of anything which disrupts a traditional way of life. They differ primarily in their concept of love and marriage. For Edith, love is not a necessary ingredient for marriage, for Jane it is the most important element in any man/woman relationship.

The grandmother's influence is an important one in Jane's life, since Jane lived with her as a child and spent weekends with her natural mother and stepfather. But together with Edith there are other figures from the past who play an important part in shaping her thinking. One is Cleva, Edith's sister, who runs away one night with an unknown actor and comes home in a coffin, the result of trying to give birth without medical aid. The baby lives, is brought up by a relative, and ironically turns into a woman whose life is a model of convention.

The other influence is George Eliot, as already mentioned, whom Jane had chosen as the subject of her Ph.D. thesis: The Theme of Guilt in the Novels of George Eliot. Though the wages of sin are death, as Edith consistently points out in bringing up Cleva's unhappy end to both Jane and her mother, Jane is tantalized and excited by the rebel Cleva. She is also awed by the courage of George Eliot, who as Marian Evans (so she chose to be called) went away with George Henry Lewes. In the face of disapproval by family and society, she achieved happiness and even acceptance by sanctimonious Queen Victoria of the Eliot/Lewes unorthodox union. Together with the figures from the past are Jane's contemporaries, women like Sonia Marks, who seem to have combined successful teaching and publishing of scholarly works with marriage and childbearing. And there is Gerda, who after a series of unfulfilling affairs (following her divorce), renounces men and becomes an ardent feminist.

In the works of Katherine Anne Porter the principal tension is provided by the necessity to change social and moral conditions and thinking. In Godwin's novel, the author attempts to generate tension from Jane's probings into the past, her speculations on the present, her clinging to objects and concepts which give her a sense of stability and identity, her fascination with great aunt Cleva and George Eliot, her efforts to establish a permanent relationship with a married man. Then, to complicate things further, Godwin places Jane on the boundary of two social classes, makes her a character more in affinity with the nineteenth century than the twentieth, and by these means dramatizes Jane Clifford as attempting to reconcile the discrepant and conflicting realities of her social and moral vision. Such an array of indecisions and conflicts might persuade the reader, but only if the author presents them organically. Here, Godwin often seems to be cataloging schematically the makings of an almost indigestibly complex situation.

As a result, it doesn't always work for the author any more than Jane's attempt to impose order on her life meets with much success. For Jane, order is "TF" (Tempus Fugit) as she affectionately calls her clock, which ticks faithfully and steadily by her side all night. But Jane suffers from insomnia and spends half the night reading or grading papers. She adores old houses, but lives in an apartment menaced by a prowler known as the Enema Bandit. When she is not in this place her time is spent shuttling between states to meet her lover, or waiting in airports for him or someone else to appear.

A believer in independence for women--both economic and emotional--she doesn't know whether or not she will have a job next year, or whether or not she will even be in America. The first is dependent on her department's reappointment of her, and the second revolves around her lover Gabriel being accepted for a Guggenheim. If he gets accepted, Jane will follow him to London, since his wife prefers not to go. She knows that it is only for a period of nine months, and after that all is in doubt. Still, she holds off putting up curtains for the apartment in anticipation of the trip.

All sorts of contradictions limn Jane's thinking. She
clings to an old silver salt shaker as a throwback to an elegant era, but this shaker serves as a prop for her book as
she eats a solitary dinner. She is convinced that family
relationships should be close, but realizes that the tender-
est exchanges between her and the family take place when
goodbyes are said at airports. She asserts her belief in
the articulation and power of words as the best way of communication, then finds herself in love with a man who stam-
mers, is given to monosyllabic phrases most of the time,
and can't bring himself to say "I love you." She is a firm
believer in the idea that one should know the exact hour of
one's birth (Mary Ann Evans was born at 5 a. m.), but discovers that her mother can't remember the hour of Jane's
birth and has kept no record. She believes that one's face
should make a certain impression on people, but is told by
various individuals that hers is so mobile that the total effect
is of a number of impressions. She wants friendship and
holds on to her friendship with her college mate Gerda for
more than a decade, only to have a rip-down fight with
Gerda at the end over their different modes of thinking and
living. She tells us that she prefers fictional figures to
live people because live people are sloppy and unpredictable,
but she wants Gabriel's living presence and seeks intimacy
with both men and women. Particularly, she wants closeness with her mother. Over and over again she maneuvers
to have a close, confidential chat with her mother; she tries
to read her mother's diary, and is chagrined when her mother takes it away from her.

It could be argued that the author is attempting to
show the formlessness and fluidity of life, which defies any
attempt to impose order on it. But the symmetrical form
of the novel, the careful plotting of characters as either
parallel or antithetical to one another, the dialogue, in which
a moral argument is set up only to be demolished by someone's counter-argument, all contradict this. Along with such
contradiction, the consistent use of flashback to put the present in perspective, as well as the rigid categories set up of
what constitutes the right and wrong social order, point to
the author's belief that both art and life must have a definite
pattern and correct structure. A good plot, says Jane Clifford, quoting Aristotle, "goes from possibility to probability
to necessity" (p. 143). In this respect, Gail Godwin, born
in Alabama and educated in the University of North Carolina
(as an undergraduate), is in the company of those Southern
writers for whom a concept of order must always be there

as a touchstone. She is very precise and articulate about
what she considers aesthetic order in writing: you must
find "the right shape for your story, " she says in The Writer
(September, 1975). Again, in the same magazine (December,
1976), she speaks of her own approach to writing: "My tools of
control are discipline, habit, intelligence, and skill. I must
work hard to sharpen them and keep them sharp. With them, I
attempt to create, out of the materials of my life, a fictional space...."

The fictional space or structure of The Odd Woman is
simple but carefully worked out. The novel begins and ends
with Jane alone, coping with insomnia, worrying about the
permanency of her job for next year, weeping over the loss
of Gabriel, speculating about the intellectual limitations of
students like Portia (who has just called her), and trembling
with fear that the sounds she hears may be the Enema Bandit attempting entry. As at the end of the first chapter,
Jane compensates for her fear by indulging in an erotic fantasy about the prowler.

It is in the author's characterization of people, where-
by characters exist as either foils or parallels to one another, that one may quarrel with the over-careful planning.
Episodes and scenes are set up to show striking similarities
or antitheses. Moral arguments are debated carefully, with
each character permitted to make appropriate rebuttal. Take,
for example, the contrast between Jane and Gerda. Jane's
upbringing is genteel, her environment sheltered, and she
goes from college (after the trip abroad) straight into graduate school, and from there into college teaching. Gerda's
people pull tobacco, are frequently hauled into court for
their stormy domestic scenes; and it is by Gerda's efforts
alone that she gets to college. Her life thereafter is one
of constant involvement in the world of action in one way or
another. She's contemptuous of Jane's reluctance to acquaint
her lover with her feelings, and finally tells Jane that she
has spent her life avoiding the "smell of reality. " Jane has
to cover everything up with "lovely old nineteenth-century
lies. " All she has had with Gabriel is "fourteen furtive
fucks over a period of two years. How's that for allitera-
tion?" she shouts (p. 398). Not to be outdone, Jane answers
with dignity that she doesn't have to listen to this street
language, and that all Gerda has been doing is blowing
around in circles and destroying everything she touches.
What she has had with Gabriel is beautiful. Both characters
are allowed equal time to refute each other's charges.

If Jane and Gerda are opposites in character, there
are similarities drawn between the lives of Jane and her
mother Kitty, both pictured as intelligent and charming wom-
en who believe they are living out of their time. Jane's
mother favors the Middle Ages and Jane, as we know, is
drawn not only to the nineteenth century but to the past in
general. The novel brings together the parallel between
Jane's love affair with an academician and Kitty's love for
a man who became a professor of literature. The two wom-
en are frustrated in their attempts to realize a permanent
union with the men they love. Kitty gives up one attempt
at happiness when Ray, her husband, ignorant of his wife's
destination, which is to join her lover, decides to accompany
her on the trip. Kitty's reason? Why risk peace and
security? Jane, her daughter, decides not to join Gabriel
for a final meeting before he goes home to his wife, because of her realization that he cannot make a decision between apples and oranges, as he refers to wife and mistress.
In essence, she is safeguarding security as her mother did
before her.

This kind of careful writing has a tendency to rob
the characters of their flesh-and-blood identity, rather than
dramatize what Doris Lessing has spoken of as the repetitive-
ness of human experience. The impression is reenforced by
the arguments pro and con on the subjects of marriage, love,
freedom, which threaten to take on a pre-digested, a priori
reasoning. When Jane cites the example of Eliot and Lewes,
Kitty is not only ironic about the idea of anyone enjoying
twenty-five years of outrageous happiness, but calls it a
myth. She got tired of myths, she declares to Jane: "they
leave out all the loose ends, all those messy, practical details that make living less than idyllic. That's why myths
can remain beautiful" (p. 169). Not only does the dialogue
have a predigested tone to it; it is also repetitious. Long
before we get to this interchange, we have noted Jane's inability to distinguish between the reality of marriage and her
romantic notions about it.

There is more of this kind of careful structuring,
which gives dialogue an overly-solicitous air and makes for
overlapping of ideas and sentiments. When Jane rhapsodizes
about Edith Wharton's old New York, there is Gerda's cynical, practical voice reminding Jane that Wharton's New York
had misery, poverty, and disease--all things of which Wharton did not write. Jane's uncertainty about asking Gabriel
if he intends to leave his wife is promptly answered by Gerda:

why don't you ask him? Gerda's voice is allowed to intrude
into Jane's inward monologues to mock her idealism and
dreams. The author's preoccupation with a neat setup, the
voice of experience versus the voice of idealism, gives the
novel a constricting quality of a fait accompli which prevents
it from moving toward a more expansive experience. The
reader has a feeling of being caged in the author's constrictions. It keeps one from getting a sense of Jane's discovery
of the difference between a fixed moral code and the moral
values that count in actual human conditions. Then, too,
while the dialogue completes a pattern or clinches an argument, it freezes the appearance of life. Godwin's Aris-
totelian idea of order seems to be invoked too arbitrarily
for the benefit of her purpose--the uncertainties of contemporary woman's life.

The restrictions in form which flaw the novel are
also present in the depiction of what the author, through
Jane Clifford, offers as the right and wrong social order.
Though the grandmother Edith is presented as not without
fault, since Kitty is allowed to point out these faults, her
set of principles is contrasted with those of Ray, Jane's
stepfather and twelve years younger than Jane's mother.
Edith is the old and settled order, as opposed to Ray, the
new order based on industrialism and "progress." He is
the disruptive element in a traditional society, and is never
happier than when he is tearing down fine old houses and
building new ones in their place with all kinds of fancy
plumbing. He relishes the demolition of old curving stair-
cases and secret rooms: "who [gives] a damn" about all
that (p. 88). He is the American Clifford Chatterley (Lady
Chatterley's Lover), who, unlike the more unfortunate Chatterley, has come back from the war with muscular legs and
arms, plus boundless crude physical energy--all devoted to
tearing down the old and installing the new. In his Mac-
Gregor shirt, hush puppy shoes, nasal twang, and indifference
to books, he is the man of the new social order.

As a matter of fact, Ray quickly changes from new
man to barbarian, in a family scene which shows Edith
quietly and regally enthroned under trees while the family
plays croquet. Ray cheats and his daughter Emily insists
he make restitution. He replies by knocking her down.
Once before he has used force on a member of his family.
Jane almost loses her hearing as a result of a box on the
ear. Edith's comment on him then and now is that some
people know how to act; others don't. The reader cannot

quarrel with this appraisal, though it has the ring of a concern more for decorum than for humanity. Jane's animus
toward Ray is revealed more cogently and in different ways,
giving us more than a hint of the extent of her dislike for
him and the reasons for it. He is condemned for using a
towel only once, for never washing a tub after bathing, for
constantly popping M&M's into a mouth of newly-capped
teeth, for installing furniture which wobbles, and for hanging mirrors which give back reflections like Woolworth's
twenty-five-cent photo machines. He awakens the family by
letting the dogs loose in the house, and opening bedroom
doors so the dogs can jump on the sleeping people.

There is nothing redeeming about Ray. Even his
father's death at the hands of a black burglar and the poverty of his family do not count for him. The tragedy turns
him into a bigot, and the former poverty now makes him
greedy and a hoarder. In an acidulous comment on Ray,
Jane theorizes that Ray has it all now: he is the father he
never had; the provider his mother had so desperately needed; "keeper of a queenly woman" who reads all night and
watches over him like a mother while he sleeps (p. 185).

Ray as the symbol of the new and bad order appears
again in the short story "Some Side Effects of Time Travel"
(DC). Here, he is again the "villain stepfather" (p. 38),
who has married an exceptional and talented woman who has
insomnia and reads all night (medieval literature and science
fiction) while the husband snores. This stepfather, like Ray,
is a successful builder. He tears down the old convent in
which the heroine Gretchen studied Thomas Aquinas and read
The Seven-Storey Mountain under the tutelage and love of
Mother Maloney. After the demolition of the convent, the
nuns move into a building which looks like a "grasshopper
about to jump" (p. 52). They bob their hair, shorten their
skirts, and throw away their veils. One saintly nun renounces her vows, goes to New York and writes an article
about her feelings during her first kiss. Mother Maloney,
who used to read Aquinas, now reads The Catcher in the
Rye.

Of course, as in The Odd Woman, the author allows
a dissenting voice to point out that the nuns' new habit is
more comfortable, etc. However, there is an obvious implication that the author is troubled by the corruptness of
what she sees as the mechanical and shifting present, in
contrast to the more idyllic and stable past. In The Odd

Woman, the author appears to be even more distrustful of
what disrupts the traditional life than of traditional stagna-
tion--which her grandmother Edith often represents for the
reader despite her granddaughter's loving depiction.

In D. H. Lawrence's Women in Love and Lady Chatterley's Lover, the values of an older and good pastoral
order in which human life held some dignity are contrasted
with the new, ugly, mechanical order in which humans are
regarded as objects. This is put into a single doctrinal
statement by the characterization of Gerald Crich (Women
in Love) and Clifford Chatterley, new masters of the new
society. Both men are represented as death presences in
this society; they destroy everything with which they come
into contact.

As we have noted, Gail Godwin's novel often looks
back to the values of a better past, but Ray as the man of
a new and bad order is no death presence in the sense that
Crich and Chatterley are. The most that can be concluded
against Ray is that he is insensitive, a bully at times, and
a man who likes new things in preference to old things.
What becomes evident is that his chief "crime" is his luck
in marrying a beautiful and talented woman who has a
daughter. This daughter hates him and seeks consolation
in literature of the past and in older men.

While the author certainly makes it clear that it is
difficult to hold on to guidelines in a shifting world, neither
Ray nor Edith can carry the burden of the Old versus the
New in The Odd Woman. The author is on safer ground
when she writes of today's academic publishing, or the act
of sex. Jane's remarks on the academic publishing of the
present as often designed to squeeze some dazed "wows"
and "cools" out of semiliterate children has a lot of truth
to it. But a more convincing insight into Godwin's quarrel
with modern civilization is in the short story "Layover"
(DC), in which she describes what modern mechanization
has done to the sexual life of men and women.

Godwin's heroine is "fed" into the airplane "through
narrow tubes with red-carpeted ramps" (p. 175). Fore-
stalling a stranger's attempt to pick her up, she goes out
and enters a room marked "For Members Only." Sitting
down on an imitation leather couch, she looks at the men
eying her and has a fantasy of endless copulation with them.
The language of commercial aviation provides a satirical

thrust (no pun intended) on the easy and uneasy transient relationships formed on these machines: "friendly" skies, "turbulence," "mechanical failure," "connection" (pp. 175-76). The title itself, "Layover," is a pun on the coarse word for sexual intercourse.

Godwin's horror at the impermanence of modern relationships and the way sex has often degenerated into an empty and sterile function is probably at the bottom of Jane's exhaustive references to George Eliot and Eliot's steady happiness and self-fulfillment with Lewes. It is the basis of her simplistic question to her mother: I want to know "whether there is eternal love between a man and a woman" (p. 167). However, without taking a Victorian stance of censure, it is hard to place much credence in the references to fidelity, since Jane herself is aware that she is mistress to a married man. The more important problem brought into focus in the novel is not the impermanence of human relationships nor instant sex, but the accommodations women make for love, or to marry, or to stay married.

It is clear from the start that Jane realizes that other people's lives, whether in literature or in real life, can offer only one vision and that one must eventually write one's own story; nevertheless, she examines these lives in relation to her own. First, she considers the paths taken by the women in her family: Grandmother, Mother, Half-Sister. The grandmother marries Hans because "he would take care of me." Kitty, Jane's mother, remarries for peace and security. Peace and security, concludes Jane from her observations of her mother, are won at the price of turning into the little woman when the husband's temper threatens to boil over. Jane watches with awe and admiration as the resourceful, talented Kitty is transformed into a weeping, clinging woman who completely disarms her husband. At another time, Jane reflects on her mother's diplomacy as she observes Mother placating both husband and daughter, who have just locked horns.

Emily, Jane's half-sister and junior by thirteen years, offers a different example of accommodation. She marries at fifteen to escape the dating game. Realizing that her husband needs to have his decisions made for him, she finds him a job designing refrigerators, and then takes herself off to law school. When not working, the two spend their time reading the funny papers, smoking, and drinking innumerable bottles of coke. Books and records are in alphabetical order, but the house is a mess of coke stains, cigarette burns, and overflowing ashtrays. Jane says she admires them for the "accommodation they have made to each other" (p. 60). There is an uneasy tone to the compliment, however, and veiled disapproval voiced in the reflection that Emily and John are like two children playing house and have no routine.

If the younger generation, and the mode of life which they represent and she cannot accept, baffle her, the lives of her friends puzzle her equally. Her colleague, Sonia Marks, appears to have it all: a good second marriage, children, an established teaching and publishing record. But there is an implication that much of Sonia's life is self-staging. Teaching, she tells Jane, is one-quarter preparation and three-fourths theater. Significantly, when Jane returns from her grandmother's funeral, Sonia asks: how did the funeral go? Then too, there is that curious reflection of Sonia's that when she thinks of Jane in connection with a man, it is with literary figures that she visualizes her: Knightly, Rochester, Heathcliff--and rejects them all. One can understand Jane's crestfallen reaction to this.

On the other hand, there is little theater about Jane's friend Gerda and much involvement in the actual world. Her solution, nevertheless, to the man/woman relationship offers little comfort to Jane. Men and women, she tells Jane (sounding like Hemingway's Jake Barnes in The Sun Also Rises), are basically creatures trying to get through the days and nights. She assures Jane that she no longer expects to be fulfilled emotionally by a man. Calling Jane an idealist, she asserts that she takes from men what she can get: a publisher's check every month for the paper she edits for him; a homosexual's companionship to the movies; and a rock singer's sex when he is in town. In the end, Gerda is seen more at home with the companionship of a woman like Eleanor, whose husband has left her for a young woman, than with men.

Of course, Jane is an idealist and she is, as usual, the first to admit it. We learn not only this fact, but everything else through her brooding solipsistic voice, which admits of no cosmic view of humanity, but only her particular humanity. For this reason, her lover, Gabriel Weeks (as his name implies), emerges not only as weak but as a shadowy figure. The author attempts to give him some flesh and blood substance by her description of him as a kind of Piers Plowman type: big, farmerish, ruddy, fading blonde. Yet he remains just a faded picture in our minds.

Perhaps this is due to the fact that despite the Piers Plow-man analogy, the writer really has Eliot's Casaubon (Middle-march) before her. There is Jane's recall of Casaubon and the way he filed his notes in pigeon holes, almost the way Gabriel files his notes in eleven shoe boxes (formerly be-longing to his wife). Then too, Jane knows from a reliable source that Gabriel's work on the three loves in the works of Pre-Raphaelites is bound to be a worthless mishmash, which is reminiscent of the adverse judgment passed on Ca-saubon's work by the omniscient narrator. However, where Eliot's Casaubon exists in a dimension of tragedy and we respond to his hidden futility of feeling, Gabriel is passion-less.

The tameness of the love affair overfloweth the read-er's cup with impatience. The fault is not all Gabriel's. Jane's constant grappling with order and control inhibits her sexually, as she herself realizes. She both wants and re-sists being carried away, and when she deliberately decides to let go, it is only by fantasizing about Aunt Cleva's illicit wedding night (on the train with her lover) that she is able to achieve sexual climax. At the end, analyzing her various reasons for entering into the relationship with Gabriel, and making a reasonable effort at detachment, she concludes that had she not met him she would have dreamed him up. The time was right. Sitting in her solitary carrel, writing her thesis on George Eliot, it was inevitable that her frozen emotions would begin to thaw with spring.

Jane's "rescue" into love ends in another confronta-tion with choice--a choice which rejects accommodation. Refusing to be Gabriel's patient Griselda and the coddler of his ego, she leaves him, but not without a lot of inward mental prodding. Godwin is making the point that an overly-controlled woman is even more vulnerable to the psychic pull of season. Nature has her own order beyond the ar-bitrarily elected. In the author's perception and projection of this, Godwin herself vividly and evocatively avoids the artificial order characterizing former scenes. Jane comes alive.

Gail Godwin's The Odd Woman is an interesting, sober, intelligent book. Technically, it is sometimes marred by the constant balancing of contrasting viewpoints. Read in conjunction with her other works, it is a happier view of the man/woman relationship and a woman's struggle to establish order in her life. There is a blur in the novel

about the concept of social order, but no blur appears about
the heroine's urge for some coherence, for some emotional
stability in a topsy-turvy modern world. She is not a
"boulder pusher" in the sense in which Doris Lessing's Anna
Wulf (The Golden Notebook) refers to herself. Imbued with
a morality derived from her Southern/Catholic upbringing,
Jane wants to believe that what is right and wrong in conduct is recognizable and unalterable. In this respect, she
sometimes sounds a little like Lessing's Molly (The Golden
Notebook), who in surveying the present is appalled at the
chaos in her generation. Molly comes to the conclusion
that the next generation will take one look at her generation,
get married at eighteen, forbid divorce, and go in for a
structured moral code.

The Odd Woman, at the same time, more than the
author's preceding and following fiction, offers an instructive
lesson in the strategies women employ to love, be loved,
to marry, and stay married. Considering and rejecting
both the strategies used and the accommodations women
make to men, Jane still clings to the idea that love between
man and woman is the only buffer against the isolation and
loneliness which bring about dissolution of identity. She
appears to echo what John Updike says in one of his essays:
"Our fundamental anxiety is that we do not exist--or will
cease to exist. Only in being loved do we find external
corroboration of the supremely high valuation each ego secretly assigns itself" (Paris Review, 1968).

Just what kind of love does Jane Clifford want? Despite her claim here and there that she would like the bored
intimacy of marriage, what emerges is that the love for
which Jane hungers is not the low-keyed domesticity she
sees about her and about which Updike writes with frequency,
nor does she want children. What she does want is sug-
gested by the love/work relationship enjoyed by some women
writers: George Eliot with George Henry Lewes, Colette
with Maurice Goudeket, Katherine Mansfield with John Mid-
dleton Murry. As for children, she sees herself as a female Charles Lamb spinning tales for her imaginary children
(it is no coincidence that Godwin's recent collection of short
stories is entitled Dream Children).

The denouement to Godwin's novel, as in all of her
novels, has an interesting twist. Recognizing and coming
to terms with being "an odd woman, " as Jane sees herself,
she sends a mental message to the Enema Bandit, whose

entry she has just feared. Make your oddities work for you, "instead of being driven by them" (p. 419), she instructs him. It is this unqualified endorsement of some kind of order which an individual must seek, that clings to Jane from beginning to end. Though fascinated by her brilliant student Howard's philosophy, she must reject it. He has told her, "life's not linear. It ebbs and flows. It's, like, Yang and Yin. It's contradictions ... People ... just flow" (p. 45). To the end, Jane believes that the tinkle of a piano in the lonely hours of the night signifies the effort of someone trying to "organize" (p. 419) beauty out of loneliness. Without question, the spirit of George Eliot hovers over the book, and Jane's motto seems to be Eliot's: "Seek a sure end" (p. 45).

CHAPTER 5

JOAN DIDION: THE HURTING WOMAN

Joan Didion is a prose writer whose vitality often
lies in the unsaid. Her style of silences between sentences,
word repetitions, short, staccato sentences, or a scene en-
compassed in one brief chapter offers a sharp contrast to
the brooding, ruminative method of Gail Godwin. The two
writers are not close either in their view of social disorder, sexual love, marriage, family, motherhood, women,
men, and life in general. Where Godwin seeks to unravel
the complexities of human relationships and to comprehend
and evaluate human experience, especially the nature of
woman's experience, Didion concentrates on the meaninglessness of existence. Godwin addresses herself to the possibilities of happiness in this life--a union between man and
woman wherein each would be free, yet find support, understanding, and happiness in the other person. Didion's young
women find no joy in family, in marriage, in affairs, in
sex, or in work. They cling forlornly to an edited dream
of family, motherhood, and domesticity. Ridden with guilt,
convinced of the enormity of their "sins," masochistically
accepting punishment for these sins, they finally reach the
breaking point in their conviction that there is no answer to the
pain in which they are fixed. They are, then, either institutionalized like Maria Wyeth (Play It As It Lays, 1972), or
they choose to die, as does Charlotte Douglas (A Book of
Common Prayer, 1977). This shift from Godwin's restrained
hope to Didion's bleak stoicism produces a very different
body of fiction.

Didion's fiction comes out of the background of the
sixties--her observations of youth cults, rock stars, the revolt against the establishment, drugs, casual sex, and runaway, lost children of fourteen sleeping on filthy floors.
Above everything, she is compassionate toward what she

87

sees as pale little children sired in a hallucinatory moment, or in a spurt of random lust. All of this is recorded in an essay, "Slouching Towards Bethlehem," in a book by the same title (1968). She shows us children left alone to chew on an electric cord, or children fed acid and peyote by mothers who are surrounded by friends on the way to some new commune. Or they are children who are handed a lighted joss stick to keep them quiet. "I start to ask," says the author, "if any of the other children in High Kindergarten get stoned, but I falter at the key words" (p. 128). For Didion, the family, social and personal disorder observed in the Haight-Ashbury district of San Francisco was symptomatic of a severe American cultural decline. Hence, children--lost in one way or another--are pervasive themes in the last two novels discussed here.

More than even a cultural dissolution, the year 1967 was for Didion a time of chaos resembling that of modern war, in which parents and children were separated, and adolescent and teen-age children became roving gangs seeking some new thrill, drug, or "happening." She catches the very taste and sound of this "war" in her essay. "This year's gonna be wild," says fifteen-year-old runaway Debbie. "We're just gonna let it all happen," chimes in her sixteen-year-old companion Jeff (pp. 91-92). "I hear New York's a bummer" (p. 87), comments a sixteen-year-old who has been drifting from city to city and has just come from Los Angeles. "I been out of my mind for three days" (p. 86), says this same sixteen-year-old who has been shooting crystal. "I just sort of know the Dead" (p. 90), giggles a pretty, little girl whose baby fat still clings to her and who has been following the rock group from place to place.

Didion records a fourteen-year-old school girl carrying her books, being picked up by cops, and given a painful pelvic examination. She tells us of young people who live in the deserted garage of a condemned hotel which they call The Warehouse. She describes the shaking hand of a twenty-three-year-old as he tries to light a cigarette. The rape of young girls on Haight Street, we learn, is as common "as bullshit" (p. 101). There are casual killings and groups of guerrillas assemble frequently for open confrontations. The author is filled with horror and dismay: "It was not a country under enemy siege. It was the United States of America in the cold late spring of 1967 ..." (p. 84). She is convinced that "we had aborted ourselves and butchered the job ..." (p. 85).

The essay is not a polemic, but an important clue to the author's future works. In the Preface to the book the author tells us that certain lines from Yeats's "The Second Coming" kept reverberating in her ears during the stay in Haight-Ashbury: "The widening gyre, the falcon which does not hear the falconer, the gaze blank and pitiless as the sun ... " (p. xi). These became her referents and images which formed a pattern to what she was witnessing. Made physically ill by the very effort of writing "Slouching Towards Bethlehem," Didion confesses that she was in such pain during this period that she drank gin and hot water and took Dexedrine to blunt the pain--but kept on writing.

In her role as reporter, Didion became convinced that the "social hemorrhaging" (p. 85) found in Haight-Ashbury was indicative of the cancer sapping the life blood of an America once sustained by the proud tradition of the Old West--family, children, parents, grandparents. It also convinced her that she herself must come to terms with the personal disorder about her. The result is not only "Slouching Towards Bethlehem" and other essays (among them one on John Wayne entitled "John Wayne: A Love Song"), but two novels. These are Play It As It Lays and A Book of Common Prayer. Her first novel, Run River, was published in 1961. It deals with a woman, Lily Knight McClellan, whose uncertain progress through marriage, incidental love affairs, and a general feeling of not knowing what it is all about foreshadow the future Didion woman for whom, in Yeats's words, "the center cannot hold."

A mood of great desolation, loss, sadness, and impending doom lies over the last two novels. Yet in Maria Wyeth's resolve to get her daughter back and her determination to endure no matter what happens, and in Charlotte Douglas's decision that death is better than flight, we also have more than a hint of what the author perceives as grace under pressure. Indeed, the name "Grace," chosen for sixty-year-old Grace Strasser-Mendana, née Tabor, the narrator of A Book of Common Prayer, is no coincidence. Living with a treacherous body which breeds pancreatic cancer, and in a corrupt Central American country called Boca Grande which breeds revolutions that change nothing, Grace is described as facing life stoically, realistically, and with compassion for the suffering and death of women like Charlotte Douglas. Judging from the many deaths in Didion's fiction, it would appear that she is in love with death almost as much as Hemingway was.

One senses the presence of Hemingway in other ways. World War I and the peace that followed convinced Hemingway that war was a metaphor for life. The sense of dark, destructive evil loose in the world, the cruelty and selfishness of people, the apprehension that there is something aberrant and unpredictable about the universe made for an existentialist philosophy of life. His view of the overall decline of society and of the values which formerly held people together dictated his themes of breakdown, violence, psychological wounding, sense of loss, and urge to escape-- all of which surround his heroes. Their response to the world was not only flight, but the formulation of a personal code of honor which, when tested, could be found to provide them with courage under stress.

The "war" which Didion witnessed in Haight-Ashbury has much to do with her clinical studies of women whose tragedy is aimlessness. However, judging from the author's remarks to interviewers about her own personal sense of loss, it seems that her bleak view of life and her general disillusionment with present American society goes even further back than Haight-Ashbury. It has to do with the vanishing of the Old West. "I come from California, come from a family, or a congeries of families, that has always been in the Sacramento Valley" (Harper's, December, 1971). She mourns: "All that is constant about the California of my childhood is the rate at which it disappears" (Harper's, December, 1971).

This kind of perspective links her to contemporary writers who examine what they perceive as an endangered environment. Like so many recent writers, she shares with them a longing for an older pastoral America not spoiled by smog, supermarkets, factories and all of the poisons of modern technology. For example, Brautigan's Trout Fishing in America and In Watermelon Sugar are whimsical exercises not only of future Edens, but also exhibit a longing "to go back to what once was." He wants to share in an idyl, a time when life was more gentle, more good; aggression and greed did not stalk the land; statistics did not clog our humanity; nor crime erupt in the streets. Rivers ran pure and strong and the trout fishing was always fine. Before Brautigan, we have Hemingway's stories of Upper Michigan in which he writes of a past which to him represents a vanished American Garden of Eden.

The romanticizing that sometimes clings to Heming-

way's descriptions of men in nature, and away from cities
despoiled by machines, dirt, crime, violence, greed, also
limns Didion's concept of the Old West. It is evident in
her remarks on John Wayne and the Western film. Despite
her attempt to mock her own school girl crush on Wayne,
she appears to see him as the prototype of the once hearty,
big, confident Western man. This was a man who was sure
of himself, of his sexuality, his world, his freedom, and
the code by which he lived. The language in which she describes the kind of Western film that Wayne makes may be
tinged with irony in the beginning, but the lyrical ending be-
lies the mockery and the impression that she is talking just
about an actor and Western films. Here are her remarks
on Wayne and his friends after she has visited them on the
set: "they could still, for just so long as the picture lasted,
maintain a world peculiar to men who like to make Westerns,
a world of loyalties and fond raillery, of sentiment and
shared cigars, of interminable desultory recollections; camp-
fire talk, its only point to keep a human voice raised against
the night, the wind, the rustlings in the brush" (p. 36).

What starts out as a comment on actors making a
Western film turns into a panegyric of these men as strong
Western types themselves. Wayne comes through as a man
who likes jokes, male camaraderie, and has that kind of
courage which enables him to face lung cancer and lick it
with the same bravery he exhibits toward a beast lurking in
the brush. He is also a man who refuses to shirk his "responsibilities" to others by working despite a cold which
necessitates an oxygen inhalator on the set. He frowns on
the breaking of rules and believes "nothing mattered but the
Code" (p. 37). Rules and a code of behavior are tremendously important to Didion, daughter of an army officer.
In her indictment of adults in "Slouching Towards Bethlehem, " she comments that between 1945 and 1967 adults had
neglected to tell children "the rules of the game we happened
to be playing. Maybe we had stopped believing in the rules
ourselves ... " (p. 123), she concludes.

Since it is not always clear to the reader just what
rules women in Didion's novels are supposed to play by, it
is important to mention the author's further comments on
John Wayne. She recalls Wayne joining his buddies, one of
whom is Dean Martin, in making "gentle, old-fashioned fun
of wives, those civilizers, those tamers" (p. 38). The encomium to Wayne ends with a description of the music of
guitars and the popping of corks from bottles of Pouilly-

Fuissé. It seems that Didion and her husband met Wayne some time after the visit to the film set. The place was Mexico and Wayne was with his wife Pilar (to whom he is no longer married?). The foursome dined together. The Duke ordered wine for everybody, guitarists appeared, and for the author, "they did not quite get the beat right, but even now I can hear them ..." (p. 41).

There are no gentle but strong types in Maria Wyeth's life (Play It ...), no past to look back on, and no future to look forward to. The town of Silver Wells, Nevada, in which she was born, is now the middle of a missile range. Maria has trouble, she tells us, recalling the past "as it was" (author's italics) (p. 5). Just one memory out of her childhood stays with her: the three of them--gambling father, pretty mother, and Maria as a child--tooling down the highway. Her mother has a wilted gardenia in her hair, her father a fifth of Jim Beam on the floor-board. From the coziness inside of the car, Maria glimpses snakes stretched out on the warm asphalt. But it's all gone now. Her mother dies alone in the desert after an accident and coyotes tear her body. Her father dies soon after Maria's marriage to Carter. When Maria tries to look up Benny, an old family friend, at the address which he has given her, she finds that no one knows him. The strange woman who answers the door becomes abusive and accuses Maria of snooping around to get some incriminating information against her.

The present for Maria, as we learn at the beginning of the book, is a neurologically-impaired child named Kate who is institutionalized. It is also a divorced husband whose parting love words to her are: "Fucking vegetable" (p. 184), and that insult which, for men like Carter, is the supreme insult: "You're going to get old" (p. 195) (author's italics). We leave Maria at the end in a state of psychological arrest: sitting in the sun, throwing an I Ching, or coins into the fountain, watching a hummingbird and telling us that she knows what nothing means.

The story is told in an accumulation of stylistic patterns reminiscent of Hemingway. Maria's present and past are presented in the first person with a shift to third person and then back to first person again. The form of the story is the episodic structure, a favorite of Hemingway's, which he made famous with the publication of In Our Time. Didion adapts his style to her own purposes and makes distinctly her own the use of tight one-line sentences, terse, cryptic exchange of dialogue, repetition of words, lack of cultivation of adjectives and verbs. She also employs Hemingway's habit of omitting things from stories in order, as he once said, to make people feel something more than they understood. One example will suffice. Carter asks Maria to come out and watch him shoot. Maria, who is now divorced from Carter, answers: "Maybe later" (p. 196). On the next page, he repeats his request. Once more Maria answers "later" (p. 197). We see her studying photographs of highway accidents, using a magnifying glass for details not easily discernible in the photograph: a rattlesnake, or false teeth on the highway. The omissions, together with the repetitions, give the reader a sense of some terrible anguish in Maria which is connected with her mother, but it is difficult to piece the story together and get at the root of her problem within the framework of the novel.

The book gives further impressions of a Hemingway-esque style in the interaction of setting and subject. In The Sun Also Rises, A Farewell to Arms, and continuing down to The Old Man and the Sea, social scene is definitely linked to character. In Didion's work, Maria's growing disengagement from life, her philosophy of nothing matters, her increasing sense of unreality, which finally culminates in breakdown, are specifically connected with the corrupt social scene about her. First, we are treated to that phenomenon of American life in which a beautiful, eighteen-year-old girl with a rudimentary high school education can go to New York, become a model and earn more than a hundred dollars an hour posing. The next step for her, as it happens to Maria, is films and marriage to an up-and-coming film director. The Hollywood scene the author portrays is one where everything is tainted and unreal, and women are treated as properties to be bought, sold, exchanged, beaten, and instructed in the proper way to give a man his sexual fulfillment. "Don't move, I said don't move" (author's italics), says the film actor with whom Maria goes to bed after her breakup with husband. The actor then proceeds to break an amyl nitrite popper under his nose to increase his sensation of orgasm. "Terrific," he says with his eyes closed, and instructs her to wake him up in three hours with her tongue (p. 152).

With depersonalized compression, we are shown a world in which the water in the swimming pool is always 85 degrees, reconstituted lemon juice is used for drinks, a

millionaire producer is a homosexual with a death wish so
strong that he finally yields to it. His wife is paid by his
mother to stay with him. Her chief interests are gossip
about which lesbian is sleeping with whom and the styling
of hair. If her hairdresser goes out of town, she becomes hysterical. The men around Maria all engage in
wheeling and dealing of one kind or another. Both men and
women feel that life is so arid that all kinds of palliatives--
drink, drugs, perversions--are necessary in order to make
life more bearable.

Didion's focus throughout is on Maria Wyeth, and
much has been written about Maria's passivity. What is
evident is that most of her ideas come from a series of
weak or worthless men and there seems to be no effort on
Maria's part to formulate any thinking of her own. She admits that she never had any plans. The passivity begins
with her father, who hands along his gambler's philosophy
to her: life is a crap game; "it goes as it lays, don't do
it the hard way" (p. 199) (author's italics). "What came in
on the next roll would always be better than what went out
on the last" (p. 3). To console her for her mother's death,
he assures her that God or "Something" is watching over
her and Maria is "holding all the aces" (p. 7). Nothing in
Maria's life gives her any proof of a deity watching over
her and her inner question is justifiable: if she is holding
the aces, what is the game?

The men she sleeps with, marries, or meets are for
the most part moral bankrupts. Her first lover, Ivan Cos-
tello, sets forth the guidelines for their relationship: he's
not going to do anything, there will be no money, no marriage, and no baby. If she makes any money, he'll spend
it. Maria timidly asks, what if she does get pregnant?
No, says Ivan with finality: "You wouldn't" (p. 141). The
next man in Maria's life is Carter, whom she marries.
He puts her into a picture featuring gang rape which his
boss views frequently in private showings. Carter is careful to remind Maria that she must make the right contacts
for him. His public image of himself is extremely important. When he learns that Maria is to have a child and that
there is a possibility that it is not his, he orders an abortion. Where Maria's father sees life as a crap game, Carter sees it as a script in which his wife has a definite role
to play. Later, we learn that her lover, Les, wants her
to view life as a joke.

Many of Maria's actions strain our credulity, but we

do come to realize that her confusion and passivity stem
from being handed a prefabricated male language in which
to think. We see her confusion when Carter tells her that
she must either get an abortion or he will take Kate away
from her. Accustomed to using the language of film when
with him, she thinks of the scene between herself and Carter in film terms. It is an "obligatory" scene and she wonders how long the scene should play (p. 50). The next day,
her inner thoughts switch from film language to the gambling
language used by her father: Carter is "confident in his
hand" (p. 54). No language works for Maria which will enable her to understand the life about her and what she is
permitting to happen to her. When she calls Les for help
and whispers over the phone that something bad is about to
occur, he laughs, assures her that something bad is going
to happen to everyone. Then he jokes, and is puzzled that
Maria doesn't laugh. There is also the language of people
with whom she comes into contact, like the man who tells
Carter: "what I like about your wife, Carter, is she's not
a cunt" (p. 26).

Living in what she sees as a world of evil and of
disorder, Maria makes various attempts to impose order on
her life. Primarily, these take the form of clinging to
Kate, cherishing a dream of domesticity, and conceiving
another child. Even after the abortion, she imagines living
with Kate and Les by the sea in a house in which every
piece of china and linen would be known to her. She would
cook, Kate would do her lessons under kerosene light, and
they would eat opalescent mussels. The dream always ends
with her realization that Les is married, Kate is retarded,
and mussels come from polluted waters. Her answer, at
one point, is to go out and buy a silver vinyl dress; attend
a party in which she has no interest, and try to forget
about the foetus she has aborted.

Before the abortion, Maria busies herself with rituals
in the desperate hope that they will stave off the reality before her. She drives on the Freeway for hours because
navigation of the difficult road gives her the illusion of control. She cleans drawers, buys a bassinet, and confides in
a parking lot attendant that she is pregnant. To convey
Maria's horror of the abortion as an unnatural act, Didion
fuses character and landscape. The night before the abortion, nature itself seems to protest the act. Not only does
the house crackle with "malign electricity" (p. 72), but
leaves fling themselves against the screens, daisies are

snapped off their stems, a drain pipe breaks, and the concrete around the swimming pool is littered with palm fronds.

Whether or not Didion is writing an anti-abortion
tract, as some have pointed out, is irrelevant. What comes
through is a woman's feeling about her body and the life she
is carrying. The huge T over the supermarket parking lot
in which she meets the abortionist's contact symbolizes the
Calvary Didion wants us to know that Maria is experiencing.
Her auctorial irony reveals itself in the guide's self-con-
gratulatory remark that he's a missionary as he hands
Maria a filter, an aid to stop smoking--as he has done himself. Irony is also evident in the doctor's consoling remark
to Maria after the abortion: just look at it as a menstrual
period. He then adds, "it's in that pail" (p. 82).

From this point on, Maria's attempts at survival
through ritual order become more and more intense. To
close off memories of foetuses floating in sewers, she
keeps changing apartments until one day she admits to herself that they all have plumbing. She agrees to a divorce
and goes through it at Carter's suggestion. Seeing an ad in
a paper from a hypnotist, she pays him a visit and realizes
that this act is as unsatisfactory as changing apartments.
She makes up an incongruous list of things she would never
do: "walk through the Sands or Caesar's alone after midnight ... ball at a party, do S-M unless she wanted to ..."
(p. 135) (author's italics).

The nadir of Maria's life is reached when she agrees
to go on location with ex-husband Carter. Here again character and landscape merge to give us a picture of utter desolation. Maria is in a motel made of cement blocks, in a
town built on a dry river bed. Hundreds of empty miles
stretch about this place. The temperature hovers between
120 and 130 degrees. There are only two trees in the
river bed, one of which is dead. To make the scene
one of even more uncompromising desolation, we learn
that it is a place in which old people await their end.
For the writer, it appears to be an appropriate place
for a woman who believes that her sins are "unpardonable"
(p. 2) and who doesn't hope for reward but only for punish-
ment--swift and personal. The typography is enlisted to
convey Maria's growing sense of alienation. As the feeling
of emptiness widens in Maria, the chapters become shorter
and shorter, with much white space about them.

Why? one asks. Why does Maria believe that she

deserves to be punished? What code has she violated? It
is difficult to find the answer in the book because of the
author's moral ambiguity. The references to the dead mother which keep cropping up give us some faint clues. The
real answer is in Didion's essay "On Morality" (Slouching ...).
If one studies the essay carefully and then returns to Play It
As It Lays, it appears that Maria's deep sense of guilt and
her conviction that her sins are unpardonable are due to
the idea that she has sinned in the ancient sense: she has
not considered kin first, not given kin proper burial. Didion
writes in this essay: "Whether or not a corpse is torn
apart by coyotes may seem only a sentimental consideration,
but of course it is more: one of the promises we make to
one another is that we will try to retrieve our casualties,
try not to abandon our dead to the coyotes" (p. 158).

In keeping with the author's concept of the Old West
and this code which she defines as "wagon-train morality,"
she defends it as the only social code that makes for survival. In life, as in war, there must be respect for the
dead, and there must be proper ritual in burying the dead--
or we run the risk of having bad dreams.

This is precisely what Didion dramatizes as happening to Maria. Maria has very, very bad dreams. She is
tormented by the fact that instead of giving money to her
mother for that trip her mother had dreamed about, she
gave it to worthless Ivan. She is also haunted by the memory of the mother's body torn by coyotes after her accident,
as already mentioned. From the careful insertion of such
facts at various points in the story, somehow one gets the
impression that in the view of the author, Maria does deserve punishment. If we look at the essay "On Morality"
once more, we see that in Didion terms Maria has deserted
her mother, abdicated her responsibilities and breached a
primary loyalty. Didion writes: "our loyalties [are] to those
we love" (p. 161). Obviously, then, since it was the mother
whom Maria loved and not Ivan (her relationship with Ivan
seems primarily sexual), then it is her mother who should
have received her utmost consideration.

The trouble with the story is that it rests on a cluster
of emotions and assumptions created around the chief character which are carried to the point where only pain is welcome and all comfort refused. We sympathize with Maria's
anguish both over her failure to carry out the mother's
dream to travel and over the circumstances under which the

mother met death. But we also discern that such clinging
to wagon-train morality is like obsession with original sin.
Maria's sense of sin and guilt leads to such hopelessness
that she is unable to do anything about her life. Believing
that there can be no possible expiation for this sin and
others she has committed, Maria can only hope for endurance
to survive. The past, then, instead of providing some guidelines for the present, becomes an eternal graveyard with an
unburied corpse in it. Instead of a woman who believes
that she has a right to some personal identity beyond that
of daughter or mother, we have a woman whose only dignity lies in knowledge of the void before her. Since the
story opens with a speculation on the evil in Shakespeare's
Iago, perhaps the final comment on Maria should be Othello's
on Desdemona: "the pity of it."

Didion's third novel, A Book of Common Prayer,
brings together the same tensions and themes found in the
second novel. Here again are the gaping holes in woman's
education which often make for vapidity and docility; relationships with men in which all the rules are set by men;
the dream of motherhood which turns into nightmare; the
clinging to family and the past, which then becomes a burden; the efforts of woman through various private rituals to
systematize and make coherent the confusion surrounding
her. Furthermore, there is the feverish editing of events
and memories by woman in order to cope with the reality
which threatens to overwhelm her. Finally, there is the
woman's stoical decision which gives her a last chance at
some moral choice and poise. The treatment of the book,
however, is more ambitious and extensive than that of the
second novel. It has to do with the religious title and use
of themes found in the Anglican Book of Common Prayer:
invocation, order in a communal sense, general confession,
rediscovery of one's soul, etc. There is also a stylistic
break with the second novel in the choice of narrator and
setting.

The choice of sixty-year-old Grace Strasser-Mendana,
née Tabor, as narrator is an interesting technical experience,
but one which ultimately makes us ask: do we close the
book with our vision enlarged and our sympathies aroused
for the particular destinies displayed, especially that of
Charlotte Douglas, the focus of the study? Is there a sense
of unfolding experience through the chief character's inter-
actions with family, husband, children, local community,

and to the whole of society, which gives us compassionate insight into her? What about the narrator and her use of irony? Is this irony sometimes self-inclusive or is it simply directed at the surveyal of the social sense?

To begin with an examination of the impressive substance of this book, we note that the narrator's method is to start with a capsule comment on the dead Charlotte. In the next paragraph she gives us her own brief biography. There is a weaving back and forth in time, sketching, at first, parallels and great contrasts between herself and Charlotte. Interposed are comments on social scene and character. The careful air of detachment and the distance between subject and narrator gradually begin to narrow, until the narrator completely identifies with Charlotte, to the point where she speaks of their relationship as almost one of mother and daughter. She finally confesses: "I am more like Charlotte than I thought I was" (p. 268). The identification with Charlotte's weaknesses is offset by the description of Charlotte's remaining in Boca Grande on the eve of revolution. The fact that she will surely be killed if she stays there gives her an aura of heroism in Grace's eyes. The reflected glory of Charlotte also casts its radiance on Grace, who ships Charlotte's body to the United States after first placing a child's T-shirt printed like an American flag (there was no flag available) on the coffin.

But the significance and purpose of Charlotte's death continue to puzzle the reader. Also, we cannot share Grace's final wholehearted admiration for Charlotte, who exhibits a certain resourcefulness in crisis, together with some interesting feats like snapping the back of a running chicken, or "field-stripping" a cigarette, or performing an emergency tracheotomy, but who is nevertheless unable to draw major inferences from experience. In summary (as the writer herself says frequently), after we have admired some of the very clever writing, the wry affects obtained by assembling incongruities ("Of course the story had extenuating circumstances, weather, cracked sidewalks and paregorina ... ") (p. 1), there is still the question: what are we to understand from this novel?

From the beginning, the narrator's terse recital of the facts of her own life are designed to project her as the champion of realism, as opposed to idealism. Colorado-born, educated as an anthropologist, she has lived in Boca Grande, a corrupt Central American country in which most

of the action takes place, since her youth. She married a
local plutocrat whose activities were largely a mystery to
her, and bore him a son who now spends most of his time
on skis, on wheels, or in the air. As a result of widow-
hood, her financial status is impressive. She has control
of 59.8 per cent of the arable land of Boca Grande, which
enables her to exercise the same percentage of control in
the decision-making process of the country.

If her financial condition is in good order, her body
is not. At sixty, she is dying of pancreatic cancer, yet
stays in this country of disorder, corruption, and disrepair
because she likes the light--harsh, flat, still--a fact which
tells us a great deal about her. Death holds no fears for
her. Essentially, she gives us the impression that she
conducts her life with discipline and moral nerve. Despite
threatening revolution, there are fresh flowers on the table,
the maids are dressed in spotless uniforms, and tea is
served at the usual hour. As for her study of anthropology,
she has long since given it up for what really interests
her--personality. Her eye is on Charlotte, who has come
to this country in the hope that her outlaw daughter will
somehow surface here. Marin, the daughter, was last
seen unsuccessfully trying to bomb a building and successfully hijacking a plane. She is now in hiding.

In keeping with the narrator's scientific training, the
reader is constantly enjoined to maintain a healthy skepti-
cism about facts and events. Grace's own method is to
sift and evaluate, with a deliberate, measured tone, the
data obtained by her own observation and from the testimony
of others. The problem of portraying a character in its
entirety can never be achieved, we are warned, nor can
the reliability of facts be determined. Having established
her aesthetic theory, Grace begins her story with the barest
of facts concerning Charlotte's death, and then moves back
and forth in time piecing together Charlotte's life. She is
scrupulously careful to impress upon us that personality is
a mystery, and that the simplest of acts has an immense
complexity behind it.

The facts of Charlotte's life present us with the in-
adequacies of woman's preparation for life, her longing for
order, and the way she goes about setting up categories of
order. We see the interaction of the private and public
person, and are asked to suspend judgment about inter-
actions between individual and society. Charlotte is the

product of an American environment which provided her with
living grandparents, a brother named Dickie, clean sheets,
orthodontia, ballet lessons, and "casual timely information
about menstruation and the care of flat silver" (p. 59). Her
thinking about revolution never took her past the Boston Tea
Party, and she still stoutly believes in the upward spiral of
history.

The narrator's sylleptical usage of ironic analogies,
such as Charlotte's simultaneous introduction to the facts of
menstruation and the care of flat silver, also adumbrates
the narrator's description of Charlotte's college education.
In college, Charlotte reads Vogue and the Brontës, buys a
loom, sleeps a great deal, and sometimes comes home weekends. An added touch to this commentary on American education is that the only time Charlotte sees the inside of a
library is to get a glimpse of the traveling exhibit of glass
flowers from Harvard. One wonders how Charlotte could
have escaped the library so completely, since students at
one time or another have to do some research for a term
paper--but maybe she availed herself of those mills which
grind out papers for students at a fee. At any rate, Charlotte's "education" ends with her elopement with an untenured
instructor, Warren Bogart, who teaches literature. They
have a child, Marin.

The narrator's laconic description of Charlotte at
this point is: "she was immaculate of history, innocent of
politics" (p. 60). It could be added that Charlotte was immaculate of everything concerning the world and her identity
as a woman. For the greater part of the book, Charlotte's
is a hermetic mind which avoids self-examination and permits little to inhabit it beyond a fixed concept of motherhood,
parents, marriage or sex. Her only way to bridge the gap
between reality and self-examination is to dream of the past
as an ideal time.

The reader perceives that Charlotte's education, like
that of Didion's previous heroine, Maria Wyeth, begins with
men. Nothing is said about Charlotte's father and his influence on her, beyond the fact that he died needing Demerol.
This latter fact continues to haunt Charlotte, like those details of coyotes tearing her mother's body in Maria Wyeth's
memory. And, as with Maria Wyeth's silence on social or
political ideas, it is not surprising to encounter a similar
muteness in Charlotte. Whatever she learns, it is from
Warren, Leonard, or other men with whom she comes into

contact. From Warren, she finds out about the Spanish
Civil War. Together with such facts, Warren (described by
Grace as having a face coarsened with contempt and a mind
coarsened by self-pity--p. 162) acquaints his wife with beating, sexual humiliation, and the premise that a man must
be obeyed. "Don't mess with me.... Don't cross me" (p.
179), he warns her, even when they are no longer man and
wife. When he comes in response to their daughter's dis-
appearance, he carries with him a bag of soiled laundry,
which he deposits on the floor with instructions to Charlotte
to have it washed and ironed. Later, his view of her as
still his domestic servant is shown again in a shout for
more ice.

From Leonard, the second husband, who runs guns
and travels extensively, arranging deals with guerrillas and
other people, Charlotte gets a sketchy knowledge of Third
World countries, whose location she cannot find on the map.
However, if her sense of geography is imprecise, she has
no difficulty understanding why Leonard married her: "I
want you. I don't need you" (p. 139), implying I'm not
clingingly dependent on you, but also: I desire you--no
less but certainly no more. Obviously, for the men with
whom she forms relationships, her red hair and blue eyes
and general seductive sexual attractiveness compensate for
her intellectual limitations. With Leonard gone on one of
his frequent trips, Charlotte drifts into affairs with Victor
and Gerardo, two Boca Grande machismos, who when they
are not skiing like Gerardo, or having nails done daily like
Victor, are playing power politics. The narrator tells us
that she prefers not to think too much about this aspect of
Charlotte's life--which is just as well.

Grace's early air of detachment toward Charlotte occasionally dips into sympathy. This warmth emerges from
an awareness that the two of them are Western Americans
and outsiders in a foreign land. Sympathy for Charlotte
also stems from Grace's perception that both of them were
given the same absurd preparations for the realities of marriage. Grace confides that upon her marriage to Edgar
Strasser-Mendana, she received twenty-four Haviland plates
in Windsor Rose pattern from her Denver aunt, who also
gave the following advice for living in the tropics: douche
with boiled water, preserve your husband's books with a
creosote solution, and set aside certain times for playing
bridge and writing letters. Since Grace's parents had died
at an early age, the aunt had taken upon herself to provide

her niece with the necessary instructions for life. Grace is also very cognizant of the fact that she and Charlotte are mothers of children whose actions result in their taking a road as useless as that unfinished road in Boca Grande, paid for with thirty-four million American dollars and now overgrown with vegetation.

After this excursion into sympathy, the narrator retreats to her role as objective observer, primarily to deflect us from her growing enmeshment with Charlotte. She is careful to indicate differences between herself and her subject. These comprise their thinking on marriage, motherhood, Boca Grande, the Mendanas, revolution, science, loneliness, and death. Where Charlotte seems to have drifted into marriage, Grace views it much as Beatrice Webb expressed herself on marriage: a waste pipe for emotion, security in old age, and a help to work when both man and wife share the same interests. We don't detect much emotion for the late Edgar Strasser-Mendana, nor any mention of his sharing a mutual interest with his wife. We do know, as already mentioned, that he left her handsomely provided for--a fact she accepts with practical satisfaction. Another area of difference on which Grace insists is that Charlotte goes from activity to activity. Grace, on the other hand, pursues an amateur interest in biochemistry, because "demonstrable answers are commonplace and 'personality' absent" (p. 12). She is ironic about the limitations of science, which can neither solve the riddle of personality nor give her any clue as to why her body breeds pancreatic cancer.

As for motherhood, where Charlotte glorifies it, considers it as a function ordained by nature and history, and idealizes her daughter Marin, Grace's attitude toward her son is that she likes him, but not too much any more. She now speaks to him as one would to an "acquaintance" (p. 20). Obviously, she takes no blame for this son, whose life is an aimless pursuit of various sports and women, with an occasional foray into the shady politics of Boca Grande. Both children, she implies, are products of a domestic and social environment which offers no personal salvation and drives them to dabble in events beyond their comprehension-- revolution, for example. There is no need to go into further differences between Charlotte and Grace, since Grace makes it clear that Charlotte insists on putting her own interpretation on everything. She believes she is the loneliest woman in the world, Grace comments ironically, and simply ignores the fact that this is part of the human condition.

This narcissistic tendency, together with her dreams of what ought to be, blind her to the making of distinctions.

Yet, after these particulars, the narrator slides back into sympathy for Charlotte by impressing upon us that Charlotte must be viewed with a certain singularity in view of the fact that she is a woman living at a particular time of history. On the day of her daughter's unsuccessful bombing of a building and successful hijacking of a plane, she returns to her San Francisco home only to face blinding TV lights, cameras pointed at her from all directions, and swarms of reporters all over her property. Her answer is flight. Of course, this arouses our pity, but we are also conscious of the fact that we are being manipulated. Despite the narrator's manipulation and having our reactions determined for us by the selectivity of detail, we begin to notice that the characterization of Charlotte is in keeping with the Didion heroine of previous fiction: the setting up of private rituals, the editing of memories to preserve illusions of the past; the drifting into sexual relationships which prove meaningless, and finally the cornering of the Didion woman, which results in some kind of stoical decision.

At this point, we cannot discount the fact that the narrator has ceased to become our link between two worlds; she has become an approving audience to Charlotte's actions. Charlotte's skillful parrying of FBI agents' questions about the whereabouts of her daughter earns her Grace's tribute: "she was not yet ready to deliver her child to history" (p. 74)--a marvelous line in keeping with the linking of Charlotte and history. The setting up of a birth control clinic in Boca Grande, because Charlotte is convinced that if she can use a diaphragm every woman can, is gently mocked, but with affection. When the authorities destroy the vaccine and Charlotte at first expresses indignation, Grace says: "I think I loved Charlotte in that moment ... " (p. 239). Charlotte's leaving her second husband to go on a strenuous trip with her former husband is explained as an action motivated by Charlotte's guilt over failing to return to the latter after she had promised she would. One's word must be kept, implies Grace. Furthermore, he is Marin's father and he is dying of cancer.

Then there is the description of rituals with which Charlotte surrounds herself to stave off the anguish of losing her daughter. First, we are alerted to her threatening inner despair by the outer disrepair of her expensive linen skirt held up with a safety pin, and the loose clasp on a $600 purse. The specificity of detail surrounding the rituals with which Charlotte arms herself is calculated to make us understand the growing disintegration which threatens to overwhelm and which, in turn, is the basis for Charlotte's great need for rituals: the daily visit to the airport, the memorizing of airline schedules, the drinking of water which has been boiled for twenty minutes, the same daily dinner of spiny lobster, the nightly query of the desk clerk concerning messages. There were none, comments the narrator; there was also no sleep for Charlotte.

The intrinsic quality of these details and the narrator's remarks are a necessary function to establish the kind of reality of the story being told. We are to understand that Charlotte's world is so terrifying that she must have rituals, must edit her memories of the past. The past must always appear ideal. The editing of memories is the only defense Charlotte has against the failure of reality to measure up to her dreams of family, marriage, motherhood. But despite the narrator's working on our sympathies, we cannot escape the fact that these are the dreams and rituals of a child. Charlotte consistently clings to a picture of Marin as a little girl in a crocheted dress, or Marin attired for Easter in a big picture hat and ruffled dress. Marin is never a person to Charlotte, only a doll baby which she yearns to cuddle once more. There is no understanding of Marin. Her feelings for her daughter are fed by dreams, not by the realities of Marin's position.

The narrator attempts to brush away webs of sentiment with touches that are often grim. Charlotte goes up to Marin's room after the FBI agents leave and looks at the swiss organdy curtains, the old valentines on the dressing table, the tray of cosmetics, the Raggedy Ann doll on the shelf. The scene would sink into melodrama if we didn't learn that Marin had removed from the room every snapshot, clipping, or class photograph of herself. Here one sympathizes, and understands the mother's anguish.

As we continue to follow Charlotte's career, we note that the brake on Charlotte's growth to maturity and moral enlargement of vision is that she is a dogmatic formulist. She keeps clinging to the belief that life has a rigid formula for happiness. Marin will always be her little girl--a child who has to stand on a stool to reach the cereal. Charlotte also believes that if one does the right thing, one

gets rewarded. Wrong doing results in swift punishment
and everlasting feelings of guilt. Charlotte encloses herself
in a narrow, cramped enclosure of principles which make
for moral myopia. She turns all of her limited insight and
small knowledge into rituals related to family, love, marriage, motherhood. She never seems to understand that
rituals alone are inadequate to the complexities of life (as
even that great ritualist Hemingway finally learned in Idaho).

I stress this because the techniques and strategies
of the narrator fail to minimize that if Marin is always
Mommy's little girl, family is a Currier/Ives post card in
which happy people gather around the festive board at Christmas time or Easter or any holiday. At other times, there
must be sharing, love, tenderness. Charlotte cannot accept
the fact that her brother Dickie is a drunk, a vulgar, preju-
diced man who keeps referring to her husband as that Jew,
and who insults his wife and just about everybody else. The
dinner scene in which his character is revealed is a horror.
More serious than Charlotte's sentimental picture of family
is her dogged belief that one must be present at the death
of a parent, say the last goodbye, close the lids over the
dead eyes. Certainly, these are emotions which we all respect. But we also know that appointments in Samarra
come at their own time--a time over which we have no control. Unfortunately, Charlotte's mother dies alone in a department store. Her father dies alone needing Demerol, we
are told. The result for Charlotte is such a sense of guilt
that she sees no other way of punishing herself except to
sleep with the first accessible man, who happens to be her
lawyer. The result is a beating by her husband in which
Marin is also hurt (since she is in her mother's arms).
Still clinging to her idea of ritual, because it is Easter,
the battered wife, bruised child and angry husband "celebrate" Easter brunch at the Carlyle. Some propriety has
been observed, as far as Charlotte is concerned. She later
edits the memory as a "happy time."

Her life from beginning to end shows a pattern of
stubborn clinging to doctrinal ritual. She marries young as
an inevitable corollary to college. She divorces one husband
who never sees her as anything but a sex object, and marries a second man to whom she is also a sex symbol, a
fact he makes adequately clear (as previously indicated).
She leaves him to go on a frenetic journey with the first
husband because he is dying, and has told her that she must
go with him. There are no stirrings of pity or tenderness

for him, only guilt that she had broken her word to him that
first time in failing to return from the trip.   She now reasons that not to go to him this time will surely invite even
more retribution from some divine source.

Nemesis always walks side by side with Charlotte.
Hence, pregnant by the second husband, and wanting this
child desperately, she jeopardizes the child's life by feverish traveling, heavy sex, including sex à trois when Warren
picks up a young girl, and beatings from Warren.   When
she finally leaves Warren because he has given the young
girl a concussion, she loses the child--final proof to her
of God's wrath.

The writing at this point is soap opera.   Charlotte
walks around a parking lot with the dead baby in her arms,
crooning to it and whispering of trips they would have taken
together.   She finally has it buried with red plastic shoes
on its tiny feet and a ribbon in its hair.   A spray of bou-
gainvillea is torn from the side of a house and placed on
the tiny grave.   However we might critically respond to the
implicit emotion of the situation and appreciate its consistency with Charlotte's nature, the author's details swamp us
and Charlotte.   Pathos becomes bathos.

Despite some very good writing, terse dialogue, easy
transition from one character to another, the fusion of landscape and emotion, the setting--even more important in this
novel than in the previous novel--suffers at times from the
same hint of melodrama which clings to the scene of Charlotte with the dead baby.   No one will deny that the narrator's picture of the Mendanas, rulers of Boca Grande, as
spoilers and corrupters of the social scene is an accurate
one, as everyday history proves.   We know that such people
exist and spread death and ugliness everywhere, kill the innocent and the weak, and are an abomination to the earth.
Placing two American women in such a setting immediately
recalls the Jamesian theme of American innocence and goodness versus European corruption and venality.   But where
James's moral norm is clear, we are not quite ready to
accept the narrator's lining up of the good guys versus the
bad guys.

Remembering the author's shift from reportage to
eulogy in the John Wayne essay, we detect the same shift
in the narrator's attempt to make Charlotte, a weak and
human woman, into a national symbol in its most honorific

sense. We are to understand in those scenes of cholera in-
jections for thirty-two hours at a stretch, and in Charlotte's
refusal to leave Boca Grande even though she has been
warned of the danger of staying, that Charlotte possesses
specific American virtues: innocence, loyalty, integrity, and
the ability to bring into being an inherent and final decency
and courage. In fact, all the Americans in this story eventually come off well: the slippery Leonard, the marginal
Warren, the revolutionary Marin (of whom the narrator is
most disapproving throughout the story, but for whom she
ultimately has some redeeming words). Leonard attends to
all the details of Warren's death, finally locates Marin, and
tells her of her father's passing. Warren, who has consistently blackmailed Charlotte emotionally, makes amends with
the note he leaves for her. Marin first denies her mother,
then ends by weeping for her. There is a bit of flag-waving
here in the constant contrast between the soulless Mendanas
and their equally soulless wives, and the Americans who
can be counted upon to do the right thing when necessary.
The impression is strengthened with the details of the ailing
Grace making a painful journey to Buffalo in order to see
Marin after her mother's death.

This brings up the consideration of how appropriate
to characterization is the moral position the narrator adopts.
Since she has considerable land holdings, she herself is one
of the rulers of rotten Boca Grande. There is nothing beyond verbal disapproval of the corrupt in-laws to indicate
that Grace herself pays any attention to the plight of the
poor, the insulted, and the injured. Her fatalistic conclusion is that revolutions in Boca Grande change nothing. She
is concerned with order in the social sense: tea at the ap-
pointed hour, fresh flowers, clean uniforms for the maids,
as already mentioned. More examples could be cited, but
they simply involve her sense of social fitness and responsibility. As for Charlotte, she sleeps first with one Men-
dana, then another. Her reward on one occasion is white
roses and dysentery. If Grace and Charlotte are to represent the norm, the touchstones or points of moral reference
by which all other characters are to be judged, specifically
the Mendanas, there is a simplification which aligns all
faulty characters (e. g. , Mendanas) on the wrong side and
the good characters (Americans) on the right side.

In any case, the antithesis does not work well. The
author's skill with narration does not disguise the fact that
Charlotte falls into the pattern of previous Didion heroines.

She is a woman who can love only as a daughter or a mother. She exudes sexuality, but is not a sexual woman. Always conscious of carrying some kind of sexual freight, as the narrator says about Charlotte, she is almost afraid to touch men. Inevitably, she is helpless to exercise any control over her body. Like a deck of cards, she is shuffled from man to man: "You had your shot," Leonard tells Warren (p. 177). She forms relationships with men who use her but don't love her, yet tell her how much she desires their sex. We never hear anything from the Didion woman except a disclaimer: I don't like it. Like the Hemingway hero always in flight from women, so the Didion woman is constantly in flight from men. And like the Hemingway man who doesn't know what to do with women beyond going to bed with them, so the Didion woman sees bed as the only answer.

There are no scenes between the author's women and men which demonstrate awareness that there can be a relationship, in which either is sensitive to mutual currents of feeling. The burden of misery concerning the inadequacy of love and marriage is fumbled with, but never carried. The men are bad and undermine women's hold on life. In woman's deepest hour of need, she can expect little help from any man--only after death does a man aid a woman, as Leonard proves with Charlotte.

Above all, the Didion woman complies with the sexual demands made on her. Maria Wyeth, as discussed, obeys Ivan, Carter, as well as the second-rate actor, and just about every man who comes into her life. The most infuriating thing about Charlotte is her passivity with men. The first meeting between Charlotte and Gerardo, Grace's son, is extraordinary in its brevity of dialogue and subsequent action. Gerardo looks at Charlotte and says: "You smell American" (p. 201). Learning that she is staying at the Caribe, he says, "I don't like the Caribe" (p. 202). The third comment he makes is: "I want you to take an apartment." And Charlotte does just that.

In sum, the kind of sensibility the author raises to fictive level in the novels is not the stuff of tragedy. Didion is a moralist in the old-fashioned style, despite her experiments with syntax, form, and language. Her women are obsessed with guilt--familial and sexual. Maria Wyeth tells us that sexual guilt is due to "bad sexual conduct" (p. 2). But the guilt burden under which the hurting Didion woman staggers is due to a concept of bad conduct revolving around the omission of some necessary ritual. Action then must take on the compulsion for punishment. The theme of ritual, particularly the stress on the necessary ritual connected with a parent's dying, is a shaky element of plot. To make a comparison, Faulkner works with the observance of proper ritual for the dying and dead in As I Lay Dying. It is the theme and substance of his book, shown to be an admission born out of human need, and has to be justified throughout the book. In the Didion stories discussed here, the theme of ritual connected with dying seems out of context, a kind of private obsession on the part of the author.

There are many narrative devices in this novel which are excellent; for example, the method of telling the truth-- or part of the truth--beforehand, or letting us know the truth simultaneously with the character's knowledge of it. However, there are also stratagems for bringing both Grace and Charlotte into perspective which make us aware of how much design and maneuvering are being used to convince us. With this perception, the characters tend to recede from vital identities to allegorical mouthpieces for the author. She wants us to believe that they are both women of some inner strength, both frontier women in the sense that Grace can shed the encumbrances of her stupid upbringing and Charlotte can give inoculations for long hours at a stretch. At the same time, living in a brutal country, they hold on to the gracious amenities and social courtesies of an age now past.

The point is dramatized in the airport scene. Charlotte, electing to stay in Boca Grande, comes to see Grace off. She brings with her perfume, magazines and candy and presses them on Grace. We are told how touched Grace is as Charlotte pins gardenias on her dress, dabs perfume on Grace's wrists "like a child helping her mother dress for a party" (p. 257). We realize that the two women, despite the narrator's precise documenting of their differences, share the same values and place the same importance on these values. This is the observance of social propriety. The emphasis in the book, then, is on social manners rather than on social injustice. There has been no growth in spiritual stature by either woman. Charlotte refuses to modify the dogmatic principles to which she clings. Grace tells us that she has changed from her neutrality of position to knowledge that the past is important, and that she is not so certain now that Charlotte's story is one of "delusion" (p. 272). But there is only her word for it. We have seen no moral struggle on her part to achieve any conviction--no sense of an unfolding experience and enlightenment. Both Charlotte and Grace, then, emerge as static figures who never gain a firm grip on our imagination and sympathies.

If there is a tragic figure in the novel, it is Marin, about whom little is written and what is written often expresses the condemnation of the narrator. Yet it is Marin who is the voice of realism as she rightfully concludes that she could never compete with the idea of daughter that both mother and father entertain of her. She knows that she is a doll baby to her mother, and a girl with a limited IQ to her father. She is also aware of her upbringing in which there have been expensive toys, steaks, Easter brunch preceded by an ugly family brawl. She grows up starved of the necessary environmental elements which nourish self-respect, intellect, and sensibility. Her search for identity leads her to the handling of Browning rifles, the making of bombs, the hijacking of planes--before she has outgrown the pink orthodonture to correct her bite. We leave her in a room in Buffalo with the knowledge that her father is dead of cancer, her mother dead of a gunshot wound in the back, and that her comrades expect her to be the household drudge, symbolized by the sink of dirty dishes.

Her predicament is tragic because she has rejected the old order, but has found no constructive basis for the new. She is caught in competing forces--love for mother and revolutionary zeal. She is a tragic figure because she teaches us of the waste of our young and their potential. Marin, like Charlotte and all of Didion's heroines, continues to play a role defined for her by others--rather than by herself. Perhaps, this is the implied warning of the book.

CHAPTER 6

WINGING UPWARD: BLACK WOMEN:
SARAH E. WRIGHT, TONI MORRISON, ALICE WALKER

The closely-textured stories of black women writers
Sarah E. Wright, Toni Morrison, and Alice Walker are
rooted in the collective history of a people regarded for a
long time as socially marginal. The nature of the response
to the black experience by these writers demonstrates that
they are not writers "who just happened to be black." The
view of life which permeates the pages has a special vantage
point--one which makes it virtually impossible for any reader
to cling to the comforting assumptions which so often under-
lie the thinking of our society. If there is pain in being
black and a woman, there is also pride in having survived
and become strong. Many of the black women we meet in
the works seem to echo what Maya Angelou voices in an interview: you "may encounter many defeats, but ... must
not be defeated."[1]

The point is worth noting, but it must also be stressed
that the writers discussed here make it abundantly clear that
both black men and women suffer from similar social and
economic pressures and restrictions. Their fiction starts
from a recognition of the intricacies of human behavior and
spotlights the social-economic political arena in which the
issues of personal freedom and happiness are to be fought.
In their deepest impress, these works compel us to reflect
upon history, economics, religion, environment, and the way
these condition the lives of men and women. The sense
these writers leave with us is of the pain behind the laughter
of black people, the absolute difficulty of human beings trying to live with one another in an environment which often
degrades, imprisons, and makes just everyday living an
agonizing contest of endurance. As Toni Morrison points
out in Sula, white society has often been oblivious to the

112

pain behind the "shucking, knee-slapping, wet-eyed laughter"
of black people (S, p. 4). She stresses that laughter which
turns on oneself is sometimes the black person's only answer to the despair which threatens to overwhelm.

In the four crucial novels discussed here: This
Child's Gonna Live (Sarah E. Wright, 1969); Sula (Toni Morrison, 1974); Song of Solomon (Toni Morrison, 1977); Meridian (Alice Walker, 1977), and in the collection of short
stories by Alice Walker, In Love and Trouble (1973), the
reader is always made aware of the astringencies of the situation of both black men and women--the uselessness of freedom unless that freedom enables the black man and woman
to buy food, educate the children, and live in clean, decent
homes. The need for social and economic change is freely
expressed by both Alice Walker and Toni Morrison. Walker's heroine, Meridian, openly voices indignation against
those who oppress the poor and calls for action. When
Morrison describes the anger of the people living in the
neighborhood called Bottom as they view the unbuilt tunnel--
symbol of their joblessness and misery--she defines with
ominous clarity the nature and composition of the ingredients of revolt.

Extensions of this kind of thinking emerge in one way
or another in the works of the three writers, and are shown
not just as the deprivations of a few people, but as the history of an entire social group. Despite differences in style,
the three writers reveal shared preoccupations and parallel
perceptions about the realities of being black in white America. Reading these writers, one is conscious of the full
meaning of that statement by Lorraine Hansberry: "Life?
Ask those who have tasted of it in pieces rationed out by
enemies"[2] (author's italics).

SARAH E. WRIGHT
This Child's Gonna Live

Sarah E. Wright's This Child's Gonna Live, particularly in its early chapters, is the most poignant response
to black suffering as it occurred in the thirties--a time also
recorded vividly by Toni Morrison in Sula. The significant
factor about Wright's book is the intensity of the effort to
register, in its own terms, the condition of everyday living

in the town of Tangierneck, a small fishing village on the
eastern shore of Maryland. The selectivity of detail, the
reproduction of dialect, the careful documenting of TB eating out the lungs of young and old; worms fattening in the
bodies of live children and crawling out of their anuses;
women in shoes without soles standing on a wet cement
floor and shucking oysters; water in oyster buckets red with
blood from cut fingers; pregnant women like Mariah (the
chief character) dragging heavy baskets down a potato row--
often impel the reader to put the book down in horror. The
impact of such documentation only too vividly dramatizes
the constant presence of death, and the truth of Aunt Saro Jane's
prophecy: "Gonna be a fat graveyard come spring" (p. 147).
Mariah keeps blue pills with which to commit suicide if she
can no longer endure. And if disease, cold, and hunger do
not succeed in killing the people, there are always the Paddy
Rollers, as white racists are called, who come to threaten,
beat, and kill.

Before considering this important novel, I want to
make the point that together with these writers' social criticism of the limitations on both black men and women, the
total effect emerging from their books is that if black men
are restricted, women are even more so. Each story involves us deeply with the realities of the black woman's
particular dilemma. Time, setting, characters may vary,
but the realities of woman's condition remain the same.
These realities revolve about the black woman living not
only in white, racist America, but in a black society which
is so tightly structured that it leaves little chance for self-
realization on the part of the individual woman.

Much of the structure of black society, particularly
in Sarah E. Wright's picture of the town of Tangierneck,
has to do with the attitudes and the moral/social codes
derived from patriarchal Old Testament religion. This religion, with its masculine, wrathful, punishing God, is the
basis for the polarization of man/woman roles, practice of
the double standard, and the concept of woman as unclean,
sinner and temptress. Such thinking, as well as superstitions about the diabolical side of woman, stigmatizes as
rebel the woman who seeks to escape the confines of the
role into which she is thrust. She soon learns that the
church, with its apocalyptic warnings, evangelical zeal,
threats of eternal damnation, brands as outcast the woman
who refuses to conform to the role expected of her.

The rebel woman is the underlying concern of all

three writers discussed here. The woman's revolt, whatever form it takes, is in a sense an upsurge from below,
an affirmation of dignity in the face of rejection and ostra-
cism. Wright's Mariah repeatedly rejects the epithet of
"whore" pinned on her by the community with: "I is so
something else. I is so" (p. 96). Morrison's Sula, considered a pariah in the Bottom, is defiant to the end in her
assertion that marriage turns women into "starched cof-
fins" (S, p. 122). With her last breath, she whispers to
her friend Nel that her own way of life was better: "I sure
did live in this world" (S, p. 143). Magnificent Pilate,
Morrison's latest woman rebel, rejects black society's view
of her as freak, something unnatural (SS, p. 143) spawned
by the devil because she has no navel, and makes a wonder-
fully self-fulfilling life for herself. It is a natural and instinctive way of life which brings contentment and peace not
only to her, but to all those with whom she comes into contact.

In short, linking all four novels are varying portraits
of women rebels who strive to create some new kind of life
for themselves and for their children, when children are involved. Stubborn individualists, the rebel women find not
only community an enemy, but kin as well. However, the
women's estrangement from communal and familial ties is
often replaced by friendship with another woman or women.
It is a friendship which helps to unburden them of the pressures under which they live. Indeed, without question, friendship for the rebel woman is more satisfying and more valuable than any relationship with man. All four novels deal
with different aspects of women friendships which allay loneliness and help to vitalize hope. When that friendship is
cut off by death, as is so movingly portrayed in Sula, the
friend (Nel) who is left behind expresses words which recall
the emotions of Pope on the death of John Gay: "How often
are we to die before we go quite off the stage? In every
friend we lose a part of ourselves, and the best part."[3]
Indeed, Sula is Nel and Nel, Sula, as will be discussed.
On the other hand, the death of Vyella in Wright's novel
bestows on Mariah a legacy which infuses her with the
strength to confront husband and community and wrest, perhaps, a new status of dignity and respect for herself.

The connection between Sarah E. Wright's work, then,
and that of the other two writers is obvious. Like them,
she tries to look beyond the familiar surfaces of life in the
black community. She examines critically and with sympathy
the social/moral code by which the community lives, and

shows its bearing on the relationships between man and
wife, mother and children, father and children, man and
man, woman and woman. To a greater and more obvious
extent, as already mentioned, she works with Old Testament
religion to bring out clearly how the belief in a stern masculine God leads to the black woman's position of social and
sexual inferiority. For men like Jacob, Mariah's husband,
largely ignored by his father and considered "boy" or clown
by white people, the concept of a strong, masculine God is
absolutely necessary. He tries to assume vicariously the
strong masculinity personified by the Old Testament God
to whom he prays. This masculinity demands that his wife
and other women be considered inferior; hence, they must
be obedient, submissive and always conscious of the separation of roles. "See, Mariah," he tells her impatiently, "it's
just a natural fact of life that men and women's business is
different" (p. 225). Though he is the father of a son by
his adopted sister Vyella, he considers almost to the end
his wife's one sexual transgression as confirming her complete worthlessness. "Decent, woman? You ought to laugh
at yourself, Mariah. You ain't even clean enough for to
touch no more" (p. 250). He sneers at her ability to be a
good mother and sums up: "You don't mean nothing, ain't
never meant nothing" (p. 233).

Vivid scenes between men and women in Wright's
novel bring out the low status of women in Tangierneck.
Mariah's father says to Vyella, who wants to get a preach-
er's license: "you aspiring to preach the Gospels, right?
Well I'm here to tell you something about those Scriptures"
(p. 178). When she challenges him, he replies: "a woman
is a mighty unclean person unless they learn how to respect their menfolks.... Supposed to obey their man" (p.
179). His attitude to his wife is one of command and contempt, and the words "shut up" are prominent in his vocabulary. Then there is Percy Upshur, Jacob's father, who
knocks a bag out of his wife's hand and orders her around
constantly.

For his daughter-in-law Mariah, who does not go to
church and who was pregnant before marriage, he reserves
his deepest contempt: "no good whore" who will give her
"cunt" to any man (p. 118). Yet Percy himself has had an
ongoing affair with Miss Bannie, an affluent white woman
who has borne him a son.

What we notice is that despite the strong religious

atmosphere and the pious stance of the men, there is a lot
of evasive sexuality going on. It reminds one of the reply
of Yeats who, when told that only a fool spent a lot of time
thinking about sex and death, retorted that only a fool spent
a lot of time thinking about something else. Obviously Tangierneck men (and women) spend a great deal of time thinking about these two factors of life, but the dark aspect to
this thinking is that the men condemn any woman who asserts
her individual ideas about self and sexuality.

But to get the author's full view of black men, one
must consider every aspect of her characterization of them.
There is the irony of Percy Upshur who remarks at one
point: "these women can't see into no future" (p. 166).
Percy's own future, like that of many black men, ends in
his murder at the hands of white racists, and a grave which
is only discovered a month after his death. The facts leading to his death have a familiar ring. Having heard that
his half-white son is in trouble because of his mother's will
leaving him property, Percy Upshur decides to go to the
sheriff and tell of his relationship with Bannie. On the way,
he is killed. His death proves to every black man in Tangierneck that white is right; black is nothing. Unfortunately,
one of the ways for the black man to acknowledge his worth
is to plant a foot firmly on the neck of the black woman--
which is what is demonstrated in Tangierneck.

The focus on Jacob, whose battered masculinity needs
always to be reenforced by an authoritarian and contemptuous
stance toward Mariah and other women (except his mother),
constantly underscores this concept. He criticizes Mariah's
method of carrying water for the family washing, but at no
point does he offer to help her, and Mariah is forced to repeat the back-breaking procedure. Despite the fact that
his children and wife are practically starving, his pride
forbids him to allow Mariah to appeal to Welfare, or to the
affluent white Bannie who seems to control most of Tangierneck's land during her lifetime. "Shut up, woman. I done
told you now. I provides for my family," he shouts (p.
14). Yet there is another side to Jacob, and the pathos
which is evoked by Mariah is allowed to flow over to Jacob.
The writer takes the reader on one of Jacob's many walks.
For Jacob, like James Joyce's Bloom, is constantly walking,
and like Bloom, though to a more exacerbated extent, he is
constantly thinking about ways to support his family.

We see him praying to his powerful God Almighty

for help--pleading with God not to forsake him. Fearful,
shivering with the cold wind which buffets his frail body,
lonely for the brothers who have left for the city, bitter
that his father has slept with a white woman and mortgaged
his land to her, wracked by stomach and chest pains, he is
a pathetic sight. Later in the story, we see him humiliated
and beaten by the white men who have killed his father.
His wife, too, is beaten and Jacob has to listen to Mariah
referred to as "your little cunting hole here" (p. 217). When
he goes to the bank to assert his claim to his dead father's
land, he is given the ominous warning that no harm will
come to him or his family providing he ceases to press his
claim.

Yet though the writer lets us recognize the abuses
and constrictions leveled on Jacob and the paucity of choices
available to him, we are also made aware that many of his
problems are due to his passivity because of the religious
conditioning. Jacob's religion, as Mariah astutely assesses,
enables him to lay his burdens on God and thus excuse himself from any responsibility for action, for most of the time.
"God's gonna send a change" (p. 113) is his usual comforting thought. Whereas Mariah, who characteristically prays
to the more gentle Jesus to help her, rather than to Jacob's
stern God, relies on herself. She's out in the potato field
or shucking oysters, or sorting strawberries, or peeling
scalded tomatoes. She's also hoarding pennies and entrust-
ing them to her friend Vyella, so that she will have a
chance to get herself and her children out of Tangierneck.
Shut out by family and by community, except for Vyella
and Aunt Cora Lou, she tries to be an activist despite the
restrictions laid upon her.

The stigma which keeps Mariah in virtual isolation,
relieved only by Vyella or Aunt Cora Lou, expands the author's broad characterization of non-conformist women and
the friendship between them. Both Vyella and Cora Lou
are suspect in Tangierneck, but for different reasons.
Vyella, as mentioned, is derided for wanting to stand up
in the pulpit, which is reserved for men, and preach. Cora
Lou arouses hostility because at forty plus she is still an
attractive woman in a place in which women look old in their
twenties. In addition, Cora Lou was at one time married
to a white migrant worker (the most despicable thing that a
black woman could do). At various intervals she has left
Tangierneck for the city instead of staying and helping her
family by working in the fields. She appears to be self-
supporting, practical, and a good friend to Mariah.

It is she who tells Mariah that her hope to have the coming baby born in a hospital won't help to save the child's life, because of the bad care given black people. She is insistent that half-black Dr. Grene (son of Bannie and Percy Upshur) will give Mariah better care, and that she herself go to enlist his aid. Cora Lou is killed on her mercy mission by white teenagers who run her down with their car, and Mariah is blamed for her death. But before Cora Lou's death, we get an impression of a woman who has no illusions about what religion has done to the people of Tangierneck. It has made them a jealous, narrow-minded lot, she tells Mariah. Perhaps the author is voicing her own opinion concerning Tangierneck's patriarchal Old Testament religion when she has Cora Lou assert: "Tangierneck'll kill anything that wants to live outside the shadows of their white man God" (p. 99). These two women are represented as life forces during their brief existence: Vyella, who dies of cancer in the end, never fails to offer Mariah sympathy and help; Cora Lou constantly bolsters Mariah's self-esteem when it threatens to sink.

Religion, as practiced in Tangierneck, attracts the author's most stringent criticism as well as her understanding of community thinking and practices. Like James Baldwin and other writers, she shows that the church or camp meeting attempts to administer to the spiritual needs of its members as well as function as a community center. An illuminating epilogue to her discussion of religion is her portraits of the older church women. These are women like Mrs. Upshur and Mariah's mother, who find in the camp meeting with its dogma a socially acceptable outlet for pent-up rage, terror, or frustration. Here is where they can divert their emotional and intellectual energies. Church is their one claim to respectability, and the religious camp meeting is evidence to visiting white people and black people from other cities that Tangierneck is a respectable community. Black people can be respectable, Mariah's mother exhorts her. The Mourner's Bench invites public confession of sin. Yet the paradox here is that if a woman (like Mariah) admits sexual transgression, she tarnishes the image of respectability--which is the only image to which the older women cling.

In other words, what we see about the older women is that eventually the oppressed turn into the oppressor. Bertha Ann Upshur, demeaned and betrayed by her husband, becomes his mouthpiece on the subject of women. She is

loudest in harping on the fact that young girls must be respectable. She addresses herself solely to the young girls,
for she has been always told that boys can control themselves better than girls. When she learns that Jacob has
fathered Mariah's child, she sends him away to avoid his
admitting paternity and marrying Mariah.

The scene in the church during which Mariah confesses her pregnancy is worthy of a painting combining the
violence and distortions of El Greco and the grotesques of
Hogarth. It is precipitated by the birth of Rosey's child.
Mother and child die and the author observes ironically that
the man responsible for her pregnancy, a deacon in the
church, hides behind his wife and is loudest in denouncing
these young girls for "living too fast" (p. 76).

There is more auctorial irony in the way the women
of the church, led by Bertha Ann Upshur, determine to
make an example of the young girl. Placing Rosey and her
dead baby, still tied to her by the cord, in the middle of
the church, they point to the "shame," predict hell fire for
Rosey, and invite any girl "in the family way" to come to
the Mourner's Bench, confess her sin of fornication, and
find her way back to God. Taking the women at their word,
Mariah moves forward and what follows is both tragic and
comic. The town's half-wit joins Mariah, which is tantamount to joint admission of paternity. The horrified Mariah
shrieks: "Get that dunce out of my sight" (p. 82) and declares that it is Jacob who is the father. The scene ends
with Mariah's mother beating her up and down the length of
the church and continuing outside.

The reader sympathizes with the young girl, but here
again the writer gives us a glimpse of the mother's side as
she grieves: "Don't want her to end up here in Tangierneck
scrounging around for whatever the devil gives up to her....
She ain't but fifteen" (p. 83). She reminds Mariah how they
tried to give her a chance by sending her away from Tangierneck (but omits the part about TB driving Mariah back).
Knowing the strict code toward women in Tangierneck, the
mother voices her fears that Mariah's chances for any kind
of life are blasted. There is also more than a personal
issue at stake here, as her next words confirm. Mariah's
mother and the other women make it abundantly clear that
it is their hope that "proving" to white people that blacks
are respectable will bring about a change in white people's
"hearts" concerning them. Maybe funds will be allocated
for a school and even jobs provided for the young people.

Nothing in this story justifies the hope to which the women cling so forlornly. What we see is that they are as much victims as agents of the System. Later, we see Mariah, too, falling into the same trap. Loving her children passionately, she is wary of showing them her affection for fear of appearing soft, which would lead to their growing up "undisciplined." Since discipline in Tangierneck is the responsibility of the mother ("Beat her ass good," Mariah's father had commanded his wife--p. 10), Mariah, too, "switches" her children, but not with the stovelid lifter her mother used on her. But we see her weeping remorsefully after she beats her son Skeeter for stealing her little hoard of money.

Mariah's mixed emotions are understandable. Unlike middle-class parents who provide their children with toys and graduation gifts, and help them to make a choice for college or a career, Mariah cannot even consider choices for her children. She, like her mother before her, thinks only about ways to keep her children out of trouble. She tries to create a tough discipline that will help her son to avoid trouble with the law and her daughter to avoid clashing with community sexual mores. For this reason, she beats her daughter Bardetta with the same passion shown toward her son when the little girl lifts up her dress to show her vagina. In essence, seared by her memories of black community's reaction to her pregnancy before marriage, she is projecting the same worries which her mother and other women in Tangierneck manifest toward their daughters. For the poor, Wright implies, harsh discipline is sometimes the only way to prepare children for "the world out there." Mariah believes that it is her duty to be stern with her children, but it is clear that ultimately warmth, affection, and the need to communicate with her children always win over the limitations she places on her love.

Despite her continuous battle with herself, Mariah keeps in mind that at no time was she able to communicate with her mother. And you, Mamma, she thinks, in so many words, never spoke a decent word to me but "whore" and "slut" and just wanted to hide me away (p. 180). She recalls how desperately she wanted to tell her mother of that spring day when she lay in the sun and felt as if its warm rays were drawing the dangerous TB infection out of her lungs. All around her was greenness and fragrance and then Jacob appeared and put his arms around her and she, Mariah, could only exult that she was alive. For one

wonderful moment, the harshness of her life was forgotten
and she felt as one with nature and the universe.

Never again is Mariah to recapture such an epiphany.
The book chronicles her harsh existence and her resulting
continued death wish, which is only rejected at the end. In
stark fact, the wish to retreat from consciousness is her
primordial response to an existence in which the props for
survival are shaky from the start. Though Jacob does return to Mariah despite his mother's efforts to dissuade him,
the two become hopelessly trapped in a poverty so bleak
that life is not a gripping pain but a constant ache. There
is always the danger of no work and the frightening slide
into hunger, sickness, and the void. At twenty-three, Mariah has no back teeth due to pyorrhea, and is pregnant
with her fifth child. A previous pregnancy has ended in the
child's death as a result of improper sterilization during
birth. Mariah is determined that the coming child will live.
The marriage relationship, we learn, has deteriorated into
a silence as gloomy as the maroon drapes in Tangierneck's
only funeral parlor.

There are clues dropped throughout the book that the
child is not Jacob's, but it is something which the author
does not enlarge on, other than having Mariah exclaim at
one point that Tangierneck is a place which would drive a
woman to anything. At any rate, Mariah seems weighted
down with a terrible sense of guilt, not only over the coming
baby but over the circumstances of Bannie's death which,
together with the terrible poverty she lives in, puts her
into a kind of psychic hell.

It is the psychological, not the physical suffering
which is most dramatized during the birth of the child. Her
nightmares--with their motifs of coiled serpents, eternal
flames, light and dark--all recall James Joyce again.
Where Wright's description of Jacob's wanderings about Tangierneck and his constant preoccupations with land, money,
and family make one think of Joyce's ambulatory Bloom,
the childbirth scene with its emphasis on Mariah's terror and
guilt feelings conveys a parallel with Stephen's frenzy of fear
after Father Arnall's sermon in Portrait. Perhaps there
is an identification in the author's mind between illiterate
Mariah and intellectual Stephen because, in one sense or
another, both are rebels against the established religion
and both want to fly. But here the analogy ends, for where
Stephen eventually accepts his rebellion with pride and suc-

cessfully makes his flight to freedom, Mariah carries her guilt feelings to the end.

Certainly, the details of her daily life encourage her to believe that she is being punished for "her sins." There is the constant worry as to what patch of ground she is going to rummage in to find some greens for her children. It is not without irony that at one point she remembers the last homemaker's visit and advice: try to make eating a "joy" for your family (p. 31). Nor does the situation improve when she leaves Tangierneck with Jacob and the children for their new destinations: Chance and Kyle's Island. The latter provides a sagging shanty for a home and work for Mariah in the oyster factory. It is on Kyle's Island that her son Rabbit dies of worm infestation and inflamed lungs. They return to Tangierneck to bury their son, just as a short time before they had come back to bury Jacob's brother (dead of TB). They come back again for Vyella's funeral.

Our last view of Mariah is of her taking part in the funeral procession for Vyella. Vyella, apparently, has achieved some status as community leader, and has the largest turnout for her funeral that Tangierneck has ever seen. For Mariah there is a letter from Vyella informing her that Ned is Jacob's son. The odyssey of Wright's heroine comes to a pause with her refusal to yield to bitterness and her forgiveness of Jacob, but not without the clearly stated intention that there is to be no servile docility on her part. In a surge of love for dead friends and their children, she decides to take in Ned, Jacob's son by Vyella, together with the orphaned children of Cora Lou. "Knows we ain't got but so much," she thinks, "but Jacob and me'll share it" (p. 268). She represents a moral poise and charity far above that exhibited by her Tangierneck neighbors. At this Easter time with which the story concludes, Mariah stands for a brief time as one woman's transcendence over the forces which threaten to force her to self-annihilation. She faces life, however, with no promise that it will be better, or that economic conditions will change to make its burdens more tolerable. Knowing that she has to work doubly hard now to provide for the enlarged family, her prayer is simple: "Help me to stay on my feet" (p. 259).

The structure of feeling on which This Child's Gonna Live is built is, then, a combination of compassionate obser-

vation of Mariah and a keen understanding of the larger social forces which make for the deep fissures between people.
It is the System which is at fault, the System which brutalizes men and puts women in a position of inferiority.   By
virtue of its sustained prose/poem effect and its frequent
incantatory rhythms, which are reminiscent of the Old Testament, together with descriptions of Jacob and Mariah wrestling with their personal devils, it recalls some of the family
stories in the Old Testament.   But this is a secular book
dealing with Mariah's refusal to submit to hopelessness and
passive suffering.   The language surrounding her is not so
much Biblical as Negro vernacular and domestic imagery.
When Mariah feels a premonition of domestic trouble, she
glances at the sky and sees that the low-hanging clouds
"huffed themselves up like dirty white leghorn roosters
ready to fly into each other over a hen" (p. 20).   After
doing the family wash, the author describes Mariah's wet
clothes clinging to her body "like the skin on a polished
Christmas apple" (p. 96).   And since Mariah is a woman
and a very poor woman at that, the language addressed to
her is often that of traditional insult: "cunting hole."

Sarah E. Wright's work, then, presents women such
as Mariah, and, to a less emphatic degree, those like
Vyella and Cora Lou, as seeking some self-definition.   On
a cynical level, it could be argued that Mariah's devotion
to motherhood and family pushes her more deeply into the
role usually ordained for women.   But it is Mariah who
exercises the power of choice in this matter, not her husband Jacob.   Her confrontation with Jacob concerning his
fathering of Ned by Vyella alerts us to the fact that she
has become a little more knowledgeable about the realities
of sexual equality and sexual subordination and will not submit to Jacob's insults anymore.   There is that last thought
of hers as she appraises Jacob's running to her: "a new
style of running.   Faster than fast" (p. 272).   It may well
be a metaphor for their new relationship.

TONI MORRISON:
Sula; Song of Solomon

In her first novel, The Bluest Eye (1970), Toni Morrison deals with children and that element of belief by many

black people, as she sees it, that an ultimate glory is possible. Pecola Breedlove yearns for blue eyes as the next
best thing to being white. Blue eyes become for her a symbol of pride and dignity. She seeks the glory of blue eyes
through prayer, through the help of the man who bills himself as "reader and advisor," and eventually through madness when, believing that blue eyes have finally been granted
her, she walks about flapping her arms like wings, convinced
that she can fly. Secure in her madness, she has no knowledge that she has become the town pariah.

The author's second novel, Sula (1974), expands the
theme of pariah by charting her heroine's odyssey from
childhood to adulthood. In addition, there is a shift of emphasis on the theme of the search for ultimate glory, as
expressed in the Preface by the following quotation from Ten-
nessee Williams' The Rose Tattoo: "Nobody knew my rose
of the world but me.... I had too much glory. They don't
want glory like that in nobody's heart." Toni Morrison develops the theme by focusing on two women and their friendship: an extraordinary friendship in which one is a rebel
who becomes the town's scandal, and the other a conformist
who does all the proper things expected of her. Analyzing
their different households at the age of twelve, Morrison
brings together the components of their lives with a fine
sympathy for a friendship which, though broken, ultimately
assumes a dramatic meaning for the story and the women.
Though it is Nel, the conformist woman, who voices the
idea that Sula had been her glory, the book ends with each
woman's thoughts centered on the other, despite the fact
that no reconciliation has taken place. "Well, I'll be
damned ... it didn't even hurt," thinks Sula as death closes
in on her. "Wait'll I tell Nel" (p. 149). And Nel realizes
after Sula's death that it was not the husband who had deserted her that she had missed all these years, but Sula.
"O Lord, Sula," she cries, "girl, girl, girlgirlgirl" (p. 174).

The typography (girlgirlgirl) enforces the idea devel-
oped throughout that the two together form one woman in
which the light and the dark, the rebel and the conformist,
exist side by side. Thus Morrison's novel, in essence,
bears a relationship to Sarah E. Wright's work beyond the
superficial resemblance of the theme: rebel woman and her
reaching out for woman's friendship. Sarah E. Wright's
pathetic Mariah clings for comfort to motherly figures like
Vyella and Cora Lou. Toni Morrison combines the psychological, the symbolic, and the philosophical in her portraits

of Nel and Sula in order to demonstrate that each comple-
ments the other. There is a hint of Dostoevsky's The
Double and the Dostoevskyan idea that in every person there
lurks a double. Morrison's fictional method is character
counterpoint, rather than the Dostoevskyan technique of en-
compassing the timid and the masterful in one figure.

Sometimes, it seems that in order to establish Nel
as the conformist woman and Sula as the rebel, the author
places her characters in settings in which the contrast is
too pat. Treating childhood as the basic experience of the
two, she demonstrates why the girls are drawn together.
Sula comes from a sprawling, untidy home always filled with
men belonging to either her grandmother Eva Peace or her
mother Hannah. Both women are described as man lovers,
and if they are not quite rebels against the existing order,
they can certainly be regarded as women out of the ordinary.
The grandmother never hesitates to use violence either
against herself or toward a member of her family when she
sees it as necessary. Almost starving with her children
when her husband deserts her, and with little over a dollar
in her pocket, Eva sacrifices a leg to a train "accident" in
order to get insurance money. She returns from the hospital, buys a big house, collects her children from the neighbor with whom they have been staying, and proceeds to take
in all kinds of strays.

The violence which is to limn Sula in childhood constantly surrounds her grandmother, and links the two together. There is Eva's shocking action when her son Plum
returns from the war a drug addict. Watching his increasing deterioration, she decides to put an end to it and does
so by setting his body afire. If he can't live like a man,
she tells her daughter Hannah, who confronts her with knowledge of the murder, then let him die like a man. She breaks
down only once: "But I held him close first" (p. 72).

Later on, throwing herself out of a high window to
smother the flames enveloping her daughter, she demonstrates once more that she considers no action as too extreme. It's a view which her granddaughter Sula absorbs
and turns back on her, as the last scene between the two
dramatizes. When a mature Sula comes back to her grandmother's home after an absence of ten years, Eva makes
no pretense of her disapproval of her granddaughter's mode
of life as well as of the lack of communication during her
absence. Fearful that the old lady may take the same

measure against her that she adopted with her son, Sula has her put into a home. It is an action which scandalizes the entire black community, to whom this is tantamount to putting kin "outdoors."

Sula's mother, Hannah, is also a woman who takes matters into her own hands. With sex as her main pleasure, she lives hedonistically during her brief life. Widowed, rippling with sexuality, as she is described, she helps herself to the men in her community like a child dipping into a bonbon dish. Where Eva's actions are allowed to speak for themselves, the author is definitely on the side of Hannah. She was not promiscuous, explains the writer; Hannah simply needed "some touching every day" (p. 44)--a delightful description of the gentle Hannah.

If Sula's home rocks with noise, music, the sound of strange men's voices, the quarreling of the Deweys (three retarded children whom Eva befriends), the staggering of Tar Baby (a white man who is quietly drinking himself to death in the house), and the hum of wheels as Eva rolls around on the chair made for her by one of her gentleman friends, Nel's homelife provides a rigid counterpoint. Her mother, daughter of a scented Creole whore, but brought up by a pious grandmother, is the essence of the striving for respectability and order. A compulsive housekeeper and a devout churchgoer, she surrounds her daughter Nel with daily do's and dont's. The author, whose presence is strong in the book, comments that the mother had almost succeeded in quenching any natural aggressiveness in the daughter, and had rubbed down to a dull glow any sparkle of imagination and creativity. That she hasn't succeeded entirely in her efforts to mold her daughter in the conventional pattern is due to Sula, with whom Nel comes alive.

However, if the plot sounds mechanistically formal at this point, Morrison deviates from the pattern to include details indicating that if the girls are drawn to each other by differences in their backgrounds, there are also similarities between them. Both girls are fatherless--Sula's is dead and Nel's father is away at sea most of the time. And since the book is primarily concerned with the non-conformist woman, the author introduces early into her narrative a view of motherhood quite different from Sarah E. Wright's. Nowhere here is the role of mother regarded with the passion seen in Wright. Eva, Hannah, and even the proper Helene (who fades from the book midway) appear to consider motherhood as but one experience--a concept finally articulated and accepted by Nel. And Sula, as an adult woman, except for the brief wavering with her lover Ajax, rejects the verities of a society which stress motherhood and marriage.

A radically fresh approach to the theme of rebellion is that the author works with symbols and the psychological to establish Nel and Sula as projections of different aspects of the same character. In appearance one is light, the other dark. Nel's skin is described as the color of wet sand, while Sula's is a heavy brown color and she has a birthmark over one eye. For Nel, this birthmark is always a stemmed rose. For the townspeople, who regard Sula as evil, it is a snake. To shell-shocked Shadrack, who lives apart from the people in the Bottom and who fishes for a living in his lucid moments, the birthmark is his beloved tadpole, and Sula is the only person to whom he tips his hat and shows friendliness.

The symbolic use of names is important. Nel (knell) connotes the pealing note of doom on which Nel's life ends not once but three times, with each separation from Sula. The first time is when Nel marries and Sula goes away for ten years. The second time is the break with Sula over Jude, Nel's husband, with whom Sula sleeps briefly. The third and most poignant is Nel's realization that in Sula's grave is buried the passion, the life, the fun, and the healthy womanhood which Sula represented. On the other hand, Sula's name suggests an abbreviation of Suleiman, The Magnificent. It may be more than coincidental that Morrison's latest book (dealing with another kind of glory) is entitled Song of Solomon. Even the Norse meaning of Sula as "sea bird" or "pillar" is applicable as symbol to the meaning of the story, since Sula takes flight while Nel stays home. Also, without question, Sula is Nel's pillar for most of the story.

In terms of psychological analysis, the actions of Sula and Nel are "figure splitting"--the separation and projection of character into component parts. Nel is calm, passive, or frightened in a crisis. Sula's emotions erupt in some action that is strong or even violent. A good example is the episode with the Irish boys who waylay the girls with the intent of harassing them. While Nel stands motionless, Sula whips out her grandmother's paring knife, slashes off the tip of one finger and warns the boys that if she can do something like this to herself, they had better consider what she'd do to them. The action has the necessary effect on the boys; they never again attempt to bully the girls.

In this scene, it should further be noted that whether or not it is Morrison's intention, Sula's action in defending herself and her friend can be viewed in Jungian terms. She is exhibiting the male side of her nature, if one accepts the Jungian concept that we are all both male and female. This masculine part of Sula is brought out in another scene, when she climbs a huge tree with a boy named Chicken Little, while Nel stands timidly on the ground watching. Sula is always pictured as thrusting out for adventure and varied experience--a role generally associated with men.

Each significant part of the two women's character-izations, both as children and as women, then, comes from the author's repeated insistence that they are one person split into two; as Sula's grandmother says, "never was no difference" (p. 169). When Sula leaves after Nel's conven-tional marriage, Nel's life, to all creative purposes, ex-pires. Sula's return ten years later revitalizes Nel, and touches her with magic. She becomes more understanding with her children, more sexually responsive to her husband, and bubbling over with fun and laughter when Sula is around. When she breaks with Sula over Sula's brief appropriation of her husband Jude, she retreats into bitterness, suffering, and barrenness. Still unaware of her real need for Sula, she is amazed that in her suffering she wants to talk to Sula, to share the anguish. Without Sula she is a woman lacking courage to make a life for herself. She becomes a ghost and is described at the end as lost in "circles and circles of sorrow" (p. 174).

In the author's structuring of Sula and Nel, then, they are less persons in their own right than representa-tions of rebel and conformist, which the author views as the black woman's intrinsic conflict. Particularly with Sula, the writer seems to be going beyond such representation, addressing herself to the idea of the great rebel--the one who exceeds boundaries, creates excitement, tries to break free of encroachments of external cultural forces and chal-lenges destiny. What, for example, does she have Sula do? Believing that an unpatterned, unconditioned life is possible, Sula tries to avoid uniformity by creating her own kind of life.

In the ten years that Sula is away from the Bottom

(officially known as Medallion), she leads what the author terms an "experimental" life (p. 118). It's not quite clear to what extent Sula experiments, but since the time span of the novel is 1919-1965, and Sula leaves town in 1927, her life in those ten years and the brief time she returns to town is certainly not that of the conventional black woman. During her absence from home, she goes to college, sleeps with a variety of men--black and white--and gives the impression that she shies away from no experience. Upon her return, she picks up her friendship with Nel, as well as with Nel's husband, and is amazed at her friend's hurt reaction. Had they not shared everything? she reminds Nel later. The term "pariah" pinned on her by the town's people does not make her blanch, and she continues to dally with their men as well as with white men.

The latter action brings her into direct conflict with social mores, and enables the author to make a stinging statement on the double standard practiced in the community. It is permissible, she points out, for black men to sleep with white women, but a union between a black woman and a white man can only be on the basis of rape. For a black woman voluntarily to sleep with a white man is "unthinkable"--there was nothing "filthier" (p. 113) she could do.

Hence Sula, by this and other acts, cuts herself off from everyday patterns of living and pays a heavy price for her independence--loneliness. But she accepts it proudly as her own loneliness, and not something created by the act of another person. It's no "secondhand lonely" (p. 143), she informs Nel. The author, however, is not just working with the idea of the importance of experience, and the acceptance of one's responsibility for experience. There are times in the book when one gets the impression that in dealing with the theme of a woman's right to an experimental life, the writer is pushing the reader to consider something much more unconventional. This is that the impulse to murder and violence in the human psyche is endemic not only to men; women, too, are capable of violence, Morrison seems to be saying. We have already noted the matter-of-fact way that the author treats Eva Peace and her killing of her son Plum. The motive is spelled out as mother love--the kind of love which will not hesitate to destroy its young in order to "save" them, even though the action puts the individual on the wrong side of prevailing concepts of good and evil.

Violence by men is not a new theme in fiction and

has been treated in different ways by male writers, notably
Dostoevsky. But it is a relatively new theme for women
writers. Violence and criminality are seldom associated
with woman's role (although Defoe's struggling Moll Flanders
is an exception). Even the prostitute who breaks the law is
victim rather than victimizer, because her act is regarded
as one of submission to the man. It is interesting that the
three women discussed: Sarah E. Wright, Toni Morrison,
and Alice Walker, all examine the idea of woman and violence, and come up with varying conclusions. Of the three,
only Morrison's women do not hesitate to resort to violence,
thereby questioning the customary assumption in our culture
that it is only men who are capable of killing.

In Morrison's novel, the moral initiative which underlies Sula's experimental life is rooted in her capacity to
initiate violence, as is illustrated in two childhood scenes.
The author hits us with the idea that Nel and Sula as women
recall the different scenes of violence with the same emo-
tion--pleasure, or more accurately, "satisfaction." Whether
or not the author is exploring repressed drives or even
pathological complexes, the following two scenes are presented boldly. As a twelve-year-old, Sula drowns Chicken
Little when she swings the child around so vigorously that
he slips from her hands and lands in the nearby river.
The act is preceded by a ritual play in which Sula and Nel
dig two holes until the holes become one, and then the two
girls proceed to throw all kinds of garbage into the hole.
Right after this the boy appears, is taunted and induced to
climb a tree, of which he is terrified, comes down, and is
drowned.

The author follows this immediately with another
scene which underscores D. H. Lawrence's idea that no act
of murder is "accidental." Sula's mother catches on fire
while tending a fire in the yard, and Sula watches her
mother's burning not with horror, as would be expected, but
with an "interested" expression (p. 78). To reemphasize
Sula's unusual reaction, the author has her recall the scene
on her dying bed. Sula looks back to the burning and remembers: "I stood there watching her burn and was thrilled.
I wanted her to keep on jerking like that, to keep on danc-
ing" (p. 147). Consistent with the theme that Sula and Nel
are one person, a prematurely-aged Nel explores the question of why she "didn't ... feel bad" about the Chicken Little
drowning. "How come it felt so good to see him fall?" (p.
170) she asks herself. The question is not pursued further,

for Nel concludes that her real feeling at that time was "the tranquillity that follows a joyful stimulation" (p. 170).

Without question, the description of the two scenes and the emotions of Sula/Nel has sexual overtones. As Mailer dramatizes with Rojack in An American Dream, the act of murder can be as orgasmic as the act of sexual love. There is more than an implication of this idea in Morrison's novel; disguised as a psychological novel, it is really a novel of ideas prodding us to think on the experimental life for woman in the vein of Dostoevsky's early thinking. In his early works there is the theme that an individual, in order to feel strong and above the cowed majority of people, must be willing to consider violence and murder. Dostoevsky works with man's contradictory drives and draws a line between what he sees as two types of humanity: the meek/ weak and the strong/ruthless. In his later novels, notably Crime and Punishment, he changes his thinking. Raskolnikov, believing himself to be part of that humanity which dares to transgress the conventional rules of society, kills an old woman whom he considers useless to society. However, through suffering, Dostoevsky has him come to the realization that he was wrong and that everyone has some innate value. Toni Morrison, as a black woman whose racial history has involved rape, torture, humiliation and death, wants us to be more aware of the heritage of hatred and despair which necessitates bravery to consider the breaking of taboos.

Yet the author does not seem at ease with her characterization of Sula, violence, and the experimental life. She steps in with an armload of explanations distributed over several pages. Sula had inherited her grandmother's arrogance and her mother's self-indulgence; she had never felt any obligation to please someone unless their pleasure pleased her; she was as willing to receive pain as to give it; she had never been the same since she overheard her mother Hannah explain that she loved Sula but did not like her; the boy's drowning had closed something off in her; and so forth.

The author soon drops this line of reasoning and turns with relief to a defense of Sula summed up as: Sula was not afraid of "the free fall" (p. 120). (It's a phrase which has a possible echo of Milton's Lucifer.) The conventional women of the Bottom were. These women had allowed their husbands to dry up their dreams, and those without men looked like "sour-tipped needles featuring one constant empty eye" (p. 122). Sooner or later, all died with their aprons on. The writer makes it clear that Sula's one lapse into conventionality, when she falls in love with Ajax and begins to dream of a commitment from him, results in sorrow and the common fate reserved for the black woman-- desertion.

Unfortunately, the literary destiny of most rebel women--death--does not spare Sula. Beginning with Samuel Richardson's Clarissa, the conventional end for the rebel woman is either death or madness. Morrison's Sula is no exception. She dies at thirty, but not without stating that her rebellion has been the natural outcome of her dialectic. On her death bed, she sustains her position philosophically by weighing the pros and cons of what is good and bad, renounces the accepted definition of goodness, and reiterates her belief that it is only life that matters. Life is important, life must be lived and duty and suffering on this earth are too high a price to pay for heavenly immortality.

All this is played out in a dialogue staged between Nel and Sula, almost like an allegory of rebel and conformist. In reply to Nel's statement that a woman, and a colored woman at that, cannot do what she wants to do, Sula's answer is characteristic. Why not? she asks. She reminds Nel that every black man they had ever known had deserted women and children--and black women had accepted it and continued to accept it. This was one reason they were dying all over the country. When told that she, too, is dying, Sula retorts that she's not going down like a "stump" but a magnificent "redwood" (p. 143). Prior to her illness, she had not hesitated to take the dizzying plunge into experience. She had really lived in this world. As for her illness, she absolutely refuses to give it the stature of tragedy.

It is inevitable that the question of good and evil come up in Nel's confronting Sula with the question: why did you do it? She has been good to Sula, she reminds her. Sula's reply is matter-of-fact: good and bad are relative. Anyway, she says, she had not killed Jude, she had just "fucked him" (p. 145) and if they were such good friends, why was it difficult for Nel to accept this? The whole business of good and bad is questioned by Sula. How do you know it was you who was good? she asks Nel, and answers her own question with: "I mean maybe it wasn't you. Maybe it was me" (p. 146). The ending has the real Russian bang, as somebody once said of that last sentence in D. H.

Lawrence's Women in Love. The ending, however, resolves
nothing; but it does make us think of the ideas posed by the
author, not as abstractions but as experiences lived by feeling women.

The novel bears the same incompleteness as Sula's
search for freedom. In the characterization of Nel and
Sula, however, Morrison does succeed in emphasizing the
duality of the mind--that part which imprisons the body and
keeps it from reaching out for new experience. Together,
Sula and Nel are light and dark--physically, mentally, and
emotionally. In her focus on Sula as the part of nature
which refuses restrictions, she fashions a central figure,
a symbol and a dialectician who renounces a conventional
morality in which suffering and the bearing of the cross is
the black woman's only consolation. Sula makes of life a
defiant gesture which liberates her to an extent, and keeps
her from self-pity. She is sustained by her pride in the
fact that she walks through life with no blinders on. Yet,
there is no happy ending. Sula collapses in the loneliness
of the search for freedom, and proves what? That love is
necessary? That the human heart cannot entertain equal
proportions of good and evil? That everything is not relative? These and other unanswered questions are given more
scope in the author's latest novel, Song of Solomon.

Before considering Song of Solomon, it should be said
that despite the trailing tendrils of questions left behind in
Sula, it is a provocative book. As a social critic, Morrison writes about blacks in their narrowness and courage,
their cruelty and humanity, because they are there, were
there in the life that once existed. The book begins on an
elegiac note, since the town no longer survives. There is
a power of evocation in the author's reconstruction of its
design--the pool parlor, the local palace of cosmetology,
Reba's Grill in which Reba cooked with her hat on in order
to remember the ingredients, the Conjure Woman with her
seven children who brought her the specialties of her trade:
nail parings, white hens, blood, camphor, etc. The people
of the Bottom come alive not only in their pain but in the
humor which enables them to sustain the threats of living:
the very name, the Bottom, laughingly deprecates the place.

The author polishes and refocuses her lens on the
people. Her individualist perspective never suppresses social connections between characters and events. The criticism of the black man that Sula voices is expanded by the

author into an understanding analysis of his situation in
white society. Without sparing the black man's frequent ab-
rogation of responsibility to women and children through desertion, she makes it clear that a determining factor for
self-development and self-esteem--a man's work--is denied
him. Ajax, the local pool room devotee, and the man who
flees Sula as soon as she shows signs of wanting to nest
with him, has a passion for airplanes, but he is not permitted to fly them (the time is 1939). Jude, Nel's husband,
yearns to be something more than a waiter carrying trays.
He wants to construct that tunnel promised to the people of
the Bottom, but the work never materializes. The idea that
men who are thwarted in their dream of better work become
brutalized and dehumanized links Toni Morrison to writers
like D. H. Lawrence, who in novel after novel explores the
results of a deprived existence on men and women. In Sula,
we come a little further in understanding the black man, and
still further in our appreciation of the black woman's problems.

Toni Morrison's latest novel, Song of Solomon (1977),
has a far greater thrust and depth than either The Bluest
Eye or Sula. In this novel, she deals not only with the
woman who breaks away from the established society to
create an individualistic life for herself, but with the black
man who yearns to fly--to break out of the confining life
into the realm of possibility--and who embarks on a series
of dramatic adventures. They prove to him: "If you sur-
rendered to the air, you could ride it" (p. 337) (author's
italics). But whether or not the hero, Milkman, as he is
nicknamed, will continue to ride the air or die at the hands
of his former black friend is unresolved. However, this
question, posed at the end for the reader, throws in sharper
focus the themes which the writer carries over from her
previous books: flight, the journey, family, friendship,
violence, the paradox of good and evil, the world of black
society: its code, superstitions, plus fable, song, and
myth.

The achievement of this novel is its willingness and
ability not only to explore these areas in further detail, but
to use black folklore, the ready acceptance of the supernatural, and magic as part of black culture. In reply to an
interviewer, Toni Morrison declared that black people believe in magic; they believe in ghosts, the way white people
believe in germs. In a sense, Morrison's fiction takes its

point of departure from Nabokov's proposition that there is
another world surrounding us from which we have closed
ourselves off.   In the words of William Blake: "For man
has closed himself up, till he sees all things thro' narrow
chinks of his cavern. "[4]

Many of Morrison's characters believe in the capacity of the mind to see through the chinks of the cavern--
even the money-hungry and materialistic Macon Dead.   But
it is Macon's sister Pilate who emerges as the most powerful figure in the book with her calm acceptance of this
world, as well as of another reality other than the fixed
one of the world.   She is thoroughly at home with herself,
and has the kind of sensibility which is not disturbed by anything she experiences or witnesses.   There is something
splendidly pagan and primitive about her, and she is represented at the time we first meet her as having the power to
evoke from others various reflections of her own kindliness
and understanding.   Implicitly, the author establishes Pilate's
capacity for placing herself in harmony with the laws of the
earth and nature.   Within the orbit of Morrison's moral vision, these laws have to do with the truths of the human
heart.   They are the necessity to demonstrate courage, endurance, sympathy, and desire to help others, while surviving with dignity.

Morrison links Pilate to the earth and nature in various ways.   Pilate makes her living by pressing grapes
into wine and distilling whiskey from grain.   Her early life
is spent in wandering from place to place, working either in
the fields or by a stream.   Like the earth turning on its
axis, she is in constant motion.   Even the description of
her lips, always moving as she chews on a piece of straw
or pine needle, helps to imply some connection with the
immemorial rhythms of the earth.   Then there is the color
of her lips: berry red; her height, like that of a tall black
tree; the scent about her of a forest.   Her deepest affinities
are with the natural world, and any detail of domesticity in
connection with her only serves to deepen the image of
union with nature.   In her home, filled with the scent of
pine and fermenting fruit, there are no curtains or shades,
and the sun streams in hot and unfettered.   At night, only
candles provide light, and kerosene supplies heat.   Above
all, her closeness to the earth is both literally and symbolically stressed by her reluctance to wear shoes.   When
she has to put them on, they are men's shoes, invariably
unlaced.

Pilate is also seen as protectress of the weak, and
skilled in arts which help the good and frighten those who
plan evil. Observing her sister-in-law Ruth withering away
for lack of "touching" (a favorite word of Morrison's for
sexual love), she mixes up a potion which awakens the husband's love just long enough for Ruth to conceive a son.
When the potion wears off in four months, the terrified and
pregnant Ruth appears on Pilate's doorstep, fearful of what
her husband may force her to do. Pilate takes her in, feeds
her all the crunchy food Ruth craves at that moment, then
goes to her brother's office. In his absence, she places
a doll on his desk. The doll has a red circle painted on its
stomach and a chicken bone between its legs. Needless to
say, the doll has the desired intimidating effect on Macon,
and we are told that he has a long and difficult time trying
to burn it.

Not always does Pilate depend on her arts. Sometimes, she displays strength worthy of an Amazon. When a
man beats her daughter Reba, Pilate seizes him from behind,
twists his arm, puts a knife to his throat, and whispers that
she is a "Mamma" and Mammas love their daughters and ...
Without question, Pilate is protean: protector, sorceress,
healer, mediator, mother, soothsayer (she predicts the day
of her nephew's birth) and many other things. She can be
regally tall or shrink to humble proportions.

The latter transformation is dramatized in the court
scene, when her nephew Milkman and his friend Guitar get
in trouble with the law. Ironically, the two have stolen a
bag from Pilate which Milkman's father tells him contains
gold; as it turns out later, it holds the bones of the father
of Pilate and Macon. Pilate ignores the circumstances of
the theft, comes to court, and immediately falls into the
shuffling, cringing, ignorant "nigger woman" role expected
of her. For to do otherwise, she realizes, would be to
challenge the cherished belief in white supremacy, and en-
danger all their lives.

Her final legacy to her nephew Milkman is a sense
of compassion and understanding. Through her and his own
efforts, he learns about his "progenitors," to use one of
Faulkner's favorite words, and to realize what Faulkner
stresses: a continuity with one's sources, with those from
whom we have come. Her life, for Milkman, becomes a
testimonial of the woman who "Without ever leaving the
ground ... could fly" (p. 336).

The story of Pilate is part of a black family history
which spans almost a century of American history.   It is
given special enrichment through the tracing of many lives.
More notably, it forms a fascinating parallel with the odyssey
of her nephew Milkman, who is the other chief character in
the story.   The fullness of the book even incorporates within
it an ironic twist on the Faulknerian theme: the collapse
of a proud, white Southern family, and the faithful black re-
tainer who continues to serve with humility and devotion.
Braided in with the lives of the black people is also a brief
story of the decline of a white family whose men killed
Pilate's father.   But no faithful Dilsey (The Sound and the
Fury) lives in its decaying mansion, only a black woman
named Circe.   She calmly revenges herself on the people
for whom she scrubbed and polished and who, she recalls,
valued their dogs more than the lives of black people. Alone
now in the big house with a pack of Weimaraner dogs, she
has them methodically and systematically rip the Belgian
silk brocade wall paper and other costly furnishings which
the owners had prized.   The dominant motif in the book,
however, is not revenge, but the proud realization by a
black family of who and what they are.   Morrison's fiction
is the opposite of Richard Wright's in this respect. Where
Wright finds no sustaining values in the past of black people,
Morrison celebrates the past.   Pilate, Macon, and Milkman,
whose last name is Dead, did not just drop from nowhere.
They go back to a long line of succession.   There was a
beginning.   A source.   It is this knowledge which gives
them a sense of renewal; even Macon experiences renewal
in a small way.

The family is dramatized, however, in ways which
permit the author to probe perspectives both unflatteringly
and sympathetically.   Consider the story of Pilate first:
it is an account of an extraordinary woman who, after twenty
years of wandering, asks herself: what makes me happy,
and what do I need to do in order to stay alive?   The question is related to her perception of the circumstances of her
birth, her name, her father's killing by white men, and the
fact that she is cut off from kin and black society.   She is
estranged from her brother Macon because he mistakenly
believes that she stole the gold he found after the father's
death.   Furthermore, she is not accepted by black society
because she is regarded as "unnatural, " since she has no
navel.

In regard to the issue of Pilate's navel, the author

appears to be aware of the arbitrariness of the kind of fiction which asks us to believe the unusual. Her method is
simply to concentrate on the idea that in a world of no fixed
reality, all things are possible. We are told that Pilate
was born after her mother died, and inched herself out of
the womb, "dragging" the cord after her. The cord eventually shriveled and dropped off, leaving a smooth place
where the navel had been. Pilate is always limned with
the unusual, as even her name testifies. After her birth,
her illiterate father opens the Bible, drops his finger on a
spot, looks down, sees the name "Pilate Christ Killer" and
decides to keep it for his daughter. He likes the illustra-
tion of the tree which appears by the name. When told the
name is inappropriate, he is adamant about retaining it and
backs it up with his logic. Had he not prayed all night for
Jesus to spare his wife and had she not died?

The husband's anguished cry at the injustice of a God
who robs him of his precious wife does not suggest that the
author has a quarrel with Christianity. Her real concern
is with the behavior aberrations of those who consider themselves "good Christians." Specifically, in connection with
the events which pursue Pilate's father, she holds up to
scorn those white Christians who cheat and kill black people
out of greed. Pilate's father is tricked into putting a mark
on a paper which gives white men the right to seize his
land. When he tries to protect it, they blow him to pieces.

The central metaphor of the book, as the author herself has pointed out in an interview, is flying. Before Pilate
can fly, however, she must run--no new experience for the
black person, as Ralph Ellison portrays in Invisible Man.
For Pilate running begins with escape from the killers'
house in which she and her brother have been secreted after
their father's murder. The wily Circe knows it is the last
place the killers would suspect as the children's hiding spot.
But before the escape, Pilate takes an important step to insure her identity--a step which throws into dramatic relief
the main theme of family, and the conviction voiced by Milkman at the end: "When you know your name, you should
hang on to it" (p. 329). Folding the piece of paper on which
her father had laboriously traced her name, she places it
in a snuff box and painfully strings the whole contraption
through her left ear. When infection develops, it is treated
successfully with cobwebs, illustrating for the writer the resourcefulness of black people and their knowledge of folk
medicine.

The significance of names to black people is stressed over and over again in black literature, and plays an important part in this novel. Toni Morrison tells us that black people get their names from "yearnings, gestures, flaws, events, mistakes, weaknesses" (p. 330). Pilate's family name is certainly based on a comedy of errors. When asked by a drunken Yankee soldier in the Union army where he was born, Pilate's father replies "Macon." To other questions, he answers that his father is dead and that he is not a slave but a free man. The soldier records it all, but in the wrong places. The name becomes Macon Dead; the place of birth: Dunfrie. As Milkman's friend Guitar remarks: "Niggers get their names the way they get everything else--the best way they can" (p. 88).

This may explain why nicknames are sometimes more important to black men than the names which were originally given them. A nickname is something that defines the person more accurately. It is picked up from the sense of the person. Milkman's name, derived from the fact that he was still sucking at his mother's breast when already a young boy, sets him apart. Prophetically, he realizes his mother's illusion that she is pouring a stream of gold into his veins, for eventually Milkman discovers he does have "gold" in his veins--the gold of his heritage (as will be explained). If black men are officially named after their fathers, then nicknamed by the community, women's names are usually taken from the Bible. Milkman's sisters are "First Corinthians" and "Magdalene called Lena," and are usually referred to in this way. Pilate, we see, has nothing but her name after her father's death; hence the symbolic marriage of name and identity by that action of hers in stringing the box with her name through her left ear--like the placing of the ring on the left finger. It is the only marriage Pilate is to have. Her move is as tactically political as it is symbolic. For to hang on to her name after her escape is to outmaneuver the killers who tried to wipe out father and children.

From here on, the story takes on aspects of the fabula and myth which it is useful to summarize. Brother and sister hide in the woods. On the third day, they see their dead father, who keeps disappearing and appearing. Towards sunset, he motions for the two to go to a nearby cave and they obey. In the early morning, Macon ventures further into the cave and finds an old white man. Terrified, he kills the man, and discovers several bags of gold

near the body. The father appears and utters the words
"sing sing" (which turn out to be the name of his wife "Sing"
and foreshadow Milkman's discovery of real "gold"--family
history). In this cave a monumental battle takes place between brother and sister. Macon wants to take the gold;
Pilate insists that it be left in the cave. Macon is defeated
when Pilate draws a knife on him--the same knife used to
kill the white man. He leaves and when he returns, discovers sister and gold gone. Believing that she has stolen
the gold for herself, his brotherly love turns to hatred.
They meet again after twenty years and, at the end, when
everything is cleared up, there is a truce, but no reconciliation.

The cave scene is an important plot ingredient because it helps to establish Macon as materialistic and
greedy--a symbol of the individual exposed at an early age
to the corruption and wickedness of the world, twisted in
the process, and becoming "unnatural." It will be a recurring reflection on various black men throughout the book.
Pilate, on the other hand, in this and other scenes, is consistently cast as nature or the good. If money becomes the
all-important factor to Macon, who at seventeen is already
pressing for wealth, it is always insignificant to Pilate.

I have gone into such detail because the writing is
rich, but not compressed. The design of the book is
sprawling and the narrative texture depends on a great many
cumulative effects. Together with the author's allusions and
indirect use of archetypal patterns about Pilate, she never
lets us lose sight of the fact that Pilate is a woman grounded
firmly in the social reality of black society. Pilate's twenty-
year odyssey, and her subsequent life in the small town in
which she finally settles not far from her brother (to his
rage, embarrassment and shame over her unconventional
life), enables the author to move further than in the previous
novel in her discussion of black society and women--married
and unmarried.

The young Pilate, alone and completely dependent on
her own resources, cannot find acceptance. She functions
harmoniously within her society until its people discover that
she has no navel. Thereafter, her life takes on a habitual
pattern. She is either asked to leave the community, or she
is deserted by these people who simply disappear during the
night, since they are migrant workers. Pilate, however,
resists any sense of permanent personal displacement.

Wherever she goes, she carries with her a geography book
she has picked up and carefully marks it to show where
she has been. She also makes sure that she collects some
rocks from each place. Obviously, both actions are part
of her continuing and sturdy effort to keep constantly before
her evidence of who she is and where she has been.

Black culture, with its classes, customs, beliefs,
rituals, its underpinning of paganism beneath the surface of
Christianity, is often treated with interest, admiration, and
affection. The belief in ghosts, the conviction that drying
and feeding to a baby the caul in which the baby is born
will prevent the baby from seeing ghosts, and other be-
liefs--all add a pungent flavor to black life as the writer
sees it. But she is too honest and realistic to avoid the
fact that there is another side to black life. Her tracing
of Pilate's journey throughout the country is arranged with
a focus on the darker side of superstitions, which have to
do with the words "natural" and "unnatural" which keep
cropping up throughout the book. The scrutiny of these
two words finally expands into social commentary on black
men and their thinking on such diverse subjects as marriage and killing, though the diversity at one point in the
discussion converges.

It is Pilate who exhibits the nature which both her
brother and society suppress and kill in themselves. As
in Sula, Morrison may be implying the Jungian idea that
we are all male and female, and that patriarchal society
suppresses the female part of ourselves. But it is safer
to assume that the author wants us to understand that Pilate
is a woman who refuses to be contaminated by narrowness
and the social diseases which plague her society at large.
Her world is the world of Nature, a world of singing, natural rituals, natural foods, kindliness, gentleness, and acceptance of all human beings.

The writer is careful not to make Pilate into a romantic Pantheist. Hence, we see Pilate appraising her
situation, the social scene, and debating the means of personal salvation available to her. She does this with no
semblance of self-pity, sentiment, and brooding introspec-
tion. Noting that men who sleep with "drunken women,"
"midgets," "one-legged women" and all other kinds of wom-
en (p. 148) are rendered impotent by the sight of her
smooth belly, she realizes that she must create a new kind
of life for herself. Like Sula, she decides to take "the
free fall," but in a different way.

She rejects the traditional image of woman by cutting
off her hair, binding it into a turban and wearing clothes
functional to her way of life. With two people now to support (daughter and granddaughter), she looks around the social scene, and realizing that throats are thirsty as long as
there is prohibition, she becomes a bootlegger, making and
selling wine and whiskey. The author stresses that Pilate
never loses her humanity, nor debases herself and other
women by allowing traffic in women flesh. She only sells
wine and whiskey (author's italics). There is no consumption on the premises. Thus Pilate soon enjoys that status
so difficult for black women (and white women) to acquire--
economic independence. As an economically-independent
woman, she is able to function outside of patriarchal values
and rise successfully above the social forces which are a
constant threat to the black woman. Hence, undisturbed by
the town's view of her as "unnatural," and ignoring her
brother's deep embarrassment and shame at the way she
lives, she seeks him out once, and that is to help his wife
Ruth.

Pilate's relationship with Ruth moves the novel further in its examination of "natural" and "unnatural," and into
more extensive social commentary on marriage, which is
as bleak as in Sula but for different reasons. This time,
Morrison discusses not only the poor man like Jude who
yearns to be something more than a waiter in a restaurant,
but the black man who, having attained some financial success, is hungry for more. Women become the leverage by
which he hopes to hoist himself to money and power--a
common practice in white society, as Norman Mailer demonstrates with Rojack (An American Dream).

We have already seen, in the author's sympathetic
structuring of Macon's early life, how the death of his
father twists him and turns all of his energies into acquisitiveness. But his marriage to Ruth, daughter of a prominent black doctor, and his subsequent treatment of wife and
daughters quickly rob his character of any sympathy we
might have felt for him. Ruth does not suffer the fate reserved for the poor black woman--desertion. Her destiny
is sexual rejection, and daily expressions of contempt from
husband.

The reason for the twenty years or more of sexual
rejection is more clearly expressed than in James Joyce's
Ulysses, in which Molly and Bloom appear to have stopped

sleeping with one another after the death of their infant son
Rudy. The basis for Macon's refusal to have sex with his
wife is given with more clarity. He had observed his wife
kissing her dead father's fingers after his death. It con-
firms for Macon his suspicions of something "unnatural" between father and daughter. After all, he reasons, the father had delivered both of his daughter's first two children.
There is a sly hint by the author that Macon's feelings may
not be due solely to these incidents, but to the fact that
his rich father-in-law had refused to lend him money to buy
property.

It is from this point on that the word "unnatural,"
pinned first on Pilate (by brother and society) and then on
Ruth (by husband, society, and even son--for a while), becomes a transcendent embodiment of the intended meaning,
rather than the accepted social meaning. It is the socially
respectable Macon (and others, as we shall see) who appears
to be unnatural. The hint of unnaturalness which clings to
Macon in the cave because of his lust for gold receives re-
enforcement from another quarter--his sexual preferences.
It seems that in the early days of his marriage to Ruth and
before he witnessed the scene between dead father and
daughter, Macon was sexually excited not by his wife's body
but by her clothes: expensive underwear, costly shoes, and,
above all, her corset with its round little holes. His preference was to undress her slowly down to stockings and
shoes, and then draw the stockings over the shoes before
he entered her and ejaculated. In all the years of marriage,
Macon had not seen Ruth's feet. Furthermore, in the years
of shunning his wife, Macon had missed only one thing--the
corset with its round holes. One is reminded of D. H.
Lawrence, another exponent of nature and the natural life,
and his view that the diverting of a man's energies into
acquisitiveness had a definite bearing on his sexual practices.

The style of reflection into which Morrison drops so
often does not minimize Ruth's deficiencies, or the incestuous feelings she may have had for her father. But without
question, the writer is sympathetic to women like Ruth and
others who marry grasping, exploitive men, and who are
rejected by these men for one reason or another. The
scene between Ruth and her son Milkman invites us to understand and value the capacity of Ruth's feelings, and the in-
capacity of feeling which her son, at this moment, shares
with his father. Yes, she tells Milkman, she had kissed

her dead father's hands, the only feature of his body spared
by the wasting disease. No, she had not been naked, but
in her slip. Yes, she had loved her father because he was
the only person in the world who had asked nothing of her,
who had loved her for herself alone. Yes, she had nursed
her son Milkman longer than was conventional. "And I also
prayed for you," she tells him. "Every single night and
every single day. On my knees. Now you tell me. What
harm did I do you on my knees?" (p. 126). This is moving,
and we respond to her impassioned pleas as her son fails
to do. But despite the compassionate handling of Ruth's
story, her tragedy is reducible to the fact that she stays
unhappily married, turns all of her energies to her son,
and ignores her daughters.

The writer marshals her materials succinctly, com-
pelling us to recognize the immense loneliness of these
daughters. Demeaned by father because they are women,
ignored by mother for the same reason, their isolation is
doubly compounded by their education, which makes them
"overqualified" in the eyes of the ambitious young bachelors
of the community. Morrison's voice explains that these
men do not want intelligent women, but women who will
sacrifice themselves to their husbands' careers--women who
will strive and strive to maintain what the man has accumu-
lated. Luckily, both Corinthians and Lena eventually break
out of the prison of their lives--Corinthians gets a job and
a man, both beneath her social status, but together they
enable her to find a measure of satisfaction in her life.
Lena's gesture is less drastic, but more symbolic. She
simply refuses to make any more artificial roses--the only
occupation permitted the women by their father all these
years.

Interestingly enough, while Morrison presents women
who eventually free themselves somehow from an unnatural
life, Pilate's daughter and granddaughter are portrayed differently. Although leading a natural life in some respects,
they are essentially weak women. Pilate allows them all the
freedom they want, and Reba does bear some relation to
Hannah (Sula). But she is a watered-down version of Hannah, and appears more in sexual bondage to men than the
symbol of natural sensuality that Hannah embodies. The
granddaughter Hagar, who is loved and discarded by Milkman, represents for the author the natural woman who cuts
herself from organic sources of life by falling into possessive
love and sinking her identity into one man. When his love
is withdrawn, Hagar loses sanity and life.

Ironically, Pilate, who is able to break out of the
enclosures of conventional thinking and make a brave and
happy life for herself, cannot inspire either woman in her
house to follow her example. The author tries to get
around it by hinting that Reba is somewhat simple-minded,
and that Hagar is one of those pretty, spoiled black women
who either want to kill or die for love. Perhaps the more
plausible answer is that Pilate exercises individual will,
whereas the others simply do not.

The explorations of the lives of these women reveal
a growth in the author's feminist consciousness not present
in the previous novel. Alternatives are possible, says the
author, and in the character of Pilate she creates a woman
who finds life worth living and lives it. Perhaps, Toni
Morrison would not care to be discussed in terms of feminist consciousness, but the fact remains that her depiction
of Pilate stresses that Pilate's pattern of living does not
follow the achievement pattern associated with successful
men. Pilate is always the humanist. Her relationships
with people are compassionate, if they are in trouble. With
others, she is polite and hospitable "within the boundaries
of the elaborately socialized world of black people" (p.
149). Morrison, here as in Sula, does not spare the shortcomings of black society. She criticizes freely that societal
thinking which brands Pilate as "unnatural" and which fails
to see that its acts: sweeping up of Pilate's footsteps, or
placing mirrors on doors when she passes, are unnatural.

The order of things is questioned and judged not only
from social and moral viewpoints, but also from the metaphysical. If Pilate is not accepted by kin and society, she
is very much at home with her dead father, who appears
before her periodically with advice. One piece of advice
is to go back to the cave and collect the bones of the dead
man, which she does. It makes for the extraordinary ending to the book: for the bones are really those of her
father. Their proper burial adds a note of the classic to
the details of family history.

What becomes evident in the story, however, is that
in the treatment of the supernatural world Toni Morrison
is an explorer into a new kind of realism. She treats of
the supernatural world, which like the material world, to
use the words of Leonardo da Vinci, "is full of countless
possibilities as yet unembodied." In accepting both worlds,
Pilate is an example for the author of the natural connec-

tions between our hearts, our reason, our mystical consciousness, our myths. At no time is Pilate's father a
Lazarus returned from the dead; he is a robust man dressed
at first in coveralls and later (as Pilate's fortunes improve)
in a white shirt with blue collar and a brown peaked cap.
Like his daughter, the father wears no shoes. They are
slung over his shoulder.

Life and death, then, hold no terrors for Pilate,
whose sense of contact with this and other worlds is a natural one. She is able to survive in a society which denies
her "partnership in marriage, confessional friendship, and
communal religion" (p. 148). The author concludes her
tribute to Pilate by commenting that Pilate makes a life
for herself in which for sixty-eight years she has shed no
tears since the day Circe offered her white bread and store-
bought jam. In return for rudeness, she extends politeness,
and her concern for troubled people ripens with the years.
Yet for some reason, as in Sula, the woman who dares to
live by her own rules must die. True, Pilate doesn't disappear from life at the early age that Sula does, but she
is rendered with such loving detail that her death from the
shot of a black killer comes as a shock to the reader.

Perhaps that is the intention of the author. In a
world in which hate often predominates, Morrison's final
irony is that the woman named "Pilate Christ Killer" and
rejected by society as unnatural has only words of love even
for those who have hurt her. "I wish I'd a knowed more
people," she whispers to her nephew Milkman as he cradles
her in his arms. "I would of loved 'em all. If I'd a
knowed more, I would a loved more" (p. 336).

Needless to say, in Pilate Morrison finds a powerful
voice that fulfills the promise of a personality who has resolved the seminal conflict between the claims of nature and
the claims of culture. However, Song of Solomon, unlike
the writer's previous novels, gives men a more prominent
place, and specifically Milkman, son of Macon Dead and
nephew of Pilate. The book is fairly equally divided between the respective journeys of Pilate and Milkman. Both
take the standard path of the formula observed in mythology:
separation, initiation, and return. The connection with
mythology is elusive. There is a literary structure which
roots both characters firmly in the everyday world, and
though their stories are rich in mythological allusions, it is
not fruitful (as already shown) to discuss the materials of

the book as taken from myth in the traditional sense of the word. This is because the mythic allusions in the author's story serve as devices to convey many aspects of meaning, criticism, irony, understanding, compassion, satire and analysis.

Certainly, one hears overtones of the Jason myth and his quest for the Golden Fleece in Milkman's search for gold and his desertion of Hagar, whose name means to forsake. But, since Morrison is working with a reality of her own which is not primarily connected with logic, science, and related fields, her language is often symbolical, and particularly her use of names. Not only does Hagar's name foreshadow her role in the book, since she is forsaken by Milkman, but her mother Reba, or Rebecca as she is formally named, recalls Rebecca of the Bible, whose son Esau sold his birthright for a mess of pottage. But Morrison's use of names is suggestive rather than definitive, for Reba has no son, and it is she who squanders herself on a series of worthless black men. And Hagar had long forsaken her identity by staking her entire happiness on Milkman.

What we have in Song of Solomon, with Milkman's story, is that constant in American literature--the undertaking of the journey to free oneself. Pilate's efforts to liberate herself from cramped conditions of living are a result of society's rejection of her. Milkman's energies are concentrated on liberating himself from the confining and bitter atmosphere of his father's home, from the role thrust upon him--being his father's flunky--and from the provincial town in which he lives.

Milkman's first thirty years are spent in the shadow of his father, and he conforms to black male stereotypes--some of the most negative in fact--just as many of Toni Morrison's men do. He discards Hagar as he would a "wad of chewing gum" (p. 277) and follows the accepted male practice in his circle of casual loving and abandoning women. Towards his sisters, he alternates between condescension and ignoring them. With his mother, his attitude is one of suspicion and accusation. Did she really make it with her father? he wonders after hearing versions of the story from both father and mother. His only desire at this point is to escape home as much as possible, which is understandable in view of the bitterness between father and mother.

The world of men outside his door is his true home,

and his true love is Guitar, his friend who is older than he
by several years. Here, as elsewhere, Morrison's allusion
to an archetypal theme, the friendship of Damon and Pythias,
deliberately neglects to fulfill early expectations. The
theme of friendship becomes still another extension of the
theme of "natural" and "unnatural." It is used to sweep
the reader to the climax of the book, there to intentionally
strand us on the question: does Guitar kill Milkman? It
may mean that already the writer is preparing a sequel to
Song.

The journey Milkman takes, which results in revelation and renewal, forms an antithesis to that of his friend
Guitar. Milkman's journey arrests his selfish egotism and
puts him on a whole new path of thinking about himself and
the world. He learns about isolation, terror, suffering,
survival, joy, triumph, and coming together. Though the
ending is deliberately ambiguous, because Guitar is waiting
for him with a gun, we get a strong feeling that Milkman
will live. Pilate has instilled in him the life-affirming
principle, and Milkman will be able to return with his new-
found knowledge and help others.

To understand why Guitar's "renewal" takes a different path--the path of the unnatural (murder to be exact)--it
is necessary to digress a bit. The author gives us bits of
Guitar's deepest internalized memories--the experiences of
humiliation, blood, troubles, and despair. They are offered
not as apology for his joining of The Seven Days avengers,
an organization devoted to the killing of white people, but
as the basis for Guitar's metaphysic for killing. The reasoning is centered around what he considers natural and unnatural.

The story of Guitar is again the story of the black
man maimed by his childhood experience, who comes to discover in murder a sense of reality and freedom based on
this childhood experience. Seared on his mind is the time
that his father was sliced up in a saw mill and the white
boss came to call on the stricken family. He brought with
him a sack of divinity candy, which Guitar's mother accepted
with a simpering smile of gratitude. The author makes no
effort to disguise her sense of shame and outrage, either in
this novel or the previous one, over the black woman who
scrapes, bows, and smiles before those who humiliate her.
In Sula there is the scene of Nel's mother smiling at the
white conductor who has just told her to "git your butt on in

there" (p. 21) when she makes the innocent mistake of entering a car reserved for white people. Song of Solomon stresses that the circumstances of his father's death and his mother's grateful acceptance of the white, sugary sweet forever fixes in Guitar's mind the ignominious status of the black man and woman in white society. He scorns the role of the black man as suffering servant, and becomes the black man who fights back. Like Richard Wright's Bigger Thomas (Native Son), he establishes his values through murder.

The change in Guitar, from an intelligent man and good friend to killer of white people and then the stalker of his best friend Milkman, forms the basis of some of the most relevant passages in the book. The theme of the unnatural now appears like a red thread in the book's design—a thread which traces the black man's complications, the muddle of rights and wrongs in which he struggles, and the memory of past injustices that haunt him. Guitar's resolve to murder is based on his conviction that white people are "unnatural killers" who desire the death of every black person. His thinking that there can be no reconciliation with white society centers on "unnatural." It allows the author to temper her sympathy for Guitar with irony on the semantic twistings of the word by him and by other black men. Black men, she comments, believe white men to be unnatural killers because they kill total strangers; whereas black men kill each other for "good" reasons. These good reasons, she points out, are: finding one's wife with another man, or violating the rules of hospitality by reaching into a pot of mustard greens and picking out the meat. Other grounds for murder are verbal insults about a man's virility or honesty, and are justified as crimes of passion. Since the book's moral focus is on Pilate, who is labeled by these men as unnatural, and since Pilate has defined death as unnatural, there is less auctorial ambiguity about violence and killing here than in Sula.

Thus, to return to Milkman, the unexpected curve to his setting out to prove himself in traditional American fashion, by finding gold and freeing himself from father and society, is the complication that he is being hunted down by his former best friend. Barring this, Morrison's tracing of Milkman's journey through Pennsylvania and Virginia can be regarded, in many places, as in the tradition of the picaresque, in which each episode brings the protagonist into contact with some aspect of black society. But, in fact, it can more profitably be examined as a journey in which each place becomes a test of character and soul, with the result that the hero grows in understanding as he learns bits of family history and starts piecing it together. History becomes a choral symphony to Milkman, in which each individual voice has a chance to speak and contribute to his growing sense of well-being.

The pattern is something like this. In Reverend Cooper's parsonage, Milkman hears that it was right in this room that Pilate's snuff box was soldered. The information makes him feel "real" (p. 231). He also learns more details about his grandfather's murder, as well as the fact that the killers were never brought to justice. It forces him to think about justice and injustice, something that as the son of a prosperous black man he has not had much occasion to do. When he visits Circe he discovers how one black woman managed to keep two children (Macon and Pilate) alive, and later revenge their father's murder in her own way. Recalling her healing of Pilate's infected ear, he reflects that had she had the opportunity, she would have been a nurse in a white hospital.

His next step is to survey the acres which his grandfather cleared single-handed, and which are now as overgrown as his grandfather found them. The sight arouses his admiration and pride in his ancestor and he feels diminished because of the life he has led personally. Later, attacked by black men, he realizes that the flaunting of his prosperity (well-cut suit, expensive luggage, good Scotch) is an affront to those less fortunate than he. Finally, faced with the unknown when he goes on a hunting expedition with older black men, he proves his manhood and achieves harmony with nature and man in the forest.

None of these episodes is fully realized, but they form a chain. Together with Milkman's increasing excited realization that he is no longer on the scent of gold, but looking for his origins, we discover the change from callous, selfish, uncaring man to caring man. In the end, the revelation that the town in which his great grandfather lived had just about everything named after him, and that there is even a legend about his ancestor, brings him exultation.

It is this legend surrounded in the romantic myth of man flying which raises some problems for me. The story holds that Milkman's ancestor lifted his arms one day and soared into space toward Africa, leaving wife and twenty children behind. He had attempted to take his son Jake (Pilate and Macon's father), but was forced to drop him. The boy landed safely, and was brought up by a kind neighbor, since the deserted wife, left with twenty children to feed and clothe, (understandably) loses her reason. The effect of the story on Milkman is electrifying: "Oh, man! He didn't need no airplane. He just took off; got fed up. All the way up! (author's italics).... No more bales! ... No more shit! ... Lifted his beautiful black ass up in the sky and flew on home ... and the whole damn town is named after him" (p. 328).

All of the events of the journey, then, coalesce in a single vision--flying. The black man must fly, thinks Milkman. The book's structure reenforces the idea. It begins with the unsuccessful attempt of a black man to fly on the day Milkman is born, and ends with the story of the successful flight of Milkman's ancestor. A question is inevitable: flight from what, one asks? Poverty? Home? Wife? Children? Yes. It is the traditional poor man's divorce, common in life and in fiction. One thinks of Thomas Hardy's Michael Henchard (The Mayor of Casterbridge), who in one swift gesture rids himself of wife and child by selling them to a total stranger, and gets a second chance in life. Or there is D. H. Lawrence's Aaron Sisson (Aaron's Rod), who abruptly deserts his family because, like Milkman's great grandfather, he is fed up with his life. Unquestionably, it is a popular male fantasy (and female), whose realization is tempting both in real life and as a theme in fiction. It is a familiar reflection in our time, even if it appears as a title on a book (Fear of Flying). It is interesting that Toni Morrison, whose attitude on desertion of family in Sula is uncompromising, should have softened her thinking.

In a recent interview (New York Times, 9/7/77), the author explains her change of ideas, the salient parts of which can be summarized. Flying is everyone's dream, she says, and as the interview continues, she makes us understand that she is speaking of escape as freedom. Her next words, however, demonstrate that she is specifically addressing herself to men. Men, she says, don't want to live in houses. Her own ex-husband, an architect, considered every house a hotel. Men want to move: "black men travel, they split, they get on trains, they walk, they move.... It's a part of black life, a positive, majestic thing.... " Despite the obvious parallels, it would be a mistake to identify the kind of movement of which Morrison speaks and which often involves desertion of wife and children as "majestic. "

The writer admits that when fathers "soar, " it is the children who pay the price. But she defends the black man and sees certain compensations as a result of his act. "The fathers may soar, they may triumph, they may leave, but the children know who they are; they remember, half in glory and half in accusation. That is one of the points of Song: all the men have left someone, and it is the children who remember it, sing about it, mythologize it, make it a part of their family history. "

The poetic rhetoric stirs us, evoking reminders of those spellbinding words of Daedalus to Icarus: "Escape may be checked by water and land, but the air and the sky are free. " But we know now that neither the air nor the sky is free. And also we cannot evade the plain, earthbound truth that abandoned children suffer, as do their mothers. There is another point to consider here. By speaking of flying in connection with the black man, the writer seems to be reversing her position on women, and the necessity for women to fly even if it means "the free fall. " We recall Milkman's encomium on Pilate: "Without ever leaving the ground, she could fly" (p. 336). This seems essentially a restatement of the doctrine that black men must try to fly, but black women must be content to stay on the ground. The social consequences of this have been spelled out for black women for ages, and have vicious implications. However, let's trust the tale, not the artist. If we look at the novel more carefully, we see that the line about Pilate flying without ever leaving the ground comes almost at the end. I prefer to believe that it signifies a return from Milkman's rhetorical fancy to what Melville enunciates about The American Dream--there is no absolute freedom for anyone. Who, then, is a better example of Melville's thinking than Pilate? Pilate lived and embraced the very texture of life, but she knew that compassion and learning to care set the limits to freedom.

ALICE WALKER:
In Love & Trouble; Meridian

Asked about her concerns in an interview, Alice
Walker replied: "I am preoccupied with the spiritual survival, the survival whole (author's italics) of my people.
But beyond that, I am committed to exploring the oppres-
sions, the insanities, the loyalties, and the triumphs of
black women. ... Next to them, I place the old people--
male and female--who persist in their beauty in spite of
everything" (New Republic, September 14, 1974).

Without question, the writer's fiction shows a dedi-
cated engagement with the resources, capacities, infirmities,
realities, consciousness, and spiritual health of black peo-
ple--particularly women. The collection of short stories In
Love & Trouble (1973), presents a varied gallery of black
women and their moves: to self-discovery; to tentative,
uncompleted exploration; to disillusionment; to recognition of
their own worth; to rage, peace, death, life. The author's
moral attitudes are explicit, though she does not assault our
sensibilities by peremptory treatment of the moral situations
discussed. Though occasionally she steps into her own
story a little unnecessarily to develop an already established
attitude on the part of the reader ("The Revenge ... "), the
total effect of the work is a sense of precise language which
consistently emphasizes the different ways in which women
(and men) take action to attain dignity.

The women in these stories do not always have a
chance or a choice, but the moral force of many of the
stories depends on characterization which portrays the wom-
en as living refutations of passivity. If these stories
possess something in common, it is the fight against resignation, victimization, loneliness, despair, stasis, "the odor
of corruption" which Joyce said hovered over his Dubliners.
In effect, this constitutes, for the most part, an underlying
theme which links such different women as Roselily; the
narrator of "Really, Doesn't Crime Pay?"; the homely hairdresser ("Her Sweet Jerome"); Hannah Kemhuff ("The Revenge ... ") and others. Together with this linking, there
is a scope of vision which moves from one woman to another, each time picking up a particular segment of the
black woman's experience.

The author is always concerned with women, what
happens to them, why it happens. The problem of marriage

and the varying expectations of women are handled with intelligence and expert craftsmanship.   There is often expressed bitterness against men--a continuing theme for the writer, as in her lines:

> Whoever he is, he is not worth
> all this.
> Don't you agree?
> And I will never
> unclench my teeth long enough
> to tell him so.

> ("Did This Happen to Your Mother?
> Did Your Sister Throw Up a Lot?"
> MS, February, 1978).

"Roselily" is the story of a woman whose name suggests the grafting on of a new identity.   An unmarried mother of four, she weds a stern convert to the Muslim religion, knowing that before her is a life of veils and robes. Against the background drone of the platitudinous marriage ceremony, the woman's body itches to be free of voile and satin; she remembers her body bare to the sun.   Under the gauze of the wedding veil, her fingers knot and unknot, paralleling thoughts on where she is going, the kind of life that will be hers, and the identity of the man she is marrying.   She knows that the man standing next to her, clasping her hand in his "iron" grip (p. 8), is the price of respectability, the price for having her children free of the "detrimental wheel" (p. 4).   He is the way to a new life.   What kind of life, she asks herself?   Babies?   Her hands will be full?   Full of what?   We realize how limited her choices have been, how little chance at living she has had.   Whether she will have any chance now is all left in doubt.

The wife in "Really, Doesn't Crime Pay?" has no such difficulty in sorting out her emotions.   Intelligent, creative, she tells us precisely in diary form what her husband expects of her.   She is to cream, scent, anoint, and deck her body.   For diversion, she is to shop, and for fulfillment she is to bear a child.   As for writing, the husband Ruel is firm in his disapproval: "No wife of mine is going to embarrass me with a lot of foolish, vulgar stuff" (p. 15) (author's italics).   Like the Muslim husband in "Roselily, " Ruel wants babies so that his wife's hands will be full, and like Roselily, but more eloquently, the wife asks: full of what?

Instead of lengthy character description, the author's few vivid sentences acquaint us with the terrible emotional and intellectual impoverishment of the woman's life, in order to make us understand why she becomes such an easy victim to her lover, a young black writer, Mordecai Rich. Though her intelligence warns her that anyone who views other people's confusions with such a cold eye cannot have much heart, she blooms emotionally and intellectually under his praise of her work--and her body. He represents life, escape. The denouement is swift. The lover leaves; there is a long absence, and one day, sitting in a doctor's office, she picks up a magazine and sees his picture. He is serious-looking, newly-bearded, and the story under his name is hers, the one he once read and praised. There is a caption below the picture stating that the author will soon issue a new book: The Black Woman's Resistance to Creativity in the Arts.

The author does not hover over her character. In a few swift strokes, she shows her breaking down, then some weeks later, gathering herself together to exercise a free choice. Like Ellison's invisible man, she will yes her husband to death--creaming, softening skin and body, shopping for more and more clothes, assuring him that the baby will be conceived. Secretly, she works out her fate by undermining her husband's plan. She takes the pill religiously. Her consciousness of freedom is not illusory. Soon, she realizes, when both husband and she are quite tired of the sweet, sweet smell of her body and the softness of those creamed hands, she will leave--leave without once looking back at her doll's house. We are aware of the psychic damage of so much attention paid to revenge, but also aware that in order to exercise free choice in working out her destiny, she is doing what seems psychologically necessary at the moment.

The unwanted, unloved, rejected woman is treated in several stories with sympathy, but with a truthfulness to individual experience. "Her Sweet Jerome" pictures a middle-aged, ugly hairdresser whose family is what is known as "colored folks with money" (p. 25). Knowing herself secretly jeered, taunted and laughed at all her life by the women whom she beautifies, she cannot resist a school teacher ten years younger than herself, "so little and cute and young" (p. 25). She tells herself she will not rest until he and she are Mr. and Mrs. Jerome Franklin Washington the third, "and that's the truth" (p. 25). Given her character's aim, the writer adapts her art to meet the exigency of the human nature she portrays. The woman masochistically submits to beating and her husband's contemptuous ignoring of her, until she finds out she has a rival. Consumed with jealousy, she questions, hunts, prowls down every street to find "the woman." Finally, she discovers who her rival is. Stacked under the bed are dozens of books on the black revolutionary movement. Her satisfaction is to set them on fire--a fire which symbolically matches the bonfire within her.

Not all the stories are of bleak marriage relationships. Some evoke the racial scene, such as "The Welcome Table," in which a stubborn, poor, black woman is ejected from a white church. Undaunted, she walks down the long road secure in the knowledge that her beloved Jesus is walking right by her side. After all, he looks exactly like the picture of him she has seen in a white lady's Bible for whom she had worked. Pouring out her life to him, she finally collapses and dies, his smile filling her with ecstasy and exultation. The woman never strikes us as an abstract figure with a delusion, but as one of the old, lonely ones whom society has forgotten. Later, her neighbors speculate why she had walked so far: maybe she had some relatives a few miles away.

Another story which evokes the relations between the races is "The Revenge of Hannah Kemhuff." It recalls Tolstoy's comment that a writer can invent anything, but it is impossible to invent psychology. Hannah Kemhuff wants justice for the insult to her spirit and body, and for the misery she had suffered from the white woman who refused her relief when she and her children were starving. The husband who deserted her has already been dealt with by God. He and his new woman were swept to their death in a flood. Two root workers assure Hannah that her spirit can be mended, and proceed to mix a potion. Demonstrating how the power of suggestion can work, Walker shows the white woman so fearful of the potion's magic that she aids in her own physical and psychological destruction.

The neglected, suffering black woman who is "not anybody much" (p. 88) becomes the theme of "Strong Horse Tea." Rannie is not married, not pretty, lives in a cold, drafty cabin and has only one thing in the world--her baby Snooks, and he is dying. At first, rejecting old Sarah's "swamp magic," she begs the white postman to summon the

doctor for her. At last, realizing that the doctor is not
coming, and told bluntly by old Sarah that Snooks is dying,
she races out to the pasture for the strong horse tea, warm
from the mare--the only thing, Sarah tells her, which will
save the baby.

Powerful characterization and language preserve the
story from sentimentality. We read of lightning crackling
around her, Rannie slipping in mud, and kicked by the horse
as she holds her plastic shoe under the mare. Language
such as: "Thunder rose from the side of the sky like tires
of a big truck rumbling over rough dirt road" (p. 96) tells
us how the Rannies of the world are pulverized by the
world's Juggernaut. What could have more concise impact
than the description of Rannie racing home, her mouth to
the crack in the plastic shoe so as not to lose a drop of
the precious "medicine?" At this moment, Sarah is bend-
ing over the child, discovering that its breathing has
stopped.

There are no careless, windy surfaces in these stories, or occasional trivializing of fact. Each detail records
the essence of the experience portrayed. The fall from
beauty into horror is handled with great skill in "The
Flowers." A child exploring the woods in late autumn,
picking ferns and strange blue flowers, steps "smack" into
the skull of a murdered black man: "Her heel ... [lodges] in
the broken ridge between brow and nose, and she [reaches]
down quickly, unafraid, to free herself" (p. 120) (author's
italics). Only when she sees the skeleton's naked grin does
she give a cry of surprise. The horror and beauty of living in the South are symbolized by the wild pink rose growing near the head and, around the roots of the rose, the
rotted shreds of a noose. Above the child's head is a
branch with more shreds of rope. We know that the girl's
education is completed that day. Summer had truly ended.

"The Child Who Favored Daughter" is a nightmarish
account of a black man who represses his rage before white
people and turns it on his women. Like Alice Walker's
Brownfield Copeland (The Third Life of Grange Copeland,
1970), he beats and cripples his wife until she escapes him
by killing herself. Learning that his beautiful young daughter favors a white man, he beats and mutilates her, all the
while realizing that she will resist him until the end. He
becomes a symbol of what has already been discussed in
the account of Toni Morrison's fiction of the unnatural man.

The author's language links the girl to nature. She is a "young willow" (p. 42); her arms are "like long golden fruits" (p. 41); her eyes, "perfect black-eyed Susans" (p. 38). Her hands are always touching the petals of some flower.

Not all the stories are somber. There is a delightful insight into the common sense and humor of black country people in "Everyday Use," in which the mother makes a choice concerning her concept of "tradition." She is a large, big-boned woman who has always done a man's work, and whose education stopped at the second grade. "Don't ask me why," she says briefly, "in 1927 colored asked fewer questions than they do now" (p. 50). Though she sometimes fantasizes being on the Johnny Carson show, and told what a fine woman she is, she laughs at her fantasies, for she has a true sense of her own worth. When her daughter Dee comes home with her black Muslim man, calling herself Wangero Leewanika Kemanjo, and informs her mother that she wants the quilt pieced by her grandmother because only she understands its tradition, the mother reacts with keen appraisal of the circumstances. She is sympathetic to the other daughter, self-effacing Maggie, who has stayed home and has been promised the quilt for her wedding, yet is ready to give up the quilt to her more aggressive sister, assuring her mother that she needs no tangible evidence of tradition. She can remember her grandmother without the quilt. Maggie gets the quilt, and the writer ends the story with language whose rhythm suggests the satisfactory tempo of the mother's life: "After we watched the car dust settle I asked Maggie to bring me a dip of snuff. And then the two of us sat there just enjoying, until it was time to go in the house and go to bed" (p. 59).

My own favorite among the stories is the one which Langston Hughes enjoyed: "To Hell with Dying." Tradition, love, the past, joy of living, a sense of black people as complete, healthy, undiminished, are all blended to convey the sense of the narrator's enrichment of her life through Mr. Sweet. For as many years as the narrator had remembered, Mr. Sweet, a family friend, has made a ritual of dying. He had been their childhood companion--a perfect companion, for he had the ability to be drunk and sober at the same time. The narrator, now a Ph. D. candidate, gets a telegram telling her that ninety-year-old Mr. Sweet is dying and could she please drop everything to come to

his bedside? Of course she could, and does. He had been
her first beau, and her tribute to him is "Sweet Georgia
Brown" plucked out on the guitar he had left her.

One criterion of the good short story is its truthfulness to individualistic experience. Alice Walker's short
stories always make us comprehend rationally the emotions
and actions of the women she writes about. When a symbol
is used, in a way consistent with the story's scope and form,
it ties the episodes to the story with organic unity. Though
in "The Revenge of Hannah Kemhuff" the ending seems unnecessarily tacked on, and we are aware that we are being
patterned in a certain way to intensify our moral perceptive-
ness, this tendency is avoided in the other stories. The
net result of the stories is an explicit comment on human
nature, which is adequately sustained and suggests not only
Walker's identification with her characters, but a genuine
love for them.

Alice Walker's latest novel, Meridian, does more
than explore the "insanities," "loyalties," and "triumphs" of
black women--her announced literary aim in previous fiction.
The story moves between the present and the Civil Rights
movement in the sixties, recreating the life of a Southern
black woman (Meridian) and the choices she makes: marriage, motherhood, education, her role in the Civil Rights
movement, her decision on the issue of violence, and her
final resolve that her place is with poor Southern blacks.
The book delves into Meridian's relationship with her mother,
a black man named Truman Held, and a white Civil Rights
worker, Lynne Rabinowitz. Though there are many characters in the story, the spotlight is always on Meridian and
the triangle she forms with Truman and Lynne. Gradually,
Meridian expands in spiritual awareness until one speculates
whether the author's intention is to present the making of a
saint. The ending pictures Meridian leaving for some unknown destination, but promising to return.

If Meridian's mysticism and affirmation of the sanc-
tity of her mission sometimes take her out of the realm of
prosaic reality, the story of Lynne Rabinowitz, which receives almost as much attention as Meridian's, pushes her
near the region of tragedy. It is in the involvement of the
two women that the novel is most richly affirmative concerning the capacity of women for friendship. The women, one
black, the other white, come together in tenderness, under-

standing, and forgiveness because of mutual experiences: violence during the Civil Rights struggle; the loss of a child; betrayal by the same man, Truman; physical breakdown; sorrow over the actions of their friends in the movement. Despite a certain amount of self-destructiveness, Lynne achieves stature in the end as a moral rather than a merely Darwinian survivor. Cut off from her Jewish family because she has married a black man, deserted by this same man who oscillates between blonde prettiness and black is beautiful, victimized by some black men, and devastated by the death of her child, she manages to summon up courage, gallantry, and humor. She could never become one of the "oppressors," she tells Meridian, and generously gives the palm to her husband Truman: he was "instructional ... besides ... nobody's perfect" (p. 181) (author's italics). Meridian responds with a wink and the bantering remark: "Except white women." To which Lynne quips: "Yes, ... but their time will come" (p. 181).

The racial gap is closed with sympathy, empathy, and ironic humor. The author gets behind the politics of race and into the different aspects of human relationships in which suffering is the leveler. Their reconciliation, which takes place in two short chapters simply and aptly entitled "Two Women" and "Lynne," penetrates the bias of black and white, and even woman and woman, demonstrating that the needs of the human heart transcend race and color. Humanists and social activists to the end, both women voice the conviction that if there is to be freedom for men and women, something must be done about the System and the inequities between rich and poor.

The lives of Meridian and Lynne are intermeshed, but the author's interest centers on Meridian. Avoiding a chronological tracing of Meridian's life, she presents a collage of events over a period of twenty-five years in which Meridian's family history, her relationship with her mother, the way motherhood came and caught Meridian, her hasty marriage, its dissolution, and her entrance into the Civil Rights movement are pieced together. From here on, we see Meridian confronted with a number of choices. Each choice is a deliberate one based on the full knowledge that the women in her family preceding her had no choice. All of these choices involve a price, for always Meridian pays with pain of body and soul. Eventually, we are given to understand that the soul conquers its spiritual ailments, and the wasted body is testimony to the great struggle which has taken place between spirit and flesh. By following the lead of the spirit, through a process of resisting the downward pull of the tyranny of the flesh, Meridian, the author implies, becomes free. She is able to soar--a feeling she once experienced as a child in the old Indian burial ground near her home. Here again is the theme of flight discussed in Song of Solomon and Sula, and handled by Alice Walker in a still different way.

Combined with the theme of flight is also the idea of "discovering gold," which coincides with the central theme in Song of Solomon--finding out who you are and what you want to do with your life. Walker's images, however, are private inventions rather than images drawn from the realm of religion and myth (like those of Toni Morrison). In a one-page chapter entitled "Gold," there is a description of Meridian discovering a heavy lump of metal. Upon scraping it, she realizes there is gold bullion beneath. Whether or not Meridian actually finds gold is unimportant. The gold can be viewed as a conscious symbolic device, used again and again in the novel with good auctorial control. In this incident, Meridian keeps digging the gold down and bringing it up, reexamining it each time. At last one day, we are told, she simply forgets about it.

The function of the gold bullion falls within the sphere of the technique to foreshadow Meridian's constant assessing of self, her gradual loss of concern for personal identity, and her final sinking of self into total commitment to working with children and the poor.

The gold, as well as Walker's recourse to the history and "destroyal" of The Sojourner tree as symbolic device, vivifies our sense of the basic theme surrounding Meridian. This is her struggle with identity, together with her thinking on the issue of violence, her conviction that she could never commit herself to use violence in order to attain social justice. The fact that a photograph shows a branch growing out of the "dead" stump of the tree convinces us that for Meridian, at this time, death and violence are to be avoided and life affirmed. The Sojourner, however, is a tractable symbol open to various interpretations; for example, the ability of black people to survive despite attempts to destroy them.

Whatever symbolic patterns the writer weaves into her story help to conceptualize the facts of Meridian's life.

The early details of her childhood and youth emphasize the leaden quality we have come to associate with the pattern of the black woman's life, already noticed in the works of the previous writers discussed. Restraining any omniscience, the author presents the rigid mother whose dignity and self-esteem revolve around duty and church; a young girl's sexual ignorance which leads to unwanted pregnancy; hasty marriage and a relationship with husband which quickly disintegrates, as the confused wife struggles with problems she is unable to sort out. At seventeen, Meridian finds herself a dropout from high school, a deserted wife, a reproach to her mother for being "fast" (p. 87), and a mother herself to a baby she cannot love, and for whose care she is responsible. Suspended in a fog of blankness, she suddenly finds some of the mist blown away by a picture on the TV screen. It shows a house on her street bombed by white racists and she learns that black children and adults have been killed. A month later, Meridian walks into the office of the Civil Rights house and says, "I've come to volunteer" (p. 80).

The writer's innovations in chronicling the story not in a straight line, but moving back and forth, allow us both an intimate picture of Meridian, at this time, and the understanding that her break out of marriage marks her first stirring of a spirit of independence. The content of the novel, however, shows that before independence is finally achieved and Meridian rids herself of what she considers the baser alloys which clog her spirit, she must confront the issue of sexual love.

Meridian's direct involvement with social change in the Civil Rights struggle brings her into contact with Truman Held, a black college man. Truman's portrait is often acidulous and in the speech, actions and contours of his character, Walker voices her own moral and feminist views. Truman punctuates his talk with French phrases, wears an imposing array of buttons on his shirt or jacket, prominent among which is a button showing a black hand clasping a white hand. On closer inspection, says the author, the hands seem not to be so much touching as sliding away--an observation which foreshadows Truman's treatment of his white wife, and the writer's scathing denunciation of such treatment.

Truman keeps bobbing up in Meridian's life and is constantly assessed by Meridian and the reader, because of the narrator's strong and complicated feelings about him. In the

beginning we see that his thinking on women is as absurd
as his thinking that people who speak French are somehow
better than those who do not. Summed up, his view of
woman is: she must be virgin but experienced, read the
New York Times, and be a port to a man. A man, like a
train, "must have a shed" (p. 141). He dates white girls
only as a matter of sex, he tells Meridian. Yet despite
this negative picture, the reader's response to Truman, at
this point, is directed by Meridian's realization that they
are drawn together through their mutual experience of jail-
ings and beatings: they were together "at a time and a
place in History that forced the trivial to fall away--and
they were absolutely together" (p. 84).

As the relationship between Meridian and Truman unfolds, however, neither character nor reader can afford to
avoid the issue that for men like Truman there can be no
common ground with the intelligent, black woman. She is
a threat to him, makes him feel uncomfortable, even sexually impotent. In Truman's thoughts on Meridian, words
such as "blade," "condemned," "guillotine" (p. 141) appear.
We learn that as he continues to ruminate on her, he feels
a retreating of his balls. It is not surprising, then, that
after one sexual encounter with Meridian, Truman goes
directly to Civil Rights worker Lynne Rabinowitz, a woman
he sees as not objecting to being his "resource" (p. 141).
For Meridian, there is not only the ironic reflection that
she had allowed herself to flounder like a "beached fish"
(p. 113); there is also the pain and frustration that at no
time had she been able to talk to him of herself--her marriage, her motherhood, her view of education at Saxon College.

Despite the writer's fascination with Truman, her
language constantly dispels the illusion that Truman is able
to regard Meridian in any terms but those of stereotype.
Learning that she has been accepted at Saxon College (near
his own) through the efforts of a white liberal family, he
tells her that she is the perfect Saxon type. Saxon College,
as Meridian learns, is an institution devoted to turning out
perfect ladies who will master the art of French cooking,
pour tea with appropriate grace, and avoid social controversy. Students who participate in the Civil Rights movement can expect no support from the college if they are
jailed. Curfew is to be observed, regardless of what is
happening in the outside world. Both Saxon College and
Truman have no confusion in their minds concerning the

role of women, and Meridian realizes at this point that were she to tell Truman of her former marriage and motherhood, she would cease to exist for him.

The author, like other black women writers, scores the double standard and that male thinking which stamps woman as damaged goods if she has "belonged" to another man. Her dramatization of Truman Held shows the explicit contradiction between Truman's twentieth-century political thinking on human rights and his nineteenth-century thinking on women. In this respect he is not singular, as the writings of black and white women engaged in the social struggles of the last ten or twelve years testify. Sara Davidson's Loose Change ... and some of the comments by Toni Cade (Bambara) illustrate that men espouse liberal political views but voice a narrow view of woman's place in society. Alice Walker's continuing scrutiny of Truman emphasizes that men like him still cling to concepts of women which are no different from that expressed by Thomas Hardy's nineteenth-century "idealist" Angel Clare (Tess of the d'Urbervilles), who rejects Tess when she confesses her one sexual "transgression."

The contrast between Truman's attitudes, liberal in his civil politics, narrow in sexual politics, is not sustained. His marriage and desertion of Lynne, the subsequent succession of young, pretty blonde girls in his life, and his final appearance as a mustached, bearded Che Guevara type wearing a Maoist jacket but driving a Volvo, close the gap between liberal and reactionary. One even considers whether there ever was a gap, for eventually it appears that he wanders from one political philosophy to another, and from woman to woman. Despite some kind words for him by the author at the end, he remains for us the man sketched in the beginning. This is one who looks good at first, but on closer examination has carious teeth and other defects. The result is a strong implication that there is a great deal of soul decay as well.

The result of the brief love affair between Truman and Meridian, his subsequent desertion of her for Lynne, is her realization that she has been betrayed not only by Truman but by her own body. She is pregnant. He had taken no precautions. It is at this point that Meridian makes one of her many harsh choices. She takes steps to rid herself of the bodily machinery which has trapped her by having her tubes tied. "Burn 'em out by the roots for all I care," she

tells the doctor (p. 115). It is a drastic choice, but it has
been preceded by an even more severe and poignant one.
To accept the scholarship offered her by the white family as
a result of her activities with Civil Rights activists, she
faces the choice of giving away her baby. Genteel Saxon
College will not consider a student with a child. We read
that seventeen-year-old Meridian (with an I. Q. of 140), who
sees her baby as a beautiful being, but one who is strange
to her, to be loved as one does the "moon" or a "tree, "
gives the baby away with a "light heart" (p. 90).

The language is studiedly ironic. For now, in college, her action exacts its price. She has nightmares. Despite feverish cramming, throwing herself into all kinds of
activities, she hears her child's voice calling, crying her
name. Thoughts of killing herself cross her mind. She
has no value, she tells herself. She had broken something
terrible--the maternal history of her family, which was of
care and devotion to children. Her slave ancestor had
starved to feed her children. Her maternal grandmother
had worked herself to death to give Meridian's mother an
education. And what had Meridian done? Given her baby
away to strangers. Headaches wrack her and she is unable
to speak without stuttering. We are told that she "distracted" (p. 92) herself with studies.

Walker's language is always subtle in various ways.
The deliberate use of understatement by the word "distracted, " when combined with the events which follow, serves
to emphasize the author's irony that Meridian could never be
distracted from what she had done, why she had done it,
and what she must do from now on. Had she kept a child
she did not love, stayed with her rigid mother, worked at
menial jobs to support herself and the child, she might have
grown to hate the baby, taken out her frustrations on him--
as her mother had done to her. Her life would have been
wasted. But the lost child continues to haunt her.

The motif of the lost child runs through the book and
is worked out in a variety of ways. Meridian's life is fo-
cused not only on helping the poor Southern blacks in lonely
rural areas, but on rescuing "lost" children. Her only act
of violence in the whole book is against Truman, as retali-
ation for the child they lost through her abortion. Some
time after the abortion (and the tying of tubes), she meets
Truman and his interest in her suddenly rekindles. In keeping with the underlying theme of betrayal and lost children,

the author has Truman suddenly lean toward Meridian with:
"Have my beautiful black babies" (p. 116) (author's italics).
She hits him three times, drawing blood. The exact numer-
ology drops us into religious symbolism (Peter betraying
Jesus three times), and into Meridian's consciousness of
the enormity of Truman's betrayal. The symbol redefines
the whole process of Meridian's thinking about children,
finally articulated in her comments on Truman's desertion
of wife and daughter Camara and the "crimes of passion or
hatred against children" ... in a society in which "children
are not particularly valued" (p. 174).

Children line Meridian's progress through life and
give the impetus to many of her actions. There is the
poor stray waif called Wild Child, who lives in the slum
surrounding Saxon College, rummages in garbage cans for
food, and is befriended by Meridian. She is killed by a
speeding car when, despite Meridian's efforts to keep her
in the college dorm, she is ordered out by the house mother
and proudly leaves. After college, Meridian's struggles to
save children take on a more dramatic form. She forces
the city fathers of a small Alabama town to do something
about the flooding of ditches in which children are trapped
and drowned. Her way of bringing the problem to the men
is starkly simple. She takes the decomposed body of a boy
trapped in a sewer for two days and lays it on the mayor's
desk. When Camara, Lynne's daughter, is raped and killed,
she mourns Camara's death with as much sorrow as the
mother.

Meridian is always among children in one way or
another. The book, which begins in the present, dramatizes Meridian facing a tank which the local officials of
Chicokema have trained on her, and from which they threat-
en to fire. Her reason for defying them is to enable the
community's black children to see for themselves that the
woman billed as "One of The Twelve Human Wonders of the
World ... " is a fake. Ordinarily, the children would get
to see the mummy on Thursday after paying a fee. They
are not permitted into the museum on any other day because
their clothes "smell" from the guano factory in which their
parents work. Meridian's disregard for her own safety is
voiced tersely to Truman: "if somebody has to go it might
as well be the person who's ready" (p. 25).

On the surface, at this point Meridian appears ready
for a saint's martyred death. She has almost destroyed the

bodily apparatus which would distract her spirit from the
flights to which it aspires. Worldly possessions have been
stripped down to a room which resembles a "cell" (p. 24).
The walls of this cell are covered with quotations from the
Bible and there is only one piece of furniture in the room--
a sleeping bag. But Meridian's light-hearted rejoinder to
Truman's question: is she ready for death?, as well as
other details of the scene just described, bind her solidly
in the world of reality. "What you see before you is a
woman in the process of changing her mind" (p. 25), she
replies in answer to Truman's query. Furthermore, the
quotations from the Bible are from her mother, accusing
her of failing to honor not only her parents, but any one
else. Then there is Meridian's feminine awareness of her
appearance: "I must look like death eating a soda cracker"
(p. 25), she remarks to Truman.

No, Meridian is not the story of the progress of a
saint to a martyr's death. Certainly, we are aware of the
strong streak of mysticism evidenced in her at an early age.
Playing in the place known as the Serpent's Coil, she experiences levitation, a sense of leaving the body's cumber-
some machinery and a strong sense of renewal--very much
like that felt by her ancestor Feather Mae in the same spot.
Though she periodically lapses out, or cannot move some
part of her body, this appears to be both a form of self-
protectiveness against the impact of the world's brutality
on her emotions, and a means of mobilizing her spiritual
resources for appropriate action.

Obviously, she practices a degree of self-flagellation,
which prompts Truman's sarcastic remark: why not put
rocks in your shoes? But this self-flagellation seems to
come out of her sense of primeval guilt concerning her relationship with her mother. The relationship between mother
and daughter is so carefully pieced together that we understand the reason for the child Meridian's shock at what
appears to be her mother's standard rhetorical question:
have you stolen anything? For Meridian understands the
implied accusation beneath the words: the mother's conviction that Meridian's birth robbed her of any creative life.
The daughter has been made to feel that she has stolen her
mother's serenity and shattered the budding self. We read
that each time Meridian hears the question, she cannot
move; the words "literally stopped her in her tracks" (p.
51). The mother had been a school teacher for whom marriage and six pregnancies became a "trap."

The characterization of Meridian's mother is not
stereotyped, but given individualizing touches. She is not
Big Momma, though Meridian often sees her as giant, nor
is she Bitch Mother. What is emphasized is that she enjoyed sleeping with her husband but found pregnancy a hor-
ror--a theme which recalls the wife Helene and her view of
pregnancy in Joyce Carol Oates's Wonderland. Meridian
realizes that there were always conditions to the mother's
love, such as her insistence that Meridian, at age thirteen,
proclaim Jesus her master. Yet mixed with Meridian's
guilt, we see that the daughter understands her mother's
limitations and accepts her.

The writer's imposing upon us a great deal of reportage concerning Meridian's mysticism does not deflect
from the book's concern with the family relationship, the
reasons for guilt, and Meridian's highly-conscious embrace
of the life-affirming principle. At an early age, she rejects the religion of her parents as death-oriented, a withdrawal from the world. Her respect for life underlines her
political convictions and her acceptance of the principle of
non-violence as a means of attaining social justice.

This is emphasized in two scenes. The first is with
her friends in New York, who consider themselves revolutionaries and insist that one must be ready to kill for the
cause. Meridian is drummed out of the organization for
her refusal to say she will kill. The second time we note
her commitment to non-violence is in a church service for
a murdered black man. She understands that the respect
she owed her life "was to continue, against whatever obstacles, to live it, and not to give up any particle of it
without a fight to the death, preferably not her own" (p.
200) (author's italics). She modifies this later, reflecting
that she was not ready to kill either herself or anyone else
for the cause. Yet the issue continues to trouble Meridian,
as it does the author. Alice Walker's recent trip to Cuba,
reported in Ms (September, 1977), tells us that she needed
to know whether the use of violence in a revolution destroyed
one's humanity. Her conclusion, at the present writing, is
still ambiguous, though she sees the lot of the poor improved
as a result of Castro's revolution.

Meridian emerges in the book as a woman frail in
body but mighty in spirit. She is the antithesis of her former college room mate, Anne-Marion, member of a revolutionary group, who is now living in a comfortable suburban

home, writing poetry on revolution for comfortable fees.
Meridian is more than a contrast to Truman Held, who can
be true to nothing, not even himself. She is a rebuke to
men like Tommy Odds, who believes his rage against white
society gives him the right to violate white women like
Lynne. The author demonstrates that there is no more re-
vealing use of force than sexual aggression. Even before
Tommy rapes Lynne, his co-worker in Civil Rights and wife
of his friend Truman, he fantasizes about hanging her by
her long black hair until the roots give way under the weight.
Truman's rejection of his "white bitch" in the chapter "Of
Bitches And Wives" alerts Tommy to the fact that she is an
easy victim now.

The story about Tommy is seasoned with language
which brings out the strong taste of bitterness and hate he
has carried within him. The author, while pointing out
that men like Tommy have been taught by their mothers
that white women are the road to death for black men, does
not let him off easily. She stresses that he selects Lynne
because she is defenseless. At no time does the writer include Tommy when she mourns for those beautiful black
men who are clubbed and beaten into nothingness by the
police during the demonstrations.

Many of the black men in the book are treated with
an eye to the brutal, hypocritical detail. We have the acer-
bic portrait of the elderly professor, esteemed by church,
school, and community, who presses sexual advances on
Meridian. An undertaker's assistant seduces young black
girls out of contempt for their gullibility. The ambitious
politician Tom Johnson has a white mistress whom he sends
to a friend's house when he entertains guests. She's his
taste in "pussy" and "good stuff. Want some?" he asks
Truman (p. 136) (author's italics). Randolph Kay sings
songs to the President, and has just exchanged his white,
blonde wife for a shiny, new, black one. In Meridian's
family background her grandfather betrayed his wife with
every good-looking black woman who would have him; forced
his wife, pregnant with her twelfth child, to do extra work
in order to pay for their daughter's education. He was
noted for beating his wife and children with more enthusiasm
than he did his mules. The young Delores sums up her
fatalism about black men deserting their wives and children:
"The last time God had a baby he skipped, too" (p. 89).

In this novel, as in the previous novels discussed,

BLACK WOMEN / 171

the strongest relationships are between women--Meridian and
Lynne. At no time does one exploit the other. Meridian
refuses to consider even remotely Truman's request that
they resume their relationship, when he makes one of his
many returns to her. "For Lynne's sake alone, I couldn't
do it" (p. 139), she tells him. As Lynne and Meridian
grieve together over the death of Camara, the author speaks
in her own voice: "They waited for the pain of Camara's
death to lessen. They waited to ask forgiveness of each
other.... They waited for Truman, Camara's father, to
come to his wife who had faced her tragedy as many a welfare mother before her had done ..." (pp. 174-75). The
writer empathizes with Lynne's excesses, her breakdown,
the suffering caused by Truman and her Jewish family who
pronounced her "dead."

Alice Walker's fiction is literary art which by means
of analysis and psychological probing brings into life contemporary moral questions on women, men, and history.
Her collection of short stories, In Love & Trouble, is an
unsentimental yet tender portrait of black women. The
novel Meridian recreates the period of the Civil Rights
struggle and the aftermath with penetrating insights into the
people engaged in the struggle and what happened to them.
She explores the life of her chief protagonist, Meridian,
her heritage, her relationship with her mother, the stumbling into marriage and motherhood, her break with both, and
her turning to the cause of social justice. Walker's understanding of black society's manners and values is essential
to the reader's understanding of characterization: for example, the stereotyped thinking of Meridian's mother. She
reasons like Ku Klux Klanners that God made black and
white, separated sheep from the goats, and that is the way
it should be. Segregation is God's will. On the other hand,
the author jolts us into thinking in different ways on the
black family through scenes like the lovely and tender one
when the dying wife asks Truman to step aside because
"You blocks my view of my husband" (p. 203).

The styles of the three women writers discussed
here--Sarah E. Wright, Toni Morrison, and Alice Walker--
share a singular blend of prose and poetry. Both Toni
Morrison and Alice Walker show the influence of Zora
Neale Hurston in their work. Their use of private myths,
authentic dialect of rural people, and the vivid metaphorical
language of black people recall Zora Neale Hurston's in-

teresting novel, Their Eyes Were Watching God[5] (1937; repr.
1969), and her language. "Pick from a higher bush and a
sweeter berry" (p. 28), is the advice on love and marriage
of the old grandmother to her granddaughter Janie. Or
there is that succinct image in the grandmother's plea to
Janie: "Put me down easy, Janie. Ah'm a cracked plate"
(p. 37).

We see the imprint of this language in Toni Morrison's description of Shadrack's sleep: "steadier than the
condor's wing; more tranquil than the curve of eggs" (S, p.
14). Or there is her description of black working men:
trudging "down the road like old promises nobody wanted
kept" (S, p. 74). We sense it in Walker's sympathetic description of Miss Margaret: "She lay on the hot ground
like a lost child, or like a dog kicked so severely it has
lost its sense of smell and wanders about and leans on the
tree it otherwise would have soiled" (M, p. 210). Better
yet is Walker's metaphor for a mother's anger and the
children's consciousness of it: "In their stiff, almost inflexible garments, they were enclosed in the starch of her
anger ... " (p. 79). Hurston's particular blend of the lyrical and the ironic is most evident in all three writers' descriptions of the place and people.

Their language has a singular quality because the
line between poetry and prose is less defined, as in Hurston's works. Poetry deals with a private imagination,
myth, a certain sensibility in regard to experience. In approaching black experience, the writers often make us feel
that the two worlds of practical experience and poetic imagination become one.

This is why I stress Zora Neale Hurston at this
point. She was one of the first black writers to identify
with the black epos in original creative endeavor. She gave
to black fiction the kind of direction which enables present
black writers to build on it and launch black literature into
its worthy place in the stream of American letters. Alice
Walker's moving account of her search for the author's un-
marked grave in a segregated cemetery in Fort Pierce,
Florida, is eloquent acknowledgment of her debt to the
writer who died of physical malnutrition and without funds,
but who left behind a rich legacy. The Zora Neale Hurston
Reader, edited by Alice Walker, is a welcome addition to
an understanding of black literature.

The many familial relationships which the authors

describe, and the means by which salvation is sought, make
the Bible (as in Hurston's work) an important influence on
the narrative quality of the writers' stories.   Sarah E.
Wright's town of Tangierneck (TC) has the sense of Old
Testament life in which everyday living unfolds with the
characters' consciousness of their relationship to God, the
issue of which is their salvation or damnation.   For Alice
Walker, transfiguration is possible only through active participation in the world.   The concern of her heroine Meridian (M) for children, the old, the sick, the lonely, the rejected is in the true spirit of the New Testament and its
treatment of the life of Jesus.   Toni Morrison's Song of
Solomon makes even more extensive and varied use of the
Bible.   The title of the novel is taken from the lush, poeti-
cal chapter "Song of Solomon," describing Solomon's achievements as well as his love for a black woman ("I am black
but comely, O ye daughters of Jerusalem ... ").   Where
the Biblical Solomon takes flight occasionally on the back of
an eagle, as legend has it, the fictional Solomon simply
raises his arms and takes off for Africa.

Not only are scenes and episodes taken from the
Bible and adapted to the writer's thematic concerns; Morrison handles names in the same way.   In the Bible, First
Corinthians is the first letter of the Apostle Paul to Corinth,
cautioning against association with immoral persons.   In
Morrison's novel, Milkman's sister, named First Corinthians, becomes involved with Porter, member of The Seven
Days avengers.   Though warned against him, she resists
the warnings and he becomes her way to emotional salvation.
Another auctorial twist to a Bible story and name are the
circumstances about Magdalene named Lena, sister to Corinthians.   The Bible treats Magdalene as the reformed sinner who spends her life in devotion and is the first witness
to the resurrection of Jesus.   In the novel, Lena endures
a life of devotion to family and then rebels, thereby resur-
recting herself from the "sepulcher" in which family has
buried her.

Drawing upon multi-layered religious references, even
the names of the men in the Shalimar hunting party, Calvin
Breakstone and Luther Solomon, suggest a special function
in the story.   It is with their help that Milkman comes to
experience self-reliance, a new concept of self, self-apprai-
sal of his former corruption--ideas associated with the Re-
formation.   Only when he questions his old values and rejects them does he experience a sense of renewal, harmony
with himself and the universe.

Along with their artistic achievement in fiction, one more thing must be mentioned in connection with the work of these three writers--the way they have restored a sense of vitality to manners. I am using the word "manners" as both courtesy and respect for other human beings--manners not as adornment to speech and action, but as an essential to good communication between people. The fiction discussed here demonstrates how much weight words and gestures carry for black people. The need for lack of artificial distances between individuals is a recognition of human dignity and autonomy. Above all, the writers' emphasis on manners and behavior has to do with the recognition that the right to respond to insult and discourtesy belongs to one's credentials as a human being.

CHAPTER 7

PIECEMEAL LIBERATION:
MARGE PIERCY, SARA DAVIDSON,
MARILYN FRENCH, GRACE PALEY

MARGE PIERCY

No one can accuse Marge Piercy of being disengaged, as was said of Virginia Woolf, a writer who although defining a woman's consciousness believed that she could not improve the world because it was man-made, and that she, a woman, was not responsible for the mess. Piercy, the author of five novels: Going Down Fast (1969); Dance the Eagle to Sleep (1970); Small Changes (1973); Woman on the Edge of Time (1976); The High Cost of Living (1978), as well as several collections of poetry, shows every indication that she has by no means totally expended her boundless energy and talent in the cause of social change. A feminist, convinced that society has indoctrinated men with a concept of manhood which is based on success in making money and in controlling women--sexually, economically, politically--her work is committed to documenting the ills of society. She centers on the man/woman relationship as it has existed, exposing past abuses of women, and suggesting alternate ways for women to live. This is the main source of the plot in Small Changes.

The book is written with authority, and knowing what we do about the writer from her article "Through the Cracks," published in Partisan Review (1974), it is reasonable to attribute her confidence to personal knowledge of what was happening between men and women who elected to break out of the System in the Sixties. In this article, the author describes her coming of age in the Fifties and her feeling of alienation in a hostile environment. Her convictions about this era may be summarized as follows: chang-

175

ing the country was impossible; there was no subculture for
women to drop into; the enclaves of hip and beat were more
piggish than the straight world; General Motors, General
Foods, and General Eisenhower dominated the world; the
only choices before her and others were conformity or exile.
Even going to college was no help. In school, she was a
"garlic among the Anglican-convert lilies" (p. 206) and
soon learned the meaning of class insult and bias. Marriage
to a graduate student brought no change. She found herself
supporting a husband through graduate school and trying not
to think about her own starved, cramped life. Finally sum-
moning up courage to leave, she was able for the first time
to appraise the social scene, the limited role of woman,
and to think about alternate ways of living for women.

One of the interesting aspects of the Fifties upon
which the author casts an appraising eye in this autobiographical article is the subject of woman's clothes. They become
for her the social indicator of the way woman's body is confined and restrained from enjoying freedom. Piercy describes the long, swaddling skirts, the tight sweaters, the
tight girdles, the narrow sheaths, the high, spiked heels,
and the padded bras. About the latter, she comments ironically: many a man believed that he was caressing a breast
when actually he was fondling Playtex padded perfect circle,
Size 34-A. Women in the Fifties, she points out, were not
bodies, but shapes. What do these costumes say? she asks,
and goes on to answer her own question: clothes of this
period jailed the woman, trained her to await babies, rape,
cancer, and made her "dumb as a centerpiece of waxed
fruit" (p. 210). As for sexual relationships, the writer admits that she found men terrified of a woman initiating sex
or expressing any honest sexual feelings, and labeled such
a woman nymphomaniac. The writer looked forward to the
Sixties as holding some hope that a woman could live like
an intelligent adult.

Small Changes, Piercy's third novel, deals with the
period of the Sixties. Her themes are conventional marriage, women's break out of marriage, their efforts at communal living, and their struggles to form relationships with
men or with women--based on mutual enjoyment and respect
for each other's minds and bodies. The author brings to
her work a reformer's zeal, which inevitably raises the
question asked so frequently about this novel (and other
novels of hers): does personal experience undergo the
transmutation into art? Critics such as Lucy Rosenthal say

no: the author makes fictional requirements secondary to
the urgency of political statement; the story has no center;
"this novel is swollen with its tangents" (Ms., September
1973).   Rosenthal concludes that the delicate balance between
ideology and fiction is never maintained, and that while the
book is an admirable document of situations which could
transpire between men and women, it is a failure as a
novel.

Looking back at the critical reception of works by
some earlier angry writers who exposed and excoriated social oppression--Charles Dickens, Richard Wright, Theodore
Dreiser, etc. --reminds us that similar charges were often
made against them.   To take one example, George Gissing
wrote of Dickens and Bleak House: though the novel demonstrates ingenuity, it also demonstrates "an almost total disregard of probability; the fitting of incidents suggests a
mechanical puzzle rather than the complications of human
life; arbitrary coincidence takes the place of well-contrived
motive, and at times the motive is glaringly inadequate. "[1]

We have by now accepted the fact that Bleak House
has numerous flaws: style; excessive heightening of characters which often gives them the appearance of caricature;
division of characters into categories of good and evil; an
exorbitant dependence on coincidence; scenes of melodrama
which attempt to coerce the reader's sympathy; a view of
life which implies that if only people would recognize their
interdependence there would be an everlasting Christmas.
But the fact remains that Bleak House (and other fiction by
Dickens) shows with tremendous power an oppressive society and how men and women are ground into "types" by it.
Dickens does this through plot and character representations
which conform to his imaginative vision and view of life.
The result is what Henry James argues as the only reason
for the existence of the novel--its attempt to represent life.

Small Changes, it should be said at the outset, does
suffer from flaws.   Frequently, the artist tries to make
the political and social perspective dominate the story rather
than tell the story.   She cannot resist putting speeches into
characters' mouths or explaining the obvious (for example,
the initials of Neil Stone's company which does work for
the Pentagon are L. S. D.).   She tries to press her own conclusions on the reader.   At times, we have a sense of wavering between documentation and fictional art because a
character simply illustrates a moral situation without the

necessary complexities of feeling. Anger spills over into
shrillness and rancor. The framework and seams of the
novel are often too patently obvious. But if the author does
not quite achieve the perilous fusion of art and politics, she
does give us a sense of the Sixties--the chaos, confusion,
indecisions, decisions, failures, successes of women faced
with men who, for the most part, are unable to break out
of their prescribed roles. Frightened by what they view as
threats to their manhood, the men are reluctant and stubborn about relinquishing the traditional role of man as woman's superior.

Men in Marge Piercy's Small Changes play a far
more important role than is usually found in the works of
women writers. Portrayed frequently as types in the Dickensian sense, they do not, however, fall into the category of
eccentrics as Dickens men (and women) sometimes do.
Piercy's male characters have a vitality of their own im-
parted to them by the writer--but a vitality which, when
directed towards women, is shown to be destructive. There
is an unrelieving no-goodness about men like Jackson, Neil,
Tom and others. Piercy seems to believe that these are
men who eventually become insensible and callous and refuse
to concede the faintest indication of a higher nature. Phil
is the one man who comes off as redeemable. He doesn't
"damage" women as much as other men, concedes Wanda,
whose own ex-husband, a radical leftist, is politically radical but traditionally narrow about women. Like Alice
Walker's Truman Held (Meridian), Wanda's ex-husband, Joe
Rosario, as Wanda explains, thinks nothing of exploiting
women sexually and in other ways--and calls it working for
the revolution.

Phil becomes linked to women by reason of being a
"hustler." One woman comments that all women are hust-
lers, constantly watching faces and gestures, trying to be
all things to all people--in order to survive. Unlike Jackson, Phil is never committed to competitive acquisition of
money, and on several occasions exhibits evidence of a social conscience. Jackson has few or no twinges of social
conscience, and is consistent in his aim to achieve economic
and sexual superiority. Phil is allowed improbabilities of
character in connection with his muddled thinking on manhood. His ultimate regeneration in forming a relationship
with Dorine, based on decent regard and love, is plausible
because we have observed his effort with Miriam to be both
lover and friend. Miriam is not just a body to him, but a

person. Unfortunately, Miriam's involvement with Jackson brings to the surface male rivalry with Jackson and some unlovely aspects of Phil's character.

The warped parts in Phil's character and the confusion about his manhood which continues to plague him almost to the end of the book, are attributed to environment and pre-vailing concepts of manhood. In Phil's youth, manhood is a gang bang on a prostitute. It was regarded as taking a leak, he recalls: "somebody was always waiting" (p. 131). Man-hood is also gang rape of an innocent girl. Years later, he tries to sort out his mixed feelings: the early excitement as they drew lots as to who would rape the girl first, and as they seized the victim and dragged her into an alley, his excitement replaced by shame as he registered her terrified eyes, bruises, blood. He recalls his own fear when he lost penis erection, the boys taunting him as just another woman, not a man like themselves, but a "cunt" (p. 287). They attempt sexual abuse of him, hold a knife to his throat, run only when the headlights of a passing car fall upon the scene. Phil, however, is troubled long after this as to whether he failed to behave like a man. Part of him, says the author, mocked such a concept of manhood, and part of him felt shame at his sexual impotency when he witnessed the girl's pain and blood.

Ultimately, Phil is the only man in the book to achieve maturity through painful self-knowledge that he must accept responsibility for his own acts. He kicks his heroin habit cold turkey (being in a Mexican jail with no alterna-tive), learns to live with his childhood and youthful mem-ories, and decides that he wants to make carpentry his work--for the time being. Despite the programmatic ring of "occupational therapy," this detail, because it is grounded in the convincing overall picture of Phil's character, does not jar. As already mentioned, he forms a union with a bright and intelligent woman (Dorine), whom he regards as comrade to be loved and trusted and not just as a "re-source" (p. 285), a view often held of the women he en-countered in the past.

Jackson, on the other hand, the second chief male protagonist in the book, becomes for the author an exemplar of the sociology of sex to which many men secretly cling or openly articulate. This is that sex is the only real means of communication between men and women, and that all mat-ters can be settled in bed. Stop talking and spread your legs, you do better that way, Jackson instructs Miriam when she tries to speak to him about their deteriorating relationship. Piercy often uses the repetition of a gesture to suggest symbolic connections. Jackson's habitual chest scratching fixes itself in our minds and reinforces the idea conveyed throughout the book that Jackson is careful not to scratch below the surface of his feelings. In Piercy's characterization of Jackson, action reveals but does not develop character. Her aim is to show a man rigidly fixed in his thinking on women, and his ideas continue to have the enameled glossiness of the furniture in his bedroom.

What we see about Jackson is that he is constantly squeezing himself into the conventional male stance--authoritative man, formulator of rules. The author does not poke into psychological states of being but presents a consistent pattern of behavior throughout. Born into an affluent, middle-class family, a corporate man and husband at an early age, Jackson's life changes only when he is drafted and sent to Vietnam. Upon his return, he seems to vent most of his rage against his wife. Accompanied by his war buddy (Phil), he systematically tries to destroy his home's furnishings. His final husbandly act is to attempt to flush his wife's mink coat down the toilet. Divorce brings him the loss of his son, and from that time on all women are "cunts" (p. 197), as he informs Miriam, his current lover. The author tries to be impartial by indicating that Jackson's wife used trickery to rob him of his son, but since he beat her and abused her in other ways, the wife's action does not seem wholly unjustifiable. Piercy's objectivity here only buttresses her portrayal of Jackson. It is apparent that Jackson's hostility is due to more than this experience. His actions are of varying importance, but if we try to fix a precise motive to them, they date back to a principle he has never relinquished: unless you control women, they will control you. In the end, Jackson is back to some degree of middle-class security with a Ph.D., a tenured teaching position, and a sex life which includes bedding young, impressionable girl students whose "marshmallow" (p. 522) yielding only deepens his contempt for women. Dour, bitter Jackson is a Dickensian character who remains the same in every respect. As with Dickens' characters, defined by their obsessions and passions, Jackson's constrictive bitterness dominates him more or less to the end. The consistency is entirely plausible because, as Piercy demonstrates, such consistent attitudes were not substantially altered by communal living.

Neil, who marries Miriam, comes in for a great deal of the author's attention. He is presented throughout as a cautious, prudent man, careful about keeping his body trim, his wife's creativity and intelligence pruned to ground level, and his finances a secret from his wife. His ideas on marriage and the wife's role are as inflexible as his sur-name--Stone. We get a hint of his duality of character in the early description of Neil as a quiet man except for the impatient moving of his hands. Fundamentally, he emerges as a brother to Jackson in the mutually-held theory that women must be controlled. In addition, both men seem to view a woman like a car which requires breaking in, polishing, and upkeep so that adequate service will be provided to the owner. With age, the woman can be turned in for a newer model. Jackson concentrates on his girl students, and Neil casts an appraising look at Miriam's greying hair, contrasts her appearance with Helen's blonde prettiness, and decides he can afford a new "car"--Helen. Stock worth $150,000 is all in his name.

Dotted throughout the book are clear indications that women, especially married women, do not pay enough attention to money. They allow husbands to write off their house-hold work as non-productive because it doesn't bring income. They do not insist on equitable control and distribution of monies in household management. They lower themselves to the status of beggars asking for every penny to buy a book, a dish, a pair of pants. "It's like being fifteen again," says resigned Miriam, "and having to ask Daddy for an allowance" (p. 410). As will be made clearer, both this "tradition" and the submission to it by women like Miriam pivot on long-held myths about women's household status.

Neil, however, is not the most unpleasant male char-acter in the book. The prize goes to Tom Ryan. Tom is a debunker not only of women but of men. For example, he refers contemptuously to Jackson as a "fringe academic character" (p. 51) and sneers at Phil's attempts to write poetry. But it is for the women that he reserves his spleen. Miriam gets her college grants "flat on her back" (p. 51). She is also a "ball breaker." Beth is not "a real woman" (p. 73) because she refuses to move in with him. His estranged wife is a nag, denies him his paternal rights, wants him to show more affection to his son, which in his opinion would certainly make the boy a sissy.

While Tom is the least savory character, he shares

with most of the men in Piercy's novel (except for Phil when alone) that conviction which was voiced by many English-men of early Victorian England. These were men who when confronted with the demands of the working class, refused to yield and saw revolution and anarchy in every attempt by the underprivileged to better themselves. Jackson, Neil, Tom, and others believe that no nostrums are necessary, and that all matters between men and women can be settled if woman will keep her place. When some of the women leave the half-way house over which Jackson presides to form a commune with Beth, Jackson, with the supporting chorus of the other men, derides the women as "the camp-fire girls" and refers to the house as "the girls' dormitory" (p. 281).

The author, however, makes it clear that it is not the man but the System which is at fault. Like the victim-ized child in Dickens' early novels, the victimized woman appears in Small Changes. The treatment of women by men is seen as the result of society's emphasis on the separation of male and female roles, and the perversion of all natural feelings between men and women. The author's women fight against institutionalized evil, as they encounter it in the world of business, in graduate school, in the sphere of love and marriage. They choose to live without men, or they choose a man or woman who is willing to accept them nei-ther as betrayers nor castrators but as decent women. Some, like Dorine, overcome social and psychological handi-caps and achieve self-esteem and dignity. Others, like Miriam, start out by liberating themselves, slide back into compromise, and find themselves stuck in the old way of living and thinking. The author's men are intelligent and strong-willed, but trapped in their view of manhood and fearful of losing power.

Marge Piercy is close to the black writers discussed in this book in holding that society in fact is to blame. So-ciety is the villain because of its stress on manhood as equated with competitiveness for money and wealth, and its clinging to a narrow dogmatism which refuses to view wom-an in any way except as inferior. True, the author lacks the visionary range of the black women writers. Her moral insistence that she is concerned with the evil of a system which brutalizes men and puts women into a position of in-feriority often hits the reader with the delicacy of a meat cleaver. Yet one cannot help remembering that this accusa-tion can also be applied to Dreiser and other writers. The

bludgeoning crudity of their address to their targets often
precluded stylistic felicity and narrative fluency, but it also
powerfully implemented their passion for honest portrayal
and reform. Like the writers just mentioned, Piercy is
angry with the spreading blight of evil and wants the blight
removed. She is adamant about the reconstitution of individual man and woman which she believes can only come
from a break with established societal patterns of living
and thinking. There must be a new way of looking at the
man/woman relationship--a way based on mutual respect
and understanding.

Along with Dreiser and Dickens, Piercy ceaselessly
realizes the negative pressures of the System as reflected
in the small theater of intimate human relations; and she
insists on the continuity of the large-scale social patterns
in the most apparently private man/woman responses. In
this respect, she is not attempting to make edifying fiction
such as John Gardner argues for in his new book On Moral
Fiction: true art is moral and seems to improve life, not
lower it. She is trying to bring home a present situation
and thereby rekindle a passion for change. That such a
mission may quarrel with the demands of art is demonstrated
in both the failure and success of Small Changes.

Failure is often due to the writer's impatience to
transmit as directly as possible her conclusions about the
situation and what she would have us feel. Such impatience
diverts her from using fully the artistic means of portrayal,
narrative rhythm, plot, etc. which would project the actual
situation with greater force. When she succeeds, however,
she in fact portrays such actuality--for example, in her
characterization of the men, especially Phil--with a richer,
more complex sense of circumstances than occurs in many
other feminist writers. In addition, there is a related
alertness to particularity: body, dress and mannerism, as
noted in her emphasis on Phil's golden blondness and his
mobility of movement; Jackson's angular body, curt voice,
and his mannerism of scratching; Neil's quiet, steely voice
slicing through Miriam's apologies or protests. However,
it would be foolish to deny that it is the women who receive
the emphasis of the author's attention.

With the women, still more than with the men, characterization depends not only on physical detail--Beth's
smallness, Miriam's body worn "like a flag" (p. 101), Dorine's bittersweet chocolate-colored hair fringed around her

face--but on the author's resourcefulness in creating patterns of response to situations and circumstances. The vitality of the women: Beth, Miriam, Dorine, Sally, Connie,
Laura, etc., is based on the belief that women have the
capacity to change--if they want to. No one woman is de-
veloped at any great length, with the exception of Miriam.
The women are often what E. M. Forster calls flat characters. Yet the feeling that the author has for her women as
types bears out Forster's amplification of his theory that
there may be more in flatness than a critic may allow.

The author's closeness to her women is apparent in
her depth of feeling for them. From this deep empathy
comes her insistence that if a woman is allowed to work
out her own life, she will eventually realize a measure of
happiness. One of the ways she shows women achieving
some kind of understanding of themselves is through talk.
Her women, unable to communicate with men, talk to each
other--a point made about Joyce Carol Oates's Loretta in
them. Loretta, however, is concerned with a new hair
style, new hair color, or expressing fear of blacks moving
into her neighborhood. She often fantasizes and the life on
the movie screen is far more real to her than the life she
is living. Oates's lower-middle-class heroine, a teenager
in 1937, admits no exits, no alternative routes. Her ultimate design for living, like that of James Joyce's Gerty
MacDowell (Ulysses), is of the kind presented her by movies
and True Romance magazines.

Piercy's women do not fantasize. There is an enormous belief in the power of language to uncover struggling
felt needs and to sever themselves from the myths men
create about them. With the exception of Miriam, women
resist the tempting inclination to idealize reality. For this
reason, Miriam becomes the most poignant figure in the
book, as will be explained. The goodness of the women depends on their personal affection for each other and their
desire to help. Along with Beth and Dorine, Miriam aids
Wanda's children to escape tyrannical grandparents when
Wanda is jailed and her children taken from her. Though
Miriam is aware of the extent of her husband's anger if he
should find out, she goes ahead with the others to help the
children rejoin their mother when she is released from
prison. Wanda has been jailed for refusing to testify against
her former husband. Despite memories of ill treatment from
her ex-husband, Wanda refuses to label him "the enemy." It
is the System which has taught Joe to use and discard women.
In Wanda, the System has an eloquent critic.

Though many women are included in the author's gallery, the novel focuses on the odyssey of two of them: Beth and Miriam. They come from different backgrounds but their lives meet, cross, and recross. We begin with Beth ("The Book of Beth"), and are given a straight linear recital of her marriage and disillusionment. Jim, her husband, expects her to work, keep house, breed children, and receive her sexual pleasure from evidence of his. The author is no pioneer in the abuses she attacks. Other writers have been aware of the difficulties of women faced with a similar marital situation. Today, of course, there is even less ignorance on the subject. But in 1973, when Small Changes was published, the author's intent was to revive the discussion of old abuses and give the subject a new perspective. She lingers over Beth's marriage, fascinated by the grotesqueries of middle-class ritual: the elaborate bridal finery; the wedding feast in the V. F. W. Hall; the double entendres which are supposed to elicit blushing giggles from the new wife. Above all, Piercy fastens on the money spent--hard-earned money which would have financed two years of college for Beth, an idea rejected by her parents.

The writer shares with us not only familiar details which all recognize, but that social-moral mood which says that once the ceremony is over and proper rituals observed, the wife must understand that the pattern of her life is now set by her husband. Beth, however, rebels, and eventually flees to Boston. From this point on, the narrative style changes, and we are plunged into the teeming world of communal living in which relationships form, dissolve, reform, or eventually disappear. As the author gets into her novel, there is an atmospheric density which is difficult to sort out: who is living with whom, what commune is Beth connected to at this point, when did Miriam, Jackson, and Phil become ménage à trois? There is the undeniable implication of the Lawrencean idea: no absolute; life flows and changes and even change is not absolute. Though Beth's metamorphosis from passive to activist is abrupt, the author finally succeeds in holding in tension the many diverse threads of the story by her insistence that Beth's singleness of purpose to free herself from dependency on man for approval, protection and love makes her strong enough to put her life in order. She does this by organizing a woman's commune in which there is no distinction between the deserving and undeserving, recognizing her bisexual nature, and dealing with her emotional and intellectual needs.

The writer's flat, deliberate tone in "The Book of

Beth" recalls Alice Walker's similar treatment of Meridian
in the early pages of her story. Tone, language and character (in both books) fuse to emphasize the deliberate way a
woman must go about casting off old ties in order to achieve
a new life. Self-scrutiny is to be avoided and feelings of
guilt diverted if there is to be achievement of purpose. For
this reason, Beth appears as a woman with less substance
than Miriam, just as Walker's Meridian lacks the psychological touches which make for the substance of Lynne Rabinowitz. The language surrounding Lynne and Miriam with
its long convoluted sentences enforces the notion of weight,
in contrast to the crisp, short prose given to Meridian and
Beth. There is a sense of Beth and Meridian stripped for
action physically and psychologically; both are pictured as
slight women and direct in thought and action. Conversely,
Miriam and Lynne, their wills distracted by excess cargo
of guilt, indulge in long dialogues and inner monologues.
They eat, they take on physical weight--a symbolic manifestation of the inner weight which impedes them and keeps them
wavering.

Indeed, there is little wavering about Piercy's Beth.
She is the author's didactic voice prodding and telling us
how one should act and think. Out of sheer loneliness, she
forms a relationship with Tom Ryan. Quickly assessing
the impoverishment of mind and spirit in him, she breaks
with Tom and the half-way house in which he lives with
other men and women. This is a house, as she tells Miriam, in which men talk to each other but not to women.
Women do the dishes, make the food appear and the garbage
disappear, and service the men sexually. It's playing
dramas with people, telling yourself they make you feel
alive. To Dorine, who sadly admits that she is the house
whore and sometimes feels as if she will go through life
without belonging to anyone, Beth's answer is tart: You're
not a dog. Why do you want to be owned? Later, when
the married and troubled Miriam confides that her husband
Neil must be provided with a quiet, orderly life, Beth retorts that no one should provide another person with a life.
Each one is responsible for his own life.

It's sensible advice and most of the women in the
book take it seriously. In the commune which Beth establishes there is sharing of work, responsibility, and time
for creativity. The author paints an idyllic picture of each
woman doing what she can best and contributing financially
according to her earning power or, as in Sally's case, by

household assistance. Connie's child becomes the special
care of each woman and we are told that he is brighter,
happier for having more than one mother. A point is made
later concerning the importance of children's games. Games
children play, Piercy believes, determine the kind of "games"
people act out as adults, recalling Vonnegut's similar premise in Cat's Cradle, with his characterization of Frank, who
puts bugs into a jar and makes them fight. The grown-up
Frank becomes a dictator, or more accurately, the power
behind the dictator of a place called San Lorenzo. Piercy's
Beth and the other women are vigilant about not creating
future dictators.

Of course, there are problems. A lesbian wants her
lover to stay overnight. Divorced Connie wants her man to
have similar privileges. Eventually, the commune breaks
up as women move on to new experiences, and we are left
wondering what happens to those children who, having enjoyed the attentions of several "mothers," now are faced
with one mother who elects to marry and presents the child
with a stranger for a father. Another interesting question
about the communal living which Piercy describes is the
casual acceptance of drugs. Beth shops not only for Tide,
soap, groceries, but also for grass, hash, mescaline and
other drugs. Piercy ironically observes that Beth finds
these drug items more available and cheaper in price at the
company where she works as typist. The company, named
Logical, does work with the Pentagon and is headed by Neil
who, despite his straight ideas on marriage and the role of
wife, expects Miriam to stock good grass as well as liquor
and wine. Yet he is angry with Miriam when he discovers
her smoking grass during her pregnancy, reemphasizing the
duality which constantly limns his personality.

There is little duality about any of the women. The
book's message is unequivocal and embodied in the ironic
title, Small Changes. Women's lives can change if women
are honest and willing to risk change from the traditional
pattern of dependency on man. Dorine, formerly chief
bottle washer, domestic, and sexual resource for various
men, goes back to school, through the encouragement of
the commune women with whom she lives, and becomes a
biologist. Later, she moves to another commune in which
there are professional people, intellectuals and artists.
When she does decide to become "a couple" with Phil, it is
with mutual recognition of her value and worth. Sally, who
never gets beyond the tenth grade, discovers (again with

encouragement from women), long secreted within her, a
talent for acting.   Beth moves on to Women's Theater and
to Wanda, a bright and talented woman, and the two women
become lovers.   Consummation takes place during grape
picking.

Here is an example of the writer's lapses into language which weakens the fiction.   Perhaps, in keeping with
the season, the author yields to purple prose which robs
the lovemaking of the lyrical which it is supposed to convey.
On the whole, however, the characterization of Beth and
her final reunion with Wanda, after her release from prison,
holds with Beth's single vision of achieving stability and
happiness in her life.   Language here has a surer touch.
"All that living, " reflects Beth on Wanda, "had gone to cure
this salty woman to just the right taste for her" (p. 499).

If Beth finds the proper saltiness in her relationship
with Wanda, Miriam finds that by constantly sweetening
Neil's life, she sours her own.   Marriage in this book, as
in previous novels discussed, is all downhill.   But then,
this is not different from the handling of marriage by two
such different male writers as Thomas Hardy and Norman
Mailer.   Thomas Hardy's Eustacia Vye (The Return of the
Native) commits suicide after marriage; Mailer's hero (An
American Dream) murders his wife and even succeeds in
escaping punishment.   Piercy elects to have Miriam stay
with Neil.   She leaves her hoping to the end that he will
love her, unaware that he is shopping around for another
woman.   She becomes for the author the symbol of the
woman who plunges into marriage as a closed response to
the events in her life, becomes caught in the restrictions
of her husband's do's and dont's, and tries to content herself with the crumbs of approval he throws to her when she
succeeds in momentarily pleasing him.

A singleness of vision underlies the writer's detail
in presenting Miriam.   At first, the fragments of Miriam's
life do not seem related or particularly significant.   We
meet her through Beth's eyes, an exotic, liberated woman
who moves with a dancer's grace and is mate of the most
beautiful man Beth has ever seen (Phil).   He watches Miriam as if making "a pane of glass" (p. 57) about them.
However, in "The Book of Miriam" and subsequent passages
which follow this, dramatic sequences are connected through
a nucleus of ideas sustained by one major theme--that Miriam is a woman who on the surface appears liberated but

who actually is anxious to please--family, friends, men--
above all, men.

The sense of wanting to be absorbed by love, and
the terror of being excluded from it, are demonstrated in
the family relationship and the relationships first with Phil,
then with Phil and Jackson--and even with women. Her
family's view of her, as a child and a woman, and her inability to meet their demands--particularly those of the
mother--give her deep feelings of guilt. Later this is mani-
fested in her view of her own motherhood--a penance to the
mother now dead. With Phil, her first lover, she is Mother
undressing him when he is drunk, tucking him in, and listening to his problems. With Jackson, she is so over-
whelmed by the fact that this man desires her that she permits him to establish all the guidelines for the relationship.
When she finally asserts herself by resuming a relationship
with Phil, she finds the two men passing her between them,
like some trophy to be wrested or stolen from the other.
Frightened by the fear that she is becoming a "twenty-five-
year-old bag of sexual tricks" (p. 381), she marries Neil.

The key phrase she weaves about Neil is wreathed
in the illusion which the author feels women so often delude
themselves with: "I know him." Ostensibly there is justification for Miriam's idea. They are in the same field--
computers; they have the same ethnic background--Jewish.
Unlike Jackson, who wants no commitment, Neil insists on
a permanent relationship--marriage. As it turns out, Miriam
and Neil are strangers who agree on nothing: politics, friends,
role of wife, role of husband, the rearing of children, the
handling of finances, etc.

Neil labels Miriam "narrowly moralistic" (p. 411) because she wants to work on computers which would replace
human drudgery and not design systems which kill and burn
people. He chides her for cuddling and kissing their son;
making a "sissy" out of him. He plays with his children,
talks to them, but gets annoyed if they lose interest:
"He grew more involved in the course of his exposi-
tion than in their reactions. His disappointment was crush-
ing" (p. 547). Ariane, the daughter, soon learns to per-
form correctly in order to please Daddy so that she will
get the reward of his smile. The last words anticipate the
final scene in which Miriam, terrified of losing Neil and
the children, plans to be more diligent in anticipating his
needs and meeting them. Ironically, Neil has plans of his

own and they do not include Miriam, but a new woman.
However, there is a vitality to Miriam which helps to miti-
gate the dispiriting ending.   We feel that Miriam will eventually get over her desperate obsession that only lovemaking
can knit a marital rent.   She will regain her confidence
that she can earn her own living doing the work she loves--
designing machines which won't kill people but will help
them live better and more useful lives.   And she will accept
the hard and unequivocal truth that marriage with Neil spells
death, and that the dissolution of the marriage is a way to
relationships with men and women which will round out her
life and make it complete.

Small Changes is both fiction and a historical document of an era.   Despite the recurrent over-insistence on
her conclusions, Marge Piercy makes us care both about
her story and about the play of historical issues.   She un-
ashamedly takes her place as a voice of her times.   Although the urgency of her conviction sometimes gets in the
way of her story-telling skill, the two frequently unite with
force.   When they do, we are urged not only to ask what
comes next, but to feel concerned with her people, and the
possibility of believing in the alternatives open to them--
men too.

SARA DAVIDSON

"Their generation changed our world forever," says
the large New York Times ad heralding Sara Davidson's
Loose Change (1977), a novel dealing with student radicals
and the social history of the Sixties and its impact on the
lives of three women who met at Berkeley.   They are Sara
Davidson herself and two other women whose names have
been changed to Susie Hersh Berman and Natasha (Tasha)
Taylor.   The author's literary aim, as stated in the Prologue, was to select women whose viewpoint of the events
in the Sixties would be different from hers because of the
divergent lives they had led.   Susie had been married to a
Berkeley radical leader and was part of the revolutionary
movement from its inception.   Tasha had moved in the art
world of New York after graduation from Berkeley and had
been involved with a famous sculptor for several years.   Sara
was a journalist who had been married to a novelist who
was also a successful disc jockey.   The author tells us that

she wants to probe character and events to find out what really happened during the Sixties and what went wrong.

Despite the stated objective, we miss the expected peripatetic inquiries into the nature of people and the reasons for their allegiances. The book has skill, but it lacks that keen perception of character and scene which arises from a vivid responsiveness to a common experience and conveys a sense of shared life. More important, we do not get a sense of history from the intricate pattern of a shifting society, nor discern a pattern and unity in the novel which would give meaning to the apparently chaotic world the author is depicting. In fact, in her effort to be objective the narrator sometimes retreats into a kind of solipsism--the belief that she alone existed.

The evident energy, receptiveness, occasional shrewd observation which the author has enlisted in this project have paid off in a way, however, of which she seems unaware. For Davidson's own self-projection in this "novel" is often that of a partisan, self-identified with, and submissive to the life she is describing in all of its confusion, futility, and fantasy. If she does not fully realize the extent of her identification, she is very alert to the delusions of the women in the Sixties that they were living a life of sexual liberation. The limitations of the author's partisanship are a major limitation of her objectivity, which does not project beyond the immediate observation of persons and situations.

The limits she sets to her story tend to rob it of the necessary range of observation and emotion which we find in Chekhov, whose arrival on the literary scene also coincided with a period of social and political unrest in his country. Chekhov's writing, whether it is a play, short story or novel, presents an analysis of Russian history in which a social purpose is always implicit, though it is not allowed to disturb the unity of the story. Loose Change is deficient not only in analysis of the social world but often in getting behind the meaning of a scene, a gesture, a dialogue. One does not need realistic saturation of detail to describe a man and woman discovering each other. But sometimes more than the following is needed to make us understand the character's action. Sara goes to interview a black playwright: "I drank two cups of coffee and he drank six beers and then I don't remember how but I was sitting in his lap and we were kissing" (p. 94).

Art is discovery, as the novels of Dickens, D. H.
Lawrence, Doris Lessing and others stress. They express
the author's conviction of the novel's viability, its function
as search and discovery of new possibilities of thinking and
acting. "The novel is the book of life," says D. H. Lawrence in "Why the Novel Matters"[2] and he goes on to explain how it redirects the reader into new perspectives,
new ways of regarding people and relationships: "the changing rainbow of our living relationships."[3] Davidson's own
characterization of her work as a novel in itself encourages
us to expect some organic shape discovered by the author,
or evolved by her. What she presents, however, is the
shapelessness of her people's lives and times, among them
her own. She fails to assert her own patterning powers
and becomes imprisoned in the shapelessness.

The writer is hampered from redirecting us into new
ways of thinking about the Sixties not only by the novel's
shapelessness but by wishful thinking, wisps of which appear
throughout the book and are finally articulated more fully in
the end. Her generation was somehow a special generation.
They had felt the great wind of change blowing and did not
succumb to conformity and mediocrity. They did eventually
effect social change: the right to abortion, for example.
The book ends in a mixture of feelings implying that something of value was lost with this generation and may not
again be found. It has the desperate ring of Julie Messinger's thinking in Such Good Friends on her bad marriage
and the husband now dead: "we were something, in spite of
each other, weren't we?" (p. 283). The effect on the reader
is the same--a sorrowful shaking of the head. The people
Sara Davidson portrays were not special in the way she
would have us believe. And if they effected some social
change, it was in spite of their lack of social values and
commitment.

Loose Change, however, has a poignant effect on us,
for it makes us recall how passionately we wanted to believe that the young were acting out what we never had.
We wanted to believe that these young people possessed the
courage to break with the whole sordid business of competitiveness, scorn the pursuit of grades and material success, and bring about a new era of humanism and social
justice. We wanted to believe that the revolt against middle-
class morality and sexual puritanism would result in honest
and fulfilling relationships between men and women. We
were, of course, wary when told about the mind-expanding

possibilities of the new (?) drugs, but tried to be open to
the idea that drugs might yield a whole new beautiful concept of consciousness.

Certainly, there is much activity recorded in Loose
Change, centering primarily on the cult of nonconformity.
But this activity only points to why the New York Times ad
on the book, "their generation changed our world forever, "
is misleading and why we now have a generation of arrested
progress--young people primarily interested in well-paying
jobs. Loose Change dramatizes that it was not so much social change that the author's people were concerned with; it
was something else: if the Fifties were the age of conformity, the Sixties were for self-expression. The young, faced
with choices, frantically tried everything: erotic sex, drugs,
marriage, body painting, meditation, Hare Krishna, Yoko
Ono happenings, tattoos. They flocked to Woodstock to chant
and sway to their favorite rock singers; they flew to India
to meet the latest guru; they sang along with the Fugs, "Co-
ca Cola Douche, " "Wet Dream, " "Slum Goddess, " "Kill for
Peace"; they bought bananas and paid a three-cent deposit
on the skins because banana peels "have a great high"; they
took psychedelic trips; they read the Bhagavad Gita, rang
gongs, and ate squash with pumpkin seeds; they went to
parties dressed in spacemen suits, African robes, cowboy
regalia, velvet gowns, or jeans topped by a velvet vest;
they listened to the Beatles in a room lined with pink fur;
they decorated rooms not only with fur, but with aluminum
foil, antlers, stuffed peacocks, railroad signals; they danced
naked with strobe lights illuminating their bare flesh. How
can I go to law class the next day and study torts? complains a youth.

How indeed, thinks this member of the older generation with a touch of envy at such hedonistic goings on,
especially remembering that sometimes one's chief excitement in a week was leaving an evening college class late
and madly chasing a bus to get home at some decent hour.
There was no lighting of joss sticks and singing while riding in a car, as Sara does prior to interviewing a great
guru. But we did dream of social change, did send a few
dollars to "Save The Children, " did vote for Norman Thomas, and did risk job security by sometimes marching on
May Day.

Obviously, since Loose Change begins with Berkeley,
the heart and nervous cortex of the student unrest which

sent its circulatory movements throughout the nation, there
are many reports of sit-ins and demonstrations. But the
interesting fact brought out in the book about the young
people engaged in these activities is that there is no conflict in values. We do not get the feeling that these young
people experience a sense of dislocation, or even the sense
of being poised in ambivalence, which many of the previous
generation had undergone. What becomes patently clear
about the people Sara Davidson portrays, including herself,
is that few of them lost sight of the dollar and the future.
Although they demonstrate and picket, they remember finals
and the necessity of good grades to get into graduate school.
They use people and rationalize exploitation as a means to
a successful end.

Jeff, the radical leader, given the most exposure in
the book, turns out to be a young man glib with revolutionary slogans, ignorant of any program for social reform,
equally ignorant of Engels' thinking on women as oppressed
by men, evident from the way he treats his wife Susie.
He is so sexually insecure that he needs constant reassurance about his sexual performance and doggedly follows his
father's advice for marital happiness: keep her laid. As
avid for the limelight as any ham actor, he rushes home
with his wife after being released by the police for demonstrating, to see if their picture and story have made the
evening TV news. A good touch on Jeff's egocentricity is
his amazement on learning that the Old Left still exists.
His amazement holds as much validity as his burning of
what he claims is his draft card, but which turns out to be
a movie pass. The total picture of Jeff and the student
revolution he heads is of confusion, inherent weakness--not
a release of constructive energy which the older generation
had inhibited.

As for his wife Susie, while her husband lives on
words, she faces diapers and keeps wondering where that
elusive orgasm is that she has been hearing about. How
is she going to survive for the next fifty years? she wonders as she reflects on her unhappiness in this marriage.
She does survive, leaves Jeff, and even gets a trip around
the world when someone instructs her how to rip off the
System by taking her ticket after each flight to an airline
company and having it rewritten. Paris-Saigon would be
changed to Paris-New Delhi-Saigon. If anything went wrong,
by the time the mistake was discovered Susie would be in
another country with another ticket. Susie even finds love

with a Vietnamese student for a while, but returns to Amer-
ica--land of opportunity, as she always views it. And her
faith is justified. A scholarship gets her into medical
school. However, there is still a fly in Susie's ointment.
Having received most of her political education from Jeff,
on hearing of Patty Hearst's abduction she exclaims, "I bet
Patty's getting a fantastic political education" (p. 359). But
as practical and resourceful as ever, she soon comes to
the conclusion that violence is dangerous and that her struggle will have to be made through the pursuit of medicine
(p. 359). Despite many problems, sexual frustrations, a
bout with TB, Susie never emerges as someone victimized
by life's tragic ironies. Her grim, humorless search for
sexual orgasm and her stress on economic and social security make her almost a caricature instead of a deeply-feeling
woman.

The outward nonconformity and the inward stubborn
clinging to forms which will not rob the young people of future security is very much due to the fact that none of Sara
Davidson's people comes from the ranks of the hungry, the
dispossessed, the jailed, the silenced, but from comfortable,
even upper-middle-class homes. There's no fall from security and order, and there is usually parental money for
tuition, drugs, wine, food, journeys. And there is welfare.
Nor do the young seem to be profoundly disturbed by the
threat of dehumanization in a machine age. After all, they
had grown up in a machine age which provided them with
those creature comforts so ironically enumerated by Joan
Didion in A Book of Common Prayer, in which she speaks
of Charlotte Douglas being provided with orthodontics, trips,
etc.

The initial exposure to the machine of the young in
Loose Change consists of long lines at registration and a
professor who is unable to remember a student's name.
When they rebel, they chant "Student Power," "Don't Trust
Anyone Over Thirty," "Turn On, Tune In, Drop Out." They
drive to demonstrations in a red convertible, as do Sara
and friends. They carry signs, "Jim Crow Must Go," and
ask (Sara again), what does it mean? I don't know, replies
her equally ignorant friend. They participate in events that
they have no desire to fathom and exhibit no central human-
istic thesis. There is little handling of ideas concerning
class war, no historical consciousness of past and present
events, no Janus looking forward and back to understand the
present in which they are living. Those who were battered

for the cause and suffered are absent from the pages of
this book. There is one brief, poignant reference to Mario
Savio who resigned from leadership because it was his conviction that an organization with a leader is undemocratic.
He went to England, had a retarded son, came back, and on
the tenth anniversary of SDS, says the writer, was reported
to be in a mental hospital. But the spotlight on Jeff keeps
us from learning more about other radical leaders, their
suffering and the struggle of moral crisis they must have
endured. Nor do we hear of protesters bumped down flights
of stairs and into paddy wagons--and not as successful as
Jeff in being released quickly.

The book evidences that Davidson's generation believed it was special and needed no past as social referral.
The young lop off family and other associations as encumbrances in order "to hang loose." A cult of rebellion pre-
vails, for there are no domineering mothers, nor fathers
as primal authority to be fought against and rejected. There
is a specific lack of family in this book, except that Sara
feels some gravitational pull to her Hungarian immigrant
grandfather, and Tasha to the father who died of a heart
attack, though Tasha's feelings are heavily laced with guilt.
The dominant idea concerning family and history is voiced
by the narrator as: we were convinced that we sprang from
nowhere.

The credo of these young people, in which the narrator shares, is: "let's not miss any piece of the action,"
and action takes them all over the United States, and to far-
flung places. But the aphorism, "you can't go home again,"
does not apply, for actually many of them never leave
"home." Two young men illustrate this. Steven Silver
wrote poetry in Berkeley about a brave new world, but enjoyed polygamous exploitation of Tasha and Sandra. He
boasts to Tasha during a chance meeting in 1972 that he is
the best gestalt therapist in Berkeley. He gets forty dollars
an hour now and his hours are all booked. He likes to work
with couples. Rob Kagan, who introduced Sara to Acapulco
Gold at Berkeley and who, together with her, put the clock
into the freezer to stop time, is portrayed in the last pages
of the book as living in what he sees as the best of two
possible worlds. He has a wife named Sun Bee who wears
baby doll dresses in white lace, clasps her hair back with
rhinestone barrettes, and puts dainty cowboy boots on her
feet. But Rob himself is all business. "Money gives you
access to perfect things, like this car" (p. 353), he says,

opening a picture book of vintage cars and pointing to a
Lamborghini. Rob is avid not only about acquiring cars,
but obtaining land--premium real estate in a beautiful setting, like Hawaii, in which there is good weather all the
year around. It would make a splendid financial investment,
he tells Sara. When asked by Sara about the high hopes of
the Sixties and the fizzle of those hopes, Rob is laconic:
"It means things didn't turn out that way" (p. 355). Rob
has no inclination to think, or to intellectualize his experience. He still doesn't understand that the hopes he had
then were no different from the goals he has now: money
and material goods as the way to happiness; motion as
progress.

Understandably, much of the activity about which the
author writes demonstrates that sex is a driving force, a
necessary release which contributes to the general restless-
ness of the Sixties. What is sad is that despite the abun-
dant use of the word love by people in this novel, deep, pro-
found love, like religion, is totally absent. Easy sex is encouraged as togetherness--love insurance against a sense of
frustration, loneliness, the isolation suffered by those de-
formed by puritanical ideas, as dramatized by Sherwood
Anderson in Winesburg, Ohio. Yet, though sex in the novel
is off-the-rack-easy-to-wear, love is complex, as the narrator admits. The book resounds with the loneliness of people, especially the women, because of their failure to establish real intimacy, comradeship, a sense of sharing in
love and in marriage. Susie is told that jealousy is bour-
geois and that sexual desires should not be censured, but
notes that "while the men could ball for lust and not get
attached, the women kept falling in love" (p. 178). As in
Marge Piercy's Small Changes, we see that the new sex
has simply made things easier for the male. One youth
sums it up in Davidson's book: "Our scene is so groovy.
It satisfies all my emotional and sexual needs without pinning
me down to anyone" (p. 127).

For both men and women, sex diffused with drugs
gives a temporary illusion that life is a winning lottery
ticket to be spent lavishly and quickly. But the illusion is
soon dispelled for the women, who are unable to find mates
who will concede them cultural equality and give some of
the reciprocal affection they desire. Women experiment
with sex for different reasons. Sara turns to sex out of
curiosity and as a symbol of independence. Various men
help her with her erotic course, giving her a varied sexual

curriculum. Carey, an SDS leader who comes "in two sec-
onds flat," explains "that's how I am" (p. 121). Gideon,
an Israeli student, teaches her touching which unleashes
pure physical joy within her. Ravi, an Indian, introduces
her to avocado milk shakes, curry, Indian music, and how
to make love to that music. Michael, who becomes her
husband, acquaints her with cunnilingus. After Michael
there is Noel, with whom she stays stoned for four days on
Angel Dust (a tranquilizer for horses) because Michael has told
her that making love to her was always "work" (p. 279).
Her lovemaking with Noel comes to a halt when their sexual
exertions make her bleed. Obviously, although there is no
mention of suffering, there is psychological as well as
physical bleeding here. Then there is Lee, with whom she
smokes grass and, as she puts it, does things which will
give her enjoyment but not cause pregnancy.

For Susie, drugs are no lever to a sexual high, least
of all with her husband Jeff. She enters into a sexual relationship with him before marriage, not out of curiosity
nor a desire to experiment, but as a response to emotional
blackmail. "I can't live like a monk" (p. 39), says Jeff,
threatening to go to another woman. What follows discloses
that contemporary Susie is fearful of losing Jeff: even as
Thomas Hardy's nineteenth-century Sue Bridehead (Jude the
Obscure). Susie quickly complies--with the same lack of
joy. Tasha, the third member of the group, goes to New
York and falls under the strong influence of a famous sculptor, twenty years her senior. Tasha is a heroine on the
Oates model. She feels that she has no choice but to yield
to male domination. Even her golden beauty, so like that
of Oates's Elena (Do With Me ...), brings her close to
Oates's characterization of Elena, not only in physical description but in Tasha's feeling about herself: "used, like a
wastebasket" (p. 201).

Tasha, who is an art dealer, exhibits her married
lover's work, arranges his apartment, accompanies him on
trips, and allows him to pick out her clothes for her--
clothes which will make her look older. Even the psychologist she goes to is Mark's. Tasha's passivity is explained
as due to the fact that she had a love affair in high school,
became impregnated when her young lover ejaculated against
her panties during petting, and eventually had an abortion. Her
father died soon after, ignorant of the abortion, and Tasha now
has nightmares about him. She also has dreams of the former high school sweetheart, in which they are always young

and always in love. But it is obvious that the father is a referential image, in a small way, and analogous to her relationship with Mark.

For the most part, whether women are married or in a relationship of some sort, that famous catch phrase of the Sixties, "doing your own thing," does not apply to women in their dealings with men. Sara tells us that Michael sets all the rules for their marriage, beginning with his refusal to let her family come to the wedding, or to have her hair cut beyond a certain length for the occasion. After the marriage ceremony, there is no talk between them, but it is tacitly understood that Sara does the domestic work, though she has a full time job as journalist. Michael comes home, retires to the green room, so called because it is painted green and the blinds are never opened, drinks Scotch, watches TV, makes telephone calls, and reads. Dinner is usually at ten or later. After dinner, Michael goes to sleep.

They are completely incompatible. He likes repetition of experiences; she is avid for new experience. She is a night person, he a day. She takes all kinds of drugs; he drinks liquor. She likes Mick Jagger; he enjoys Frank Sinatra. Sara is fair about reporting that Michael is supportive of her journalistic aspiration to be published in the finest and most prestigious publications. She is also scrupulous about reporting that he beat her on occasion, gave her a concussion once, and at the beginning of their relationship exacted a promise of fidelity. It would mortify him, he explains, to learn that she had slept with other men. They must "trust each other" (p. 207). Sara learns, after filing for separation, that Michael has been unfaithful from the early days of their marriage--even sleeping with some of her friends. After many trials and separations, the two agree to a divorce. Sara takes cash, leaves Michael the apartment, books and appliances--except the dishwasher, symbol of her former drudgery. She manifests a characteristic sharp eye for priorities and intent dismissal of the past as encumbrance. Even as we acknowledge her practical sense in this, we realize that for Sara, as for her friends, the "encumbering past" covers a range of history: not only impeding institutions and memories, but essential knowledge of causes and precedents.

As for Susie and her marriage, there is considerable tension between social events and the way women who take

part in the revolutionary movement are treated. Susie soon
discovers that she and other women are reenacting the traditional role: picking up after their men, cooking, washing
dishes, taking care of the baby, cleaning up--in addition to
typing and distributing pamphlets. She runs to hear her
husband make an impassioned speech against the System,
hears him proclaim, "this generation sees the world differently than its predecessors" (p. 78), and then runs home
to finish domestic chores and also to be ready to prove to
Jeff that his view of himself as a virile revolutionary leader
is correct--one who can "ball" three times a day (where
was the time?). She hates sex with Jeff with the aversion
attributed by myth to Victorian wives--but in her case the
aversion is real because Jeff has no attraction for Susie as
a man. She is proud that they are pointed out as a show-
case couple, but her marriage is devoid of joy until she
discovers some happiness with a vibrator. Unfortunately,
the writing (even if it is Susie's voice, as the author says
in the Prologue) sometimes sounds like soap opera and purple prose: "She [Susie] wanted to hit bottom.... What
stopped her from going to the depths was Sam" (p. 255).
However, another example from Susie's life restores a degree of pathetic actuality. We learn that her one attempt
at identity, to have a tattoo, is taken over by Jeff who decides that she will have a red and green rose tattooed on
her chest.

For a long time, until the tattoo is removed and
Susie takes some other steps, she moves, speaks, acquies-
ces to the life Jeff maps out for her, as countless wives
in the generation before her had done. One wonders why?
The background Davidson sketches for us allows us to draw
some inferences despite, not because of Davidson who
sometimes edits her material as sentimentally as Joan
Didion, though with inferior finesse. We see Susie in
high school as infatuated with power. She can love and
pity in the abstract but is cruel to the individual. For
example, she spreads vicious rumors about one of her class-
mates in order to set people against the girl. She vacil-
lates between manipulating people for her own ends and
dreaming of Messiah-like powers: the poor would be fed;
the lame would walk. She transforms this longing for power
to Jeff when she hears him speak against Kennedy and for
Castro. But Jeff, like Alice Walker's Truman Held (Meridian), proves conventional in his view of women and erratic
in politics. He is last mentioned as joining the Communist
Party because his new wife and her family are members of
the party.

Men in this novel, as in Marge Piercy's Small Changes, are characterized as self-centered, expecting their wives or the women they live with to take on their values, become alter egos, work in the home and out in the world-- but soothe them when at home, baby them, love them--act in accordance with the traditional role. Susie, like Sara, takes the way out through divorce, and finds some kind of new life for herself. But that comment of hers on Patty Hearst's "fantastic" education with the Symbionese army demonstrates how accustomed she is to the fact that women are to get their political education secondhand. Other educations, too.

The lives of all three women--Sara, Susie, Tasha-- and their search for self-knowledge, autonomy and self-definition, while taking different routes, end on the same muted chord. Sara and Susie, both divorced, seem to choose aloneness at this point in their lives and appear almost asexual. Sara lives in a house by the sea. The house has a cactus garden and is decorated with Mexican tile. Susie now occasionally shops for clothes with her mother in Saks (where she used to steal as a teenager). She occupies an apartment with young son Sam. The place vibrates to the sounds of a stereo played by the black psychiatrist overhead. Susie comments: "he runs women through by appointment ... likes to fuck to environmental sounds" (p. 325).

Tasha finally breaks with her sculptor lover, sleeps with a Tai Chi instructor, writes a book, tries meditation, cuts her hair, colors it brown to look ordinary, studies the Talmud, dances with women on Friday nights until her feet bleed, and then marries "a big honey bear" of a man (p. 363). They move to the suburbs with his fourteen-year-old son by a previous marriage. The woman, once described as a devastating beauty whose long, blonde hair hung in a golden cape to her waist, and who loved the world of art and other creativity, now stocks her pantry shelves with a year's supply of dog food, family-size bottles of catsup, cartons of Pepperidge Farm cookies, and exchanges endearments with her husband, of which the principal one is "love" (p. 364). She appears to have come to rest. The move seems motivated more by sheer weariness than by the love she proclaims for husband, in view of her former life and tastes. Also, like Susie and Sara, hers is an attempt to make a complete break with the past. To break with an imprisoning domestic past is right and commendable. But

we are faced here as elsewhere in the book with a total denial of the past--not merely its morbid, useless elements--
which amounts to a denial of history.   The three women
have cut off that sense of process by which we learn to deal
with experience, and to recreate our experience.   By failing
to make connections between themselves and their history,
they also fail in other essential connections, as between politics (or history) and their personal lives.

In addition to Sara, Susie and Tasha, the author gives
us snatches of other women's lives--women who play out
their men's dreams of returning to the land and living the
simple life.   These women bake bread, grow plants and food,
have babies with different males, turn the clock back by
wearing sun bonnets and long skirts in order that the men
can stride around in overalls and boots and view themselves
as stalwart pioneers.   Although it is not Davidson's intention, in view of her historical myopia (as she herself admits), this is as far as a sense of history goes for these
women and men.   It's a matter of costume and posture and
as real as an Errol Flynn movie of Dodge City.

The women in these communes are careful about diet:
they eat brown rice, beans, fruit, but like Sara will smoke,
or swallow any kind of drug: grass, mescaline, peyote tab-
lets, acid, hash.   Not too much is known as yet of what
happened to these women, but we wonder about children like
the infant, called Blue Jay, who is left in the care of a
young man.   When the two come back, the man exclaims to
the mother: "What a mellow day ... I dropped mescaline
and we were lying in the garden and ya know what?   Blue
Jay started playing with my dick and I sucked his cock" (p.
241).   The mother is at first scandalized ("a baby can't
handle that"--p. 241) and then begins to laugh so heartily
that she ends on the floor, still laughing.   This scene is
handled with restraint, giving us the powerful impact that
the author intends.

The same cannot be said for the narrative style,
which reconstructs the events of the Sixties and the lives
of the three women with a montage of newspaper headlines,
popular songs, political oratory, flashes of assassinations,
Beatles, Timothy Leary, Richard Alpert, etc. --reminiscent
of John Dos Passos in U.S.A.   The book certainly is not as
ambitious as U.S.A., nor does it pretend to be.   Dos Passos
wanted to give us a total history of public moods and social
and political changes through the biographies of twelve dif-

ferent Americans: Debs, Edison, Rudolf Valentino, Hearst,
and others.   He fused all of his sociological indicators--
songs, headlines, the man on the street, the politician in
the Senate or Congress--to form a panoramic view of our
culture and what was happening.   The result was an artful
pattern which reproduces the felt experience and goes beyond
the event recorded.   Disparate episodes are brought together
by a pervasive theme--greed loose in the land and the
threatening disintegration of society.

Dos Passos was a student of history and politically
committed to what he was writing about.   No Marxist, he
was convinced that something had to be done about social
injustice.   He staked personal security more than once by
such actions as trying to help striking miners in Harlan
County, Kentucky, or publicly supporting the Spanish Loyalists,
and Sacco and Vanzetti.   He was not a writer who stood aloof.
A solid atmosphere of history is created in U.S.A. , and the
political analysis is astute, more astute than in his previous
works.   Event and character meld when he enters the mind
of his character, especially with some of the women.   One
remembers the career of Janie Williams, timid, genteel
secretary to the advertising tycoon, J. Ward Morehouse.

Sara Davidson's Loose Change exhibits considerable
energy and journalistic craftsmanship and we do see what went
wrong in the Sixties, with a little less reassurance than is
expressed by the author that it was all for the best.   Neither she nor the people she portrays have values or any
sense of history.   Her style of reportage whirls the reader
through the lives of the three women as she records sit-
ins, draft card burnings, Altamont, Woodstock, the Miami
Republican Convention, Mick Jagger singing "I Can't Get No
Satisfaction, " the Hippies, Hell's Angels, Svetlana Alliluy-
yeva's defection to the United States, Boston's reaction to
a concert by the Rhinoceros, Groupies, and other events
too numerous to put down here.   The result is a blur, both
in the reader's mind and for the narrator.

She tells us in conclusion that she knows she will be
criticized "for copping out. ...   But the truth is, I have not
found answers and I'm not sure I remember the questions"
(p. 367).   Susie has a similar blank concerning the questions.   Here is a conversation between Susie and son about
a photograph he views.   What is Daddy doing? he asks.
Making a speech, his mother replies.   What is Daddy saying? Susie tells him that Jeff is angry about something

"wrong" the United States is doing. What? persists Sam,
and Susie wrinkles her forehead and answers, "I don't remember" (p. 323). We don't expect many answers, but to
forget the questions?

The narrative bears out that Sara and her friends
never did know the questions. Narrative tempo gives prior-
ity, like the characters' careers, to slam-bang imagery and
effect, abandoning that awareness of background which gives
weight and richness to the writing of Dos Passos. Davidson
unreels scenes quickly, but we miss the swift illumination
of a public mood which would tell us what we want to know.
Why, for example, did a concert by the Rhinoceros, in
which skinny, seventeen-year-old rock singer Danny with
his lacquered, sprayed, teased, long blonde hair, touch the
city of Boston with "magic" (p. 208)? What does the author
mean by magic? What accounted for it? Why did youth
gatherings in which, at first, the password was love and
peace turn into scenes of ugliness and even murder? What
about other political leaders of the student movement? Were
they all like Jeff? There must have been some who never
lost sight of their human values and future hopes. They
could have been faithfully and movingly portrayed. Instead,
we are pelted with facts that develop no ethical forms,
shape no discipline of experience. Man and woman's en-
tanglement with social history is an important theme, but
the author is unable to transliterate the conflict into some kind
of universal terms. The novel lacks a set of moral and
social values which can be applied artistically as the unify-
ing principle of the novel's design.

The problem lies with the narrator herself, as is already obvious, and with the people she has chosen to portray. We don't have to judge whether her version of the
student conflict, such as the scene in which demonstrators
protest a store's bias against hiring minorities, coincides
with or deviates from available evidence. Such a test of
the novel's mimetic accuracy would in itself be a tool for
defining rather than passing final judgments. Furthermore,
what we actually find thrust upon us by Loose Change is that
despite the author's conviction that her selection of the three
women portrayed would give the reader three different viewpoints from which to survey the Sixties, we find the opposite. All three women, while pursuing different lives and
outwardly differing in other details, are united not only by
one purpose--to be successful--but by what seems to be one
level of consciousness. This is submission to trends and

to traditional success imagery. Tasha's protestations of
happiness in suburbia without the striving to which she is
accustomed are difficult to take seriously and seem but a
temporary break with her former life.

It is Sara, however, who emerges as the touchstone
of the success philosophy. Her story becomes an American
success story right down to the wistful ending which fiction
has made so popular: finding herself with achieved ends
that have no meaning. But since she is a contemporary
heroine, not a Sister Carrie, content to rock and meditate
with bittersweet ruefulness on the meaning of success, the
only solution for Sara is to move on. It is another way
out, popular in life and in fiction, as the heroes of Hemingway, Mailer and Bellow demonstrate. Bellow's hero Hen-
derson, whose "I want, I want" echoes through Sara's rhetoric (as she goes about planning her success), comes back
realizing that one must be committed to something--some
vision of life: to keep on moving is to escape the threat of
moral obligation.

Somewhere toward the end of the book, Sara wonders
about her frenetic activity and pursuit of success. "And
then what?" she asks herself silently, as she and her husband and father-in-law celebrate the young couple's newest
achievements in publishing and the father predicts still more
glorious publishing ahead. The answer to Sara's question,
"and then what?" is the novel Loose Change, which is alive
and doing well on the best-seller list at the present moment.

Without question, Sara Davidson has talent, and though
the novel suffers from many flaws it also exhibits some excellent touches, such as the writer's juxtaposition of the
trite and important side by side to illustrate how complacent
and inconsistent the young people's image of themselves can
be. Sometimes, a brief impressionistic picture captures a
decisive moment, such as Sara's opening her eyes to see
the arc of the sun glistening on the rim of the gorge where
she has been sleeping, and her decision not to see her psychiatrist any more. We get a good insight into the sexual
"revolution" and learn that by exculpating "freedom" from
commitment without attacking the stricture of man/woman
relationships, the "revolution" merely diverted the exploitation of women along another more superficially alluring path.

The writer possesses a great rage for living, and
this rage is communicated to us. But we also understand

that despite her confession of being a "neurotic, Jewish overachiever" (p. 277), she is not ready to get out of the bell jar of competitiveness, click off her tape recorder and make an effort of the imagination to construct some kind of pattern for the materials with which she is dealing or intends to deal. Make an affirmation of life! When she does, she may give us a story with that subtle mingling of pathos and humor which is an outgrowth of the disparity between human hope and reality.

MARILYN FRENCH

Marilyn French and Grace Paley have several things in common: they belong to an older generation of women, they teach in college, and they write about women: deserted, divorced, neglected, struggling to be father and mother to their children, searching for some meaning to their lives, and turning to other women for comfort, sympathy, and understanding. Here the similarity ends. The two writers differ from one another in use of genre, in narrative technique, and in their views of age and of the world in general.

Author Marilyn French has published The Book as World: James Joyce's "Ulysses" (1976). For her first major work of fiction, The Women's Room (1977), she has chosen the genre of novel. Her settings are suburbia and Harvard University (where she has taught); the method of narration is long and discursive, in the manner of the nineteenth-century novel; her view of women and society is tragic.

Grace Paley writes only short stories. Her settings and characters in her second collection, Enormous Changes at the Last Minute (1974), are the same as in her first book, The Little Disturbances of Man (1959)--the city and city characters. She illuminates a segment of experience in language which reflects a tragi-comic view of life. Where French's women often respond to experience with bitterness, hopelessness, and sometimes madness, even the old in Paley's stories, like Mrs. Raftery, manage to summon up some jaunty courage. You "slippery relic," says Mrs. Raftery to the husband who deserts her for a Ukrainian lady with a huge cross on her bosom. "I'll send your shirts by the diaper-service man" (EC, p. 23). So too with Paley's younger women, who huddle together for psychological warmth and comfort with other solitary women in parks and playgrounds, while their children play; the writer has only admiration for the way these women ride the stormy currents of their lives without being swamped.

Marilyn French mourns over women, particularly aging, lonely, discarded women who see nothing before them but life left over to kill and the inevitable physical death. To paraphrase the words of Camus' young Caligula: men die and are not happy; the overall impression of French's book is: women die and are not happy. The writer pities the young women who lack confidence and remain in sterile marriages only to suffer slow psychological deaths. Those who survive are viewed as standing in a bombed-out terrain. Grace Paley, on the other hand, is proud of the way her women survive by holding on to rituals and habits which give them some comfort without subordination of personality. She focuses on men and, of course, to a greater extent on women: their pain, their laughter, and their rueful acceptance of the crazy world in which they live.

Both writers are concerned with a moral imperative. In Paley, it is the ways women manage to cope which compel her respect. For French, the time for coping is long past. Women, she implies, must free themselves from the tradition of dead generations of men, whose roles for women are contained in one statement: conform and obey. Yet her book's ending leaves us not with the flavor of revolt: the urgent need for women rotting in rebellious acceptance (as the author often views them), or in Christian-Judaic resignation, to do something. The cry of the heroine (Mira) at the end is of bitterness and even despair. Her anguished vision of self is that of the non-conformist woman--a stranger and exile in an unchanging culture. Indeed, the author might as well have chosen the title of one of George Gissing's works, Born in Exile.

The Women's Room has received a mixed response. One reviewer describes it as a marathon soap opera destined for a TV series. Publishers Weekly (1977) hails it as an "extraordinary" book which "speaks from the heart to women everywhere," and from that stronghold of feminism Ms magazine (January, 1978) comes the voice of critic Sara Sanborn, who asks if Marilyn French is "A Feminist Jacqueline Susann?" She answers her own question by informing the reader: "rest assured; this book is devoid of sur-

prises.... The whole action unfolds with the tragic in-
evitability of a melodrama. "

For me, the book suffers from over-simplification of
issues, a grim insistence that all women are victims and
that man is the enemy--a view summed up by Val, one of
the most important characters in the book. The writer also
risks a too-pat structure, in which a moment of tenderness
or happiness is inevitably followed by disillusionment, betrayal, or tragedy. For example, Mira experiences an un-
accustomed softening towards her husband; he immediately
comes in with a request for a divorce. Val bustles around
her kitchen humming and cooking. The phone rings. Val's
daughter cries that she has been raped. Sometimes, the
language is bad: "Mira flung her face away from Val" (WR,
p. 405). But there is also good writing. The narrator
comments on Mira and her ambitions: "She brushed them
away, but they stuck like threads of cobweb that get trapped
in a shred of broken plaster even as you try to dust them
off" (p. 183). Or we read that Mira's heart "felt like a
bruised prune" (WR, p. 334). Many of the scenes ring
true, and we get to understand the chaos and confusion
which confront the woman not treated in any fictional depth
by contemporary American writers--the woman on the brink
of middle age, who after years of coping and adjusting finds
herself labeled "the geritol woman" by an age-conscious culture. But unlike the smiling husband in the TV commercial,
who assures his audience that he will keep his wife, the
husbands in French's novel find younger women--women with
the necessary iron in their blood, and personality with the
required softness and yielding.

Nor do lovers behave differently. Mira, the discarded wife, meets a new love and discovers that the "liberal" man, Ben, is as ready to abandon her when she fails
to meet his plans for marriage and children as was Norm,
her former husband. As for Val, she suffers double jeopar-
dy, and finally loses irreparably any notion of men and women
understanding each other, together with the sense of herself
as a member of a far-flung community.

The author is a very angry woman and she sets out
to prove through her narrator, who turns out to be Mira,
why she is angry and why every woman needs to be angry.
Her indignation stems from her conviction that Woman has
little or no chance in our present male-dominated society,
in which men are sexual Kiplingesque imperialists who cling

to the fiction of absolute control that finds its political justification in the rhetoric of dominant and dominated.   When
women like Val reject pinning their hopes on slow possible
changes and become revolutionaries, the outcome is death.
Val and others attempt to rescue a black woman sentenced
to prison for defending herself against rape by knifing her
rapist. They are blown to bits by police machine guns.

As for Mira, her lover takes himself to Africa with
the prospect of a new job and a new woman when Mira refuses to lop off her life to fit his.   He returns with lots of
bounty: wife, children, and a prestigious, well-paying job
awaiting him.   Mira, on the other hand, finishes her Ph. D.
dissertation and finds a meager job market cool to forty-
year-old women.   She finally gets a teaching position in a
small community college in Maine.   Here she walks daily
along the Maine coast and watches the waves dash themselves
against the rocks--the author's implicit view of Woman in
our society.   And like those unwanted, unloved women in the
novels of Gissing, Mira seeks the companionship of the brandy bottle.

Marilyn French is not "a congenital novelist," but a
writer using fiction as a vehicle for ideas.   This is a "talky"
or "discussion" novel like D. H. Lawrence's Women in Love,
or Aldous Huxley's Antic Hay and Brave New World.   It has
the same ponderous elaboration of ideas, but often lacks
Huxley's balance or Lawrence's brilliant analysis of the complexities of modern emotional reactions and responses.   As
in Huxley's works, it is not plot which is important, but the
contribution of each character to the action by some assent
or clash of opinion.   Thus, the setting for much of the book
is suburbia (Meyersville/Beau Reve), chosen for the purpose
of bringing together a group of young housewives with growing children and with husbands in a variety of occupations:
medicine, aviation, business, law, teaching, labor.

After Mira's divorce and her admission to Harvard,
the setting is the university.   It becomes the place for a
group of educated women: some young like Kyla, Clarissa,
Iso, and some not so young: Mira and Val.   The setting
changes, but the problems remain the same.   The young
university wives combine domesticity with graduate work and
find themselves constantly bruised by their husbands' inability to take seriously their personal needs or the work in
which they are engaged.   Though, like their husbands, they
are involved in the Ph. D. discipline, they cannot get past

the dialectic of the myth that man's life and work must take
precedence over woman's. The entrenched ethos of the importance of man's work is so powerful that an intelligent
woman like Kyla wonders aloud if she has the right to intrude on her husband's time with any problem of her own.
Yet she is aware (like the other women) that her husband
regards her as his resource, and his home as a place of
solace and privacy on which to draw sustenance for his
work. The Harvard wives, like the author's suburban
wives, realize that wives are supposed to get their nourishment from the sight of their husbands' well-being and contentment.

Kyla's husband Harley constantly makes it plain that
he considers his field of physics much more important than
the one Kyla has selected--literature. Clarissa finds out
that her husband Duke, who is in military work, expects
all kinds of concessions if he tries a little dabbling in her
values. The divorced wives, Mira and Val, wrestle with
the complexities of getting a degree, and coming to grips
with a new love relationship. Mill's On The Subjection of
Women (1869) and Engels' The Origin of the Family, Private Property and the State present a vehement gallery of
past thinking on the need to redefine the man/woman relationship, but the basis of marriage is still (Mira, in particular, discovers) largely paper theory, as far as men are
concerned.

Then there is Iso, divorced and a lesbian, who struggles for the purity of an inner life in the face of an un-
comprehending and sometimes hostile outer world. The
character of each person, whether in Meyersville or Harvard, is implied in the idea for which she is the spokes-
woman. Mira serves in a dual role as narrator/commentator,
and third-person character in the novel. As narrator, she
speculates, philosophizes and comments on a variety of top-
ics: suburban life and loneliness ("loneliness is not a longing for company, it is a longing for kind"--WR, p. 141);
women (despised species); university administrators (pale,
unapologetic racists and sexists), etc. Her tone towards
Mira is often a mixture of pity and contempt, but finally
becomes completely sympathetic.

On the subject of men her attitude is unequivocal.
There is no trace of the compassion or understanding of
George Eliot. Nor does she drop into that sympathy found
in the works of Doris Lessing or Tillie Olsen. The writer

is frank that her view of men is one-sided, and advises the
reader concerned with learning about Man's suffering to con-
sult the works of Bellow, Roth, Mailer, or Hemingway.
There was a time when she would have considered Man in a
more favorable light. No more. He is not her concern in
this book. Her involvement is with women: their frustrations, urgent needs, inner desires, and the disparity between these needs and Woman's prescribed social role.

Time in this novel is not pulverized as in Joyce or
Faulkner, but weaves between the present and the past--a
period somewhere between the Fifties and the Sixties. The
narrator begins with thirty-eight-year-old divorced Mira
cowering in the women's lavatory of Harvard University, a
room in the basement of Sever Hall. Mira has retreated
to this place because of her feeling of isolation, invisibility
to the people about her--mostly young people who pass her
with unseeing eyes. She looks at her mirror image, applies
lipstick, straightens clothing, notes the thickening body,
though her weight has not changed, and sees that nothing
coalesces.

Nothing ever coalesces for Mira, and our last image
of her walking the beach, an outsider to outsiders, strength-
ens the impression the author wishes to make. Like Camus' Meursault, Mira is now truly the stranger to those
around her. By her refusal to play by the rules of society,
accept the social destiny offered Woman by Western patriarchal society--follow Man to the place of his choice, bear
his children (though she already has children by a former
marriage), wedge her creative work in whatever cracks of
time are available--Mira becomes the stranger in society.
Unlike Meursault, however, Mira finds no consolation in
the past, nor does she accept with equanimity the prospect
of her coming death, symbolized by the beach on which she
prowls: emptying day by day, the sky ever paling "toward
the north ... white, moving to stark immaculate whiteness"
(WR, p. 470). Mira's cry, at the end, is that she doesn't
want to forget what has happened to her: "Forget: lethe:
the opposite of truth." No, she tells us: "I have opened
all the doors in my head. I have opened all the pores in
my body. But only the tide rolls in" (WR, p. 471).

To make the reader aware of what has brought Mira
to her present state, and what it is she wants us to know,
we are taken from that opening scene of the women's room
in which Mira has sought sanctuary, to her childhood. We

learn that Mira was an independent child who loved to explore the world outside the confines of her yard, to take off
her clothes and venture out. Her mother tied her to a long
rope, and when Mira persisted in taking off her clothes the
mother withdrew her affection. It worked, says the narrator. On her wedding night, Mira had problems with removing her clothes. Mira's youth consisted of being trained
not to climb trees with boys, not to play tag in the alley,
and not to ask questions about sanitary napkins and the meaning of the word "fuck."

Unfortunately, the picture of Mother in the fiction of
Marilyn French and others does nothing to dispel the image
of a monstrous Mom created by Philip Wylie and his statement about the consequences: a generation of vipers. But
again, we must keep in mind that women like Mira's mother
are convinced that they are only doing their duty. A deeper
reason (shown throughout this book) is that ignorance and
oppression breed further ignorance and oppression. Phyllis
Chesler in her new book, About Men (1978), speaks of her
now-ended Iranian marriage and some of the Iranian women
she knew--women locked up by men for most of their lives,
turning cruel and abusive to female servants and daughters-
in-law.

Woman's education at home, in school and elsewhere,
with its contradictory elements, is condemned with even
more intensity in French's book than, for example, in Lois
Gould's or Joan Didion's. Young Mira is depicted as a
very intelligent girl who is put into an advanced class with
older and more emotionally sophisticated students, with the
result that she is ignored by them. Loneliness turns her to
the world of books and magazines. She picks up a range
of information which she is unable to reinterpret.

From Jane Eyre she learns that a woman is virgin
until marriage. Shakespeare's Petruchio informs her that
he views Kate as his dog, his horse. Nietzsche condemns
all women as liars who are out to dominate men. Seventeen magazine advises what makeup to use in order to attract
boys who will become nice men. Some day one of these
nice men will pick her out and marry her. Neighborhood
sounds reveal that all men are not nice men, even though
outwardly pleasant. Some beat wives. Those without wives
get drunk and come home and beat their daughters. Ad-
mittedly, the selected indictment of men is just more auctorial proof that the writer's literary aim is to stress the

dichotomy under which Woman labors as part of a minority culture with no redeeming vision in the past, or for the future.

It is not surprising to learn that the author looks with even more contempt than the writers discussed previously, on the extent to which Woman is taught to despise her body. Mira is told that menstruation is a process of poisons built up by the body, which have to be expelled. Together with instruction on menstruation, Mira is given a girdle which encases her body tightly, in order that her bottom will not wriggle, with the result that she takes to walking stiffly-- all facts familiar to us from Feminist fiction, but which the author feels can never be over-stressed. Familiar, too, is Mira's experience in college, when her date deserts her and she is left alone--a sign to every male, says the narrator, that she is nobody's property and fair game. Yet we realize that this is a truism not dissipated but reinforced by fiction and current conditions: not too many women feel sanguine about being alone in public places. Mira's near rape so terrifies her that at nineteen she marries the first man (Norm) who shows her some respect, and what Kate Millett defines ironically as manly guardianship.

True to form, Norm proves that beneath his cloak of chivalry and protection and his lofty panegyrics on Mira's pure moral nature, there is only oppression. You're safer on a bus, he tells Mira when she asks for the car in order to get to her job. You don't want to work in the city with all those men. You don't know men like I do, he implies, with a knowing air. Mira takes a dull job nearby, grateful for Norm's concern: "I couldn't bear to live if anything happened to you" (WR, p. 41). As for their sex life, it is a study in emotional frustration for Mira. Norm puts on a rubber, sucks her nipple, enters and ejaculates. "No healthy male could or should try to hold back" (WR, p. 41), he informs Mira when she demurs at the speedy timing of his needs to his sexual alarm clock. Mira stays tolerant because Norm is a medical student and "knows" all about these things, with the result that she concludes she is frigid. This gives the author an opportunity to point out more of Norm's limitations. He is not displeased at Mira's reluctance for sex. Now he can play out his fantasy of angel/whore/rape, etc. The two children she soon bears him make her angel mother, and her unwillingness in the bedroom gives him the illusion of rape.

Motherhood brings Mira into the company of suburban

wives/mothers like herself--all united by motherhood. They
sit on benches, bathed in the good fortune of their maternity,
a concept with which the narrator identifies. Mother love,
says Mira, who later defends it, is more irrational than
sexual love. Harvard University Val agrees and has no
doubt that being a mother kept her "human" (WR, p. 374)
after leaving her husband. Motherhood, though, has its
price. Suburban wives/mothers talk about diapers, steriliz-
ing bottles, formulas, washing, chopping baby food, as well
as a tedious day illuminated by a child's endearing remark
or a surprising spurt of independence. The narrator makes
it clear that she does not minimize the work connected with
child-raising, nor the status it lacks and deserves: "the
tender of a child is the priest in a temple" (WR, p. 68).
Tenders of children, she points out, do not receive priestly
respect; their lives are unnoticed.

The wives' remarks on husbands provide illuminating
perspectives: husbands exist only as idiosyncratic beings
who have special preferences as to the way coffee should
be brewed, or cling to some peccadillo such as not fixing
a drawer against which the wife constantly bangs her head.
Even taking into account the plethora of domestic duties with
which the writer saddles her women characters, French's
wives are appallingly helpless about picking up a hammer
and fixing something. It is the author's contention, however, that the central quality of their lives is the infinite
role playing: man's and woman's, and the terms of the
difference must never dissolve. Hence, as already discussed elsewhere, French sees two cultures existing side
by side, but she uses the idea with an excess of polemical
intensity. Women confined to the home, self-deprecating
and self-immobilizing concerning anything that smacks of
Man's work, talk to each other solely about children and
domesticity. Men who go out in the world talk to everybody, have occasional expensive company lunches, make
sure that they play tennis or squash to keep trim, acquire
a healthy tan, keep a close watch on money, demand peace
and harmony when they get home, don't neglect to appraise
other women, and are not slow to move on to a new woman
and a new marriage when they deem it necessary.

This is what happens to Mira, but before this we
get a compilation of the fates of some other women. Some,
like Lily, end in breakdown; others, like Adele, keep having
babies in keeping with Catholic decree, while husband Paul
enjoys his current mistress. Samantha's husband leaves

her with $60,000 worth of debts which she eventually pays
off. Martha goes to law school, falls in love with her
teacher, believes that he will divorce his wife, follows his
advice to leave her husband, only to find out that her lover's
wife is pregnant. And Mira, who has allowed Norm to dic-
tate the pattern of their life and has almost absorbed the
bland poison of his ideas on children--don't cuddle or hold
a boy on your lap: you will make a "faggot" (WR, p. 214)
out of him (recalling Marge Piercy's Neil Stone), is faced
with Norm's demand for a divorce.

The facts detailed here may be the basis for many
current or future soap operas; nevertheless, they have the
innate journalistic truth of many soap opera situations. Ac-
counts more "extreme" or "incongruous" than those in The
Women's Room fill the records of Family Courts and divorce
courts: and, as we have already noted, part of French's
function is a kind of journalism. Such detail is indispensable to the on-going discussion of past and still current history concerning men and women. Neither is the tone about
Woman's victimization inconsistent with the Fifties, when,
as against the evidence of court and welfare records, the
women about whom French writes were taught the idealized
virtues: humility, softness, timidity. One could wish, however, that the data were dappled with more light. In fact,
the writing is opaque, without depth, and it prompts us to
an unkind reflection. We tend to drowse as the author sets
up character and situation with mechanical regularity. Yet,
despite the lack of that artistry which would leave a paragraph or phrase lingering in our minds, her handling of
marriage is sound and punctilious, for many women. We
recognize that for these women marriage was the core of
aspiration, and the wife's duty was to do everything which
would insure her husband's love for her--a silly ethos
preached by Victorian Eliza Lynn Linton and now by Marabel
Morgan, as I have already pointed out. What the novel
demonstrates is that the Meyersville/Beau Reve (Beautiful
Dream) women, having lost irreparably any concept of identity, sit and chirp about their children and husbands, creating out of this the illusion of community and family. It is
reinforced by the once-a-month neighborhood socials to which
wives and husbands come--wives with teased hair, high heels,
and maybe a new dress; husbands wearing a sports jacket.
Wives sit in the living room and talk about children and a
new way to prepare hamburger. Husbands stand in the
kitchen and talk sports. It secures the women, for a while,
implies the narrator, against the emptiness of their lives.

It is at this point that we feel a bit uneasy. Despite the author's construction of various doctrinal and moral brick walls between men and women, and her magnification of woman's sorry plight, we can make certain assumptions of our own. These include, that women contribute to their own ignorance. For heaven's sake, what was there to prevent Mira or some of the other women from joining a Great Books discussion group; read, think. We are told that Mira reads, but does not think. Marriage has dammed up all thought. Why? Could even hers (and many an average married woman's throng of domestic duties) really crowd out her ability to <u>know</u>, to draw intelligent conclusions?

Mira has been exposed to some education; she has a good mind. Why does she accept Norm's ideas as if they were the only reality she could imagine, and air them to her neighbors? Does it take going to Harvard to understand that Tupperware parties and the visit of the Avon Lady are not the greatest experiences in a woman's life? Why does she fall into a pattern of running around the house waxing with Lemon Pledge, pushing the vacuum cleaner up and down the stairs, finally treating herself to a scented bath--and ultimately the brandy bottle to be sipped in solitary bedroom comfort (because Norm is sleeping at his mother's). The author refuses to have women accept responsibility for perpetuating their own ignorance and childishness. Woman exists to be crushed by Man's ego.

The narrator anticipates some adverse reader reaction and attempts to answer it. She warns us at the beginning of her story that Mira had no concept of reality, lived in a fairy-tale world, and had a head full of fairy-tale images. What this means, she doesn't elaborate. We do know, however, that Mira often seethes with anger and resentment against Norm, but does nothing about it. And we further note that as her financial security increases with the purchase of a larger home, and her leisure time is augmented by the children going to school, Mira becomes apprehensive about losing these new comforts. She has been reduced to what Freud describes as psychical infantilism (though he attributes it to religion). So Mira decides to trot even more docilely around the domestic paddock Norm constructs for her until he puts her out to pasture. Her only act of defiance during their entire marriage has been to lend her neighbor $300.00 (against Norm's objections) when the husband deserts wife and family. But we

note that Mira is worried over Norm's anger, and decides
that she and husband must get to know each other more in-
timately. Predictably, at this point Norm gives her the
bad news. It is a reality of a sort, but too many hints
have robbed it of any surprise.

Are all men bad and all women good? asks Phil in
Marge Piercy's Small Changes. Piercy allows a man like
Phil a measure of humanity, but the answer to this question
in French's book is a resounding yes--men are bad. Norm
and other husbands are given no distinctive traits to relieve the blackness with which they are pictured, because
they are always dramatized as sharing in the same philosophy of marriage. We may recognize this as the one articulated and criticized by Mill and Engels (in different ways), as
the subjugation of one sex by the other. Engels extends
the humanism of Mill by pointing out that marriage in Western capitalistic society depends upon the inferior status of
women and the supremacy of the man in his family. The
Women's Room emphasizes that whether the man is Norm,
Paul, Roger, Carl, Simp, or any man, he is the power
figure, firm in his conviction that woman is his property.

But even power figures are sometimes human. Although the book is a novel, it falls short of the novel's capacity and responsibility: to lead the reader into further
conclusions about experience, and, in turn, encourage further questions. The book suffers from an unrelenting procession of men who are devoid of interest in, or loyalty to
their wives. Every man is brutally insensitive and every
marriage lacks honesty, tenderness, and mutual respect.

While the novel has its limitations, the sadistic Carl
and his pathetic wife Lily are credibly drawn. Lily says:
"We all come out of nothing, you know? Brutality was the
way of life. Without it, the men felt like they were nothing,
you know?" (WR, p. 171). We learn that Lily's immigrant
father beat his wife and children with the same ferocity attributed to the grandfather in Alice Walker's Meridian. The
deprived and dispossessed often take out their frustrations
on women, as already noted. Though Carl is neither poor
nor dispossessed, he still clings to a culture distinguished
by its contempt for women. His attitude towards his sensitive wife is that she can do nothing right, though she holds
down a job and does her own housekeeping. He punishes
her by withholding affection, and with constant complaints
("the kitchen floor is filthy," p. 152) and long silences at

any infraction of his domestic rules. Lily breaks down when
a crisis occurs concerning their son. At the end she is a
woman old beyond her years, yellowed by pills forced on
her by doctor and husband, and trembling with fear that she
may be returned to the mental institution for more electric
shock treatments if husband and doctor have their way. Her
life does not precisely exemplify what Robert Frost implies
in some of his poetry on women--domestic entrapment may
lead to madness. She is, however, a terrifying example of
the woman beaten down and caged, before she has a chance
to live, by circumstances beyond those of familiar domesticity alone.

The Harvard section of the book leaves us with hope
that some women can change through experience and crisis,
and by talking to other women. Iso comes to terms with
her sexuality, publishes her dissertation, travels to England,
lives with a divorced woman, and accepts impermanence as
a way of life. Kyla rejects her handsome, brilliant, but
self-centered husband with his think-tank philosophy and goes
to law school. We leave her about to be graduated and
ready to embark on a new life. Clarissa gives up Duke because he simply wants to make a housewife out of her.
She is so successful in producing a Chicago program that
there is talk about putting it on national TV. Only Val and
Mira, the two older women, are losers.

Throughout most of the book, Val exudes a great
vitality, bristles with self-confidence, and gives us her
thinking on such matters as love, marriage, and a new kind
of architecture which would make for successful communal
living. Common sense and love seem to be the touchstones
of her character, almost up to the end. She loves her
daughter and warms to and sympathizes with old and young
alike. She refuses to accept the idea that only women
should be selfless, insisting that everyone should have some
selflessness. Her creed is that men and women should
both tend children. She agrees with Freud that fear and desire for pleasure are the mainsprings of behavior, but is
adamant that aggressiveness should be controlled. Has a
John Wayne movie ever been censored? she asks. She
describes how new ways of building houses would provide
adequate space and facilities for communal living in which
old and young would share and have equal rights. She not
only believes that relationships are important, but in her
relationships with women and with men stresses openness
and loyalty as ruling motives in her actions. Operative in

the characterization of Val are basic human feelings uncor-
rupted by malice, self-seeking, and artificial social values.
The narrator's encomium of her is not excessive: "glowing
and laughing and gay. Ah, indomitable Val" (WR, p. 385).

It is precisely her very human feelings which en-
mesh Val in tragedy. What pushes Val over into action
which destroys her is her final confrontation with a legal
system which has given Woman few legal rights in the past
and still persists in depriving her of justice. Marilyn
French's feud with the legal system centers on rape and
those male concepts of rape as: "wild disturbance of the
female mind, " or "she asked for it." Val's daughter, raped
while coming home, is regarded by the police as so much
genitalia to be prodded and examined, always with disbelief
that she is innocent. One of the state's officials, who questions her, sneers that a lot of "white princesses want to
try a little black meat" (WR, p. 422)--the rapist is a disturbed black youth. Another official advises Chris not to
press charges, or she will be in for a harrowing time
during the trial. His colleague has already laughed at him
for even attempting the case: "Come on, you're not going
to try this one.... This chick had hot pants" (WR, p. 426).

Val and her daughter Chris are given to understand
that rape and wife-beating are two of the old stock griev-
ances of women--troublesome women. The scene is strong
but the author is unable to resist the fascination of blowing
it up still more by her description of policemen walking
"swaggeringly, " pants sagging with the weight of holster and
gun they look, she says, "like a pair of balls and a prick" (WR,
p. 421). The deeper emotional and social implications, though,
are not lost in the strident rhetoric. The result for both
mother and daughter, unfortunately, is estrangement, when
Val decides to send Chris to a place where she will receive
help that she, the mother, is unable to furnish. Chris objects to going, clings to her mother, ends by complying,
but refuses to communicate with Mother thereafter. Val
suffers and characteristically takes action. Realizing that
the ways she has challenged the social molds have changed
nothing, as she sees it, Val disconnects herself from her
former life, declares that all men are the enemy, turns to
militant action with other militant women, and is killed.

If Val's body is destroyed by bullets, it is Mira's
belief in Ben as the new man that is riddled. She learns
that his love has limits. He will love her just as long as

her choices are his. Despite the author's sympathy and justification of Mira's bitterness, we draw our own conclusions. Mira has been faced with that old dilemma: dream and reality--and is unable to accept reality. Ben, approaching forty, like Marge Piercy's older man Jackson, is not able to develop a new way of thinking about women.

The Women's Room is concerned with dramatizing what Marilyn French considers the central disease of the Woman's condition in our society, symbolized by that recurring nightmare of Mira's at the end of the story: a white man with vacant, empty, unseeing eyes entering her room, pipe and penknife in hand, proceeding to take off the inner door knob on her front door. The author is convinced that men are blind to Woman as a person. This is the common denominator in the work--Woman's search for some autonomy, her insistence on being recognized as a person in her own right, and the blankness with which she is regarded. The author's strong presence leaves no doubt that the older woman is no better off after her break for freedom than she was in the circle of her oppressive marriage. In reality--so says the message of the book--as the situation stands today, there is no freedom for any woman in this male-dominated society. You either play by the rules, or you will end alone. Younger, educated women get along despite men, through available jobs which eventually burgeon into careers. The older women, like Mira, squeezed into inferior work and solitude, become "the stranger."

The most striking aspect of this book is the author's lack of confidence not only that Man can or will change, but that men never experience hells of their own. She rejects the compassion of a Mrs. Gaskell or Doris Lessing. Her men are middle-class individuals invariably portrayed as smooth of face, unlined of brow, freshly-barbered, trim, spruce--regardless of any crisis. Indeed, there is no crisis which is not satisfactorily resolved to the advantage of Man. With Val's death, her ex-husband gains his daughter back. Our last view of him is his leading Chris off with a proprietary gesture. It is difficult to determine whether French believes with Marge Piercy that scarred men (like Phil) are going to change, for there are no scarred men in French's fiction.

The novel makes it clear that the author feels committed to speak for women--vocal or silent, especially those silenced by various forms of tyranny. She wants action against the forces which threaten to stifle women--forces which push women like Mira into isolation. It is not the kind of isolation which George Orwell writes of as "the happiness of quietness," but simply exclusion.

The future which the writer paints is bleak, and it is with this that one must take issue. Surely the new generation--Mira's sons, for example, pictured as becoming friends with their mother, trusting her, helping her, talking to her--will have a different outlook on the man/woman relationship. In fact, one must go further than depend on the new generation. It is disadvantageous for women to view the present situation as a tragic impasse and Man as the enemy. More women, too, must take responsibility for contributing a balanced, qualified statement of a complex theme--the new relationship between the sexes. In fact, it is sensible to join in the words of George Gissing, that champion of women: "My part is with the men & women who are clearing the ground of systems that have had their day & are crumbling into obstructive ruin."[4]

The new day of new relationships has yet to come, but its possibility is now, at least, being voiced increasingly: so that a novelist like French who elects to speak for women of this generation seems, by insisting on a note of hopeless resentment, to be selling reality short. Nevertheless, for an emerging older generation of women (second-career women), the tone is both familiar and all-too-justified. The Women's Room, by projecting both the mood and the conditions which still give rise to it, provides an often vigorous and accurate voice for many women. They and we can still wish, however, that French might have gone the extra distance of the total novelist: not only voicing what we feel, but liberating our ability to feel and imagine more.

GRACE PALEY

In her two collections of short stories: The Little Disturbances of Man, published first in 1959 and reissued in 1969, and Enormous Changes at the Last Minute, 1974, Grace Paley writes about the old, the young, politics, street life, Jews, Irish, Blacks, the city, men and women--specifically of women, in most cases, who are deserted wives. Her second book carries over some of the characters we

meet in the earlier book: Faith and her two children,
Richard and Tonto; Mrs. Raftery and son John; Virginia/
Ginny with her four growing children. All sorts of other
interesting people enter the author's stories, but always she
returns to the women deserted by men and refusing to make
a tragedy of it. "When will you look it in the face?" (EC,
p. 167), begs the eighty-six-year-old father of Faith. He
urges her to do something with herself, write a story in
the mode of Chekhov, de Maupassant. When she tries to
oblige him by improvising, he snorts in disgust: always
making jokes.

The dominant quality in the writer's works is the
way people joke, laugh, make a cheerful comment or a rue-
fully-humorous remark to ward off pain, fear or loneliness.
The author's language belongs to the same comic vein as
that of Jane Bowles. It unites and expands the individual
rather than dividing or dwindling. Charles C. Charley
("don't call me Charley"--LD, p. 109) responds, in the
narrator's words: "quick as nighttime in the tropics" (LD,
p. 106). Although Charles installs air conditioners for a
living, his tone is buoyed up everywhere by a jubilant
awareness of his heroic role in solving the limitations of
cross-ventilation.

The author has an unerring ear for the proper reflection. "From Coney Island to the cemetery.... It's
the same subway; it's the same fare," observes one of her
characters (LD, p. 55). "If there was more life in my
little sister," says plump, cheerful Rose, defending her
love affair with Volodya Vlashkin, chief actor with the Yid-
dish Theater and the Valentino of Second Avenue, "she
would know my heart is a regular college of feelings and
there is such information between my corset and me that
her whole married life is a kindergarten" (LD, p. 9). The
same Rose tells us how she was fired: "I said to the fore-
lady, 'Missus, if I can't sit by the window, I can't sit. If
you can't sit, girlie ... go stand on the street corner.'
And that's how I got unemployed in novelty wear" (LD, p.
9). When asked about her health by her former lover, she
replies: "My health, considering the weight it must carry,
is first-class" (LD, p. 19). Rose is one of Paley's first-
class characters.

Nor are the Irish neglected by the author. Mrs.
Raftery, sturdy and assertive, appears in both collections
of short stories and is not easily forgotten. Speaking of

the lady for whom her husband deserted her, she observes, with characteristic acerbity: "a skinny crosstown lady ... wears a giant Ukrainian cross in and out of the tub, to keep from going down the drain, I guess" (EC, p. 23). However, despite the author's skill with Mrs. Raftery, the voice is frequently more Jewish than Irish, as when Mrs. Raftery refers to her son as "Mr. Two-Weeks-Old" or "Mr. Just Born" (EC, p. 24), recalling the idiomatic speech of the old Jewish couple in Tillie Olsen's "Tell Me a Riddle." Yet though the author's language has its limits with Mrs. Raftery, it enlarges the confines of Mrs. Raftery's characterization in the way Joyce's language transforms his characters. It has punch and is so well-suited to the people she describes that the reader cannot help but chuckle over the absolutely right image: "eat your ice cream, Claudie," says the young mother Leni, who is one of the few street whores in the neighborhood, "the sun's douchin' it away" (EC, p. 146).

In certain passages, the author's humor is honed to a cutting edge, as in her characterization of Mrs. Hegel-Shtein, president of the Grandmothers' Wool Socks Association in The Children of Judea Old People's Home. Mrs. Hegel-Shtein is mistress of the supreme put-down, in the manner of the woman who, when told of the achievement of astronauts landing on the moon, comments: when you have money you can travel. For Mrs. Hegel-Shtein, Faith, the daughter of a couple in the home, is a special target to be singled out for her barbs: "So it turns out you really have a little time to see your mother.... What luck for her you won't be busy forever" (EC, p. 37). Even her own children do not escape the flick of her tongue. Commenting on their habit of closing their bedroom door when she visits them, and thus depriving her of "necessary" ventilation, she complains: "For a ten-minute business they close themselves up a whole night long" (EC, p. 38). Mrs. Hegel-Shtein is a needler, a meddler who at 9 a.m. knocks on the doors of the other occupants' apartments and rolls in noiselessly on her oiled wheelchair, distributing orders like a commando raider. But the story's effect is far from caustic, simply demonstrating how people allow their lives to be manipulated by a kind of super-Jewish mother.

The author is not above an occasional hazard with language to see how far she can skate on thin ice. The narrator in "The Immigrant Story" (Faith again, who seems to be the author's alter ego) tells us of her morose friend

Jack, who was a Marxist and a Freudian at the age of
twelve. He blames all of his troubles on society and on
his parents, and mocks Faith for her rosy cheerfulness. In
the sixth grade she had brought three American flags to
school and made a speech eulogizing 172nd Street and its
glories: a grocery store, a candy store, a shul, and two
doctors' offices all on the same block. "A pile of shit,"
says Jack, referring to the same neighborhood (EC, p. 173).
Faith tells us she "continued to put out more flags. There
were twenty-eight flags aflutter in different rooms and windows. I had one tattooed onto my arm. It has gotten dim-
mer but a lot wider because of middle age" (EC, p. 174).
It's difficult to make the necessary transition between one
dialogue and another, because of the language and the handling of time sequence. Yet the imagery is vivid, and the
characterization of Faith, allegorized in name, is sustained
in different stories throughout the two collections, as she
appears and reappears.

Paley's language, with its sensitivity to nuances of
dialect, offers an assortment of stories in these two books,
mixing yarn, monologue, dialogue with very little comment,
allegory, anecdote, the tale of pointless garrulity, the
character Faith as wife/mother/deserted woman, the comedy
of the man/woman encounter, the delusions and illusions of
women about men, and the love of women for children. Surprise, coincidence, burlesque, hyperbole, understatement,
flippancy, and certain liberties with language combine to
give her stories a variegated texture which seldom fails to
hold the reader's attention. The language is always portrayed in its function within the people's lives: as solace,
as defense against what so often threatens to be intolerable.
Yet, at her best, Paley--so keen and firmly concrete is
her realism--does not let the language blur for us the genuine stresses of her characters' lives.

She leans upon a thread of theme--women and children living in neighborhoods where roaches scuttle over the
kitchen table when the light is put on (and when it is off);
where ceilings peel and drop calcimine which is nibbled by
children; where mothers have constantly to petition city
officials about the necessity of a fence on the playground to
keep out junkies, winos, and perverts; of mothers sitting
on park benches and singing the praises of their offspring
as they watch these same children climb trees, play in
sandboxes, or snatch each other's toys.

On the darker side, there are stories of boys who

ride railroad cars and get killed, of fourteen-year-old run-
aways coming to the city who are raped and then killed.
But the author comes back frequently to the same chief
characters: Faith, Mrs. Raftery, Ginny/Virginia and their
children, repeating the identical pattern of story with more
fluency.   What becomes clear is that Grace Paley may write
of age, adultery, going back to the past, men, sex, immi-
grants--but her great theme is motherhood.

More than anything else, motherhood links the young
Ginny and the older Mrs. Raftery.   We meet them in an
early story, "An Interest in Life," and then a later story
from the second collection by Paley, "Distance."   The first
is told from the perspective of the young wife and mother,
and the second story is narrated by old Mrs. Raftery.   Both
women are concerned with the same man, John, Mrs. Raftery's son, but for different reasons.   Ginny's story (or
Virginia as she is sometimes called) opens with, "My husband gave me a broom one Christmas" (LD, p. 81).   The
young wife already knows that her husband, sick of domesticity, is about to leave her and the apartment he calls a
"fucking pissoir" (LD, p. 95) and join the army; make a
clean sweep, she thinks in Paley fashion as she contemplates
the broom.   Like most of Paley's heroines, she finds something to console herself.   At least the broom has a fancy
dust pan attached to it.   Hers is not a husband to shop in
bargain basements or January sales.   Then she sits down
to total her assets--$14.00 and the rent unpaid.   Still un-
daunted, she goes to Welfare and finds that they are recep-
tive only to lies.   Mrs. Raftery, who is always on hand
with advice, points to some truckers eating their lunch
across the street and suggests: "Look around for comfort"
(LD, p. 84).

Comfort, however, turns out not to be a hefty trucker,
but Mrs. Raftery's son: devout Catholic, leader of the Father's Club at his church, and active in all the lay groups
for orphans.   A man who sends out The Ten Commandments
as a Christmas card each year, he doesn't hesitate to jeopar-
dize his immortal soul by bedding down with Ginny.   The
young woman observes that he gets quite adept at buttoning
and unbuttoning despite any lingering moral scruples concerning his own wife Margaret, who is constantly with child.
John tells Ginny piously: "Children come from God," to
which Ginny retorts: "You know damn well where children
come from" (LD, p. 88).   Ginny accepts John as lover, not
out of passion but so that her children will have a "father."

For John combines filial devotion to his mother together
with presents for and activities with Ginny's children. Both
women are fulfilled as mothers through John, who functions
as a good-will ambassador between the generations. His
coming, observes Ginny, occasions loud singing in a "girlish
brogue" by Mrs. Raftery and a public advertising to the
whole neighborhood through the open window about John's
virtues: "Ask the sisters around the corner.... They'll
never forget John" (LD, p. 87).

For Mrs. Raftery, as for Marilyn French's Mira
(The Women's Room), mother love is irrational, more irrational than sex and a greater force. "I need the sight of
him, though I don't know why," she confesses to us in the
later story, "Distance" (EC, p. 26). Even though she has
to share him with Ginny, she is tranquil and accepting.
She knows exactly what Ginny wants of her son (a married
man with children of his own)--a father for her children.
And she's right. Ginny's pride in motherhood is that of a
woman who "counts her children ... acts snotty, like she
invented life" (LD, p. 94). So Mrs. Raftery, aware of
what is going on and sympathetic to the young mother, waits
on the stoop summer nights for a brief talk with John,
proud of his success in the building trade and his children:
"Every kid of his dressed like the priest's nephew" (EC,
p. 18).

This story presents both another view of the impro-
vised domestic scene and another distribution of sympathies.
In "Distance" (EC), old Mrs. Raftery recalls the girl Ginny
as competitor for her son's affections, a possible candidate
for wifehood, and the drastic measures she took to prevent
John from marrying Ginny. Seizing a kitchen knife and taking delicate aim, she pierces just enough skin to unloose
blood and John's guilt. Now, in retrospect, she is willing
to reappraise her action, realizing that with her rather dim-
witted daughter-in-law Margaret, communication is like that
of "a crazy construction worker in conversation with fresh
cement" (EC, p. 25). Ginny would have been more interesting.

She takes the long, second view from amidst a ka-
leidoscopic scene: relationships including herself and her
husband and the young Italian with whom she spent time
"mashing" the grass in Central Park (EC, p. 19). With
her husband, life was a time-table: dinner at 6:15 when
she got home from her cashier's job; sex at 7:45 ("he liked

his pussy. Quick and very neat"--p. 19); his shower, evening paper and sleep--but there is no such timetable for
her. Mrs. Raftery's thoughts reveal a sense of pride in
her own self-renewing capacity as she recalls that she never
went to bed until the last commercial. Like Paley's other
characters, Mrs. Raftery is always discovering ways and
means of refreshing the well-springs of life, or of coming
to perspectives which give a philosophic twist to the past.
Remembering the straying of her husband, she thinks of
him as now "stalking the innocent angels" (EC, p. 26).

The author sees mothers, old or young, especially
mothers with very young or growing children, as survivors
of families which have been reshuffled and revised because
of the men who desert. But Paley's women do not consider
themselves survivors looking over a bombed-out terrain, as
do Marilyn French's heroines (The Women's Room). They
see themselves, together with other women in similar circumstances, as so many water tributaries flowing into each
other and strengthening one another. The children, in the
meantime, bob on the waters and push their own skiffs along.

There is little over-protectiveness, especially with
Faith and her children, in such stories as "Faith in the
Afternoon, " "Living, " "Faith in a Tree, " "The Long-Distance Runner" (EC). Children are allowed to have experiences of their own. In turn, the mothers take spark from
their children, for children act as enlargers of life's possibilities. Faith's son visits young people in mental institutions on Saturdays, and returns with his own sense of community reaffirmed. We don't know who these young people
are, but they might well be the casualties of a neighborhood
drug culture.

Children not only have some autonomy of their own,
but participate in their mothers' lives: peace marches,
distributing petitions for better neighborhood facilities, going
down to City Hall in protest against some infringement of
rights. They act as friends and advisors to their mothers,
and often seem to have more worldliness than their mothers.
This is evidenced in many of the stories concerning Faith
and her two boys. Richard and Tonto, the sons, exhibit
common sense, a grip on reality, scepticism without cyni-
cism--something the harsh world around them might easily
breed. They are not unique in this attitude. The son of
Faith's dead friend politely refuses her offer to live with
her and the boys, knowing she can't easily provide for him

and is making the gesture out of duty.   He's going to his
uncle's in the country, he tells her, and will be O. K.
Faith is relieved, but sorry that she will probably never
see him again.   The last lines of the story suggest her
emotion that this obligatory offer emphasizes the barrier,
the finality of her friend's death, which now separates her
from the boy.

Faith is a Salinger character who sees children as
special, loves them all--but she doesn't feel they need sav-
ing, as Holden Caulfield does.   They take care of themselves, to a certain extent.   She even identifies with young
street hoods who whip out knives or boards to which nails
are attached, seeing these potential felons as brick city
Huck Finns.   Faith is always on the child's side, for in
this neighborhood many a mother does the wash before rush-
ing off to work, and many a child must cope as he/she best
can.   Above all, she identifies with her own children; their
achievements are her achievements.   She views them as
more than flakings of herself.   They represent diffusion,
moving out, the centrifugal motion of the world.

It should be made clear that Faith's boys are not
placed in the position of surrogate husbands.   She is not
parasitical, just very scrupulous (like Toni Morrison's
Pilate in Song of Solomon) in letting her children know that
they are loved.   The extent of this love is defined in an
early story, "A Subject of Childhood" (LD), in which Faith's
younger son Tonto climbs into her lap.   Faith tells us: "I
held him so and rocked him.   I cradled him.   I closed my
eyes and leaned on his dark head.   But the sun in its
course emerged from among the water towers of downtown
office buildings and suddenly shone white and bright on me.
Then through the short fat fingers of my son, interred forever, like a black and white barred king in Alcatraz, my
heart lit up in stripes" (LD, p. 145).   There is a lot of
Marilyn French's Mira with her son Clark in this description.

The precise imagery of Grace Paley's language tells
us that motherhood imprisons with its demands.   Like Richard Lovelace, however, Paley believes that stone walls do
not a prison make.   The constraints of motherhood simply
belong to the various constraints of the world which have
to be encountered.   A number of the author's stories, however, imply that the women, like women everywhere, wish
that some of these constraints would be shared by men.

Nevertheless, despite the lack of permanent fathers, the
ambience of love with which Faith surrounds her boys pays
off.   They know who they are.   Nothing deflates them.
Their response to a remark or situation which threatens to
whittle them down reminds one of the story of the Texan
who stopped for a drink of water at the tiny house of a Jewish family.   After being served, he asked how large was
the property.   "Well, " said the husband, "in front it's a
good sixty feet--and back it must be a hundred and ten. "
The Texan smiled: "Back home on my ranch, I get up at
9 a. m. and drive and drive and drive.   I don't reach the
end of my property until six in the evening. "   "Ah-h, "
clucked the householder sympathetically, "I once owned a
car like that. "

Mothers and children are bound together by love,
kinship, and proximity.   Yet mothers are women in their
own right, with a cumulative courage that is impressive.
Faced with so many swirling headwaters--separation from
husbands, the wanderings of their own children, the withdrawal of parents' approval--they keep their often eccentric,
fairly erratic, but flexible and intuitively-right course.   They
try to avoid drifting by holding on to certain values, rem-
nants of habits which give life some order.   Their will to
survive is not opposed to these values, but takes life from
them.   Faith and her friend Ellen bring their children to
Central Park, play ball, picnic, row.   Faith visits her aged
parents in the old people's home.   Mrs. Raftery looks forward to her son's visit, keeps a sharp eye on the street,
likes it all: "the dirty kids and the big nifty boys with
their hunting-around eyes" (EC, p. 26).   She puts a drop of
burgundy on her ice cream on Sundays, the way her father
permitted them as young children, and she saves a drop of
consolation for Faith and Ginny.

In fact, it is the communication and help between
women which sustains them.   The strong bond of affection
between women is articulated by an old grandmother in the
early story, "A Woman, Young and Old. "   "Women, " says
the grandmother, "have been the pleasure and consolation
of my entire life" (LD, p. 28).   Faith and Ellen share
apartments, jobs, and "stuck-up studs" (EC, p. 61).   When
Ellen dies, Faith mourns for the "sister" who was so much
a part of her life.   To return to Mrs. Raftery again, it is
she who counsels Ginny when the husband leaves: "tell the
Welfare right away....   He's a bum, leaving you just before Christmas.   Tell the cops....   They'll provide the toys

for the little kids gladly. And don't forget to let the grocer
in on it. He won't be so hard on you expecting payment"
(LD, p. 84).

If women are dusted lightly with praise everywhere in
these stories, down to the two young whores who dutifully air
their children in expensive prams and dress the children in voile
and ribbons, men are given a special treatment. The view
of men is a good-natured one: they are embodied as without principles, but sometimes delightful company. Beneath
the surface, however, one senses a bit of Marilyn French's
criticism. In the early allegorically-heightened view of
Faith's life, "The Used-Boy Raisers," Faith's two husbands
(one ex), Livid and Pallid, complain that they are disappointed by their eggs, by the absence of liquor in the house, and
by the way Faith is bringing up the boys. Then they leave
together: call me, says one, if you need anything. The
story concludes with Faith's reflection on these "clean and
neat, rather attractive, shiny men in their thirties" going
off to "the grand affairs of the day" and the prospect of
"dark night" and "pleasure" ahead of them (LD, p. 134).
She contemplates her future: the making of peanut butter
sandwiches and the reward of a roast at the end of the week.

Another story, "The Pale Pink Roast," with its reference to cannibals who, once tasting man, see him thereafter as "the great pig, the pale pink roast" (LD, p. 48),
leaves no doubt concerning the woman's feelings about her
former husband. He sends her $8.50 a week for support,
and is so conscious of maintaining the strength and beauty
of his own body that he spends $12.50 on vitamins alone,
plus other necessities to keep his body "the dwelling place
of the soul," as he grandly refers to it (LD, p. 48). Men
not only fail to hold up their share of the financial responsibility of raising children, but they whittle women down, an
idea encountered already in the works of Lois Gould, Marge
Piercy, Sara Davidson, Marilyn French, and others. "How
do you know you're the father?" asks Alexandra, trying to
be sophisticated. "Come on," says Dennis, "who else would
be" (EC, p. 134). Faith's ex-husband always referred to
her as "Baldy," though she had a plentiful head of hair.
His shapely mistress was "Fatty" (EC, p. 34), and another
was "Bugsy"--not exactly a misnomer, as it turns out.
Faith explains that after Ricardo, her husband, "helped"
Bugsy through several abortions and some bad winters, she
became an alcoholic and a whore for money.

Men are always leaving. "First grouchy, then gone,"

says the old woman of her son (LD, p. 29). Deserting husbands, on the other hand, may be grouchy, but they pause
just long enough for some parting advice. "The city won't
let you starve," says Ginny's husband, as he adjusts his
duffel bag. He assures her that people like her are half
the population; they are keeping up the good work, and without her the race would die out. "Who'd pay the taxes?
Who'd keep the streets clean? There wouldn't be no Army.
A man like me wouldn't have no place to go" (LD, p. 85).
Men in Paley's stories make stopovers, give advice to women
on how to cope, and then skip.

In D. H. Lawrence's pastoral novel The Rainbow,
which already evidences the beginnings of industrialism, wom-
en are the restless ones, trying to picture what lies beyond
the spires of the town's church steeple. Indeed, Ursula
Brangwen does venture out and discovers the pressures of
job and a new relationship. Paley's city men (like Bellow's)
choke under what they regard as the yoke of urban life:
squalid domesticity, uninteresting jobs. They break with
wife and children. The young Ginny philosophizes that children make women happy; men want money and success. In
the later story, "Wants" (EC), the woman makes it clear
that she has specific wants of her own beyond that of being
the mother of children. She wants to be a responsible individual, an effective citizen who can influence the Board of
Estimate on necessary neighborhood and city changes; she
wants to stay married to one man.

It's not sex that Paley's women miss when their husbands desert them, but the illusion of family and together-
ness. The women often appear asexual in their brave play-
fulness. Sometimes, they regard the appetites of the flesh
with jocular relish or ruefulness. A woman imagines her
missing husband returning to her and tricking her into getting down on the floor. Before she can even make herself
comfortable on the polka-dotted linoleum, she says, they
would be making love--without taking precautions.

Like Mark Twain, the author often ridicules the body,
with excursions into occasional bawdry. She attempts no
analysis of the chemical affinity between men and women
beyond the habitual bedding down. There is no probing of
desire. Sex is an activity with a kinetic vocabulary of
"thud" (EC, p. 124), "noisy disturbance" (EC, p. 124),
"rattling shivers" (EC, p. 26), "thumping" (EC, p. 97). It
is Nature swishing quarts of blood to wherever it is needed
for action.

Underneath the language is a sense of sex as a great
force--a force against which woman is often helpless. This
is expressed in Ziggie's poem, which speaks of girls as
flowers whose legs are petals "nature would force open no
matter how many times" the girl said no (EC, p. 186).
The concept is given a more sinister twist in "The Little
Girl." A fourteen-year-old "baby," as the old black man
Charlie regards her, follows a young dude into an apartment
and is told to rest herself: "she lie down," says the sor-
rowing Charlie, "Down, right in her coffin" (EC, p. 154).
Both boy and girl pay for their folly. "Never seen free
daylight since" (EC, p. 156), says Charlie: the youth in
jail for rape and murder (though it is not clear who murdered the girl); the girl in death.

Sometimes, sex is regarded as establishing "tenancy"
for the man (LD, p. 50). But in the key story of the second
collection, which bears the same title as the book, Enormous
Changes ..., the author has her heroine disprove this.
Though the young Dennis tries to establish tenancy with the
middle-aged Alexandra by moving in, making her pregnant,
inviting her to his commune, etc., she rejects him and his
offer, and decides to bear her child alone and live with
three girls. Her action bears some resemblance to women
in Marge Piercy's Small Changes and their solution to tenancy.

"Change is a fact of God," says the indomitable Aunt
Rose. "From this no one is excused" (LD, p. 9). Grace
Paley's women change. They become more resourceful and
more aware of what they want ("Wants"). They can look
back on the past as Mrs. Raftery does and recall that
"Tuesdays and Wednesdays was as gay as Saturday nights"
(EC, p. 15), and that the present is not bad. She has no
complaints "worth troubling the manager about" (EC, p. 15).
Old Mrs. Raftery is unflaggingly attuned to the velocity of
her own life in all its complications and turnings. Her
serenity is not that of numb resignation or indifference; it
is the product of her energy and fortitude.

Women like Faith change to a degree. They learn
that their habits of dependency on men are dictated by the
circumstances of their upbringing: clean up the house, put
on a steak, do your hair a different way, and he'll come
back, says Faith's mother when she learns that the husband
has left. Faith's mother concludes that before Faith will
even know it, the husband will be in the living room turning

on the hi-fi. Faith replies: "Oh, Mama, Mama, he's tone deaf" (EC, p. 36).

For the most part, with the exception of sturdy old men like Faith's father, the men are tone deaf to the music which sustains the women--family and other relationships. Grace Paley writes of these women with an impudent, pungent, resilient humor which never wavers. Hers is an anti-establishment wit which hits the reader when least expected (he "took long walks. That's what killed him, I think"-- EC, p. 23). What we witness, however, everywhere in Paley's stories concerning these tone deaf men is the kind of humor which Mark Twain explained as: everything human is pathetic. The secret source of humor itself is not joy, but sorrow. There is no humor in heaven.

Are Grace Paley's women losers, as Michele Murray claims (The New Republic, March 16, 1974)? In one sense, no. They are concerned with survival--physical and emotional. They find in their survival a sense of pleasure, comfort with their children and other people, without idealizing the picture. They are kin to all, webbed together by pain, suffering, and laughter. In another sense, they are losers, and this is where a certain thinness appears in the writer's stories. They are like the little boy who comes home from his first day at school and tells his mother that he can write. "Wonderful, " exclaims the mother, "What did you write?" "How should I know, " replies the child, "I can't read. "

The lives of Paley's women are limited to motherhood, desertion of husband, and a procession of transient lovers. Lovers are taken out of a preoccupation with the necessity of keeping an illusion of the centrality of marriage and family. They also testify to the human need for intimacy, love, some commitment, emotional and other kinds of support. Written mostly in the last two decades, Paley's stories bear witness to the upheaval in society caused by war, social and economic conditions, and the way men, unable to make adjustments and yearning for simplification of their lives, just leave. On a lower economic and less sophisticated level, they go back to the line of Hemingway heroes who, chafing at domesticity and responsibility, take off to ski, travel, fight, pick up a new woman, a new life. In contemporary fiction we perceive something of the same in the works of Brautigan and others, though the sporting life men desire is presented in different terms.

Beneath the banter, the jokes, the jocularity of tone, Grace Paley is concerned with the breakup of family, and the ways women try to hold the family together. In the struggle to do so, those who have hidden talents have little time to do something with them. After a while, the urge to create becomes like the scratchings of an old record-- and nothing more. Granted all this, Paley's stories are conditioned by her eye on bankrupting American families and her conviction that there is some hope of solvency--in children and in some men.

The concluding story, "The Long-Distance Runner" (EC), with its narrative technique of seemingly disconnected experience and Faith's air of comic disproportion, leaves us with a small measure of positive feeling concerning the family. Faith makes a journey back to her old neighborhood and returns after a stay of several weeks with a black family. She is greeted with affection by sons Richard, Tonto (now taller than she), and Jack, whose status in the family seems to be friend, as in "The Immigrant Story." They all listen to her experiences, while continuing with their chores: Richard and Jack vacuuming, Tonto getting ready to visit his friends in Bellevue.

It's not much, but it's a start. We have an air of reconciliation, a soothing perspective, a breakthrough to something better. Paley resists the temptation to idealize just the young, demonstrating that there is hope that men like Jack can alter and that both men and women can resolve their blunderings for freedom.

CONCLUSION

Surveying these twelve writers and their works presents us with a general sense of renewed, rediscovered perspective: the very thing that all serious fiction is traditionally expected to supply. These stories portray women
examining past and present with intentness and resistance,
ranging from passive to militant, regarding assumptions
which Society has taught them to make. This awakened
alertness permeates all classes of women and all degrees
of mental and emotional maturity. Jong's and Gould's Jewish, upper-middle-class women; Didion's and French's as-
sorted upper-middle-class women; Godwin's academic woman;
Oates's white, blue-collar and other women; the black, ven-
turesome, dauntless women from various levels of society
in the books of Wright, Morrison, and Walker; the young
radicals of Piercy and Davidson; old people and the lower-
middle-class Welfare mothers of Paley--all are animated
in different ways to see the world anew and take true account of their lives in it.

Even Joan Didion's Charlotte Douglas, for the most
part submerged in fantasy, reassesses her life and comes to
a decision. It's an affirmation that she will not retreat further, will no longer try to dissolve in dreams. Gail Godwin's Jane Clifford ultimately dismisses her cosmeticized
image of her relationship with middle-aged Gabriel and
chooses to hold out for her own certainty. This certainty
is that she will face even the possibilities of not marrying
or having children. She will assert that individuality which
the society around her identifies as ill-fitting, inconvenient,
and "odd." Although she still seeks love, she will no longer
ransom her individuality to the idea of love. An exception
to the range of heroines in this book is Lois Gould's Jessie
Waterman. Refusing to remain a helpless woman, as she
views her past history, she perversely becomes the ultimate
victim by sacrificing womanhood to assume maleness. Yet
viewed in another way, it can be argued that her action is

235

like that of Toni Morrison's Sula--an attempt at the "experimental life."

Nowhere, throughout these works, do we find men's sensitivity to change keeping pace with women's. Even when professing sympathy or identification with women's new thinking, the majority of men quickly retrace their few faltering steps back to the reassuring Valhalla/Mohammedan Paradise in which women serve and defer--and men decree. The new sexual revolution, treated by Marge Piercy and others, simply enlarged Man's options concerning sex and marriage. The emerging openness turned into polygamous exploitation of women and signified just another expression of male domination. It was a tipping of balance in favor of men, ultimately becoming the license for men to loosen ties and responsibilities.

The upheaval of family, home and relationships in which the black woman and Paley's woman perennially find themselves is not essentially different from that which the poor have encountered from time immemorial. The depictions of the poor and working-class women by Oates, Wright, Morrison, Walker, and Paley underscore, as do Piercy and Davidson in their exploration of the sexual revolution, that a change of mores and ways is not the major issue in a true revolution. There must be a revision of behavior and attitudes toward women. Together with this, a total overhaul of prevailing society's values is needed.

Such a revolutionary change must include a recasting of language by both women and men. Women writers adopting a male sexual vocabulary of cunt and cock are also implicitly adopting the situations and conclusions sustained by this language. In contrast, the language of Toni Morrison and Grace Paley, for example, with its fresh, inventive verve and spirited precision, shows how the revitalization of language can follow upon the reappraisal of the world and of oneself. And, as Morrison and Paley further remind us, the dislodging of Woman from old assumptions about her body and the world outside it can be instrumental in reawakening language.

If male writers are wrestling with a sense of dissolution, things running down, as Tony Tanner says (City of Words ...), women writers discussed here are occupied with that dissolution which Gissing hailed as clearing the ground of obstructive systems. In these terms, work after

work by our twelve writers (with some exceptions) expresses
a concern with order which is humanly relevant and organic,
rather than arbitrary and confining--as it has been in the
past. On the whole, these women's self-extensions as
writers manifest the refusal by women to be confined to the
cubicles of home-making, raising children, self-subordination
to husband, and economic dependence. If the roles of wife
and mother are important, these women are saying, they
are important enough to warrant being defined in their own
terms as free beings. The writing by contemporary women
writers speaks of Woman's insistence that the space of the
human universe far outreaches the cubicles allocated to
women. The reachings out, which I try to describe here,
are toward the new boundaries of that universe--no less.

NOTES

Preface

1. Ellen Moers. Literary Women (New York: Doubleday & Co., 1976), xi.

2. Lois Gould. A Sea-Change (New York: Simon and Schuster, 1976), p. 143.

3. Vern L. Bullough (with the assistance of Bonnie Bullough). The Subordinate Sex: A History of Attitudes toward Women (Chicago: The University of Illinois Press, 1973), p. 336.

4. Eliza Farnham, in Duncan Crow, The Victorian Woman (New York: Stein and Day, 1972), pp. 174-75.

5. Michael Korda. Male Chauvinism! How It Works (New York: Random House, 1973).

6. Bullough, p. 335.

7. Our Bodies, Ourselves: A Book by and for Women, by The Boston Women's Health Book Collective (New York: Simon and Schuster, 1973).

8. Michael Korda, pp. 43-64.

9. Cheryl McCall, Ms., May 1977, p. 31.

10. Molly Haskell. From Reverence to Rape: The Treatment of Women in Movies (New York: Penguin Books, 1975), p. 119.

11. Ibid., p. 120.

12. Irving Howe. The Critical Point on Literature and Culture (New York: Dell Publishing Co., 1975), p. 203.

13. Ibid., p. 204.

14. Ibid., p. 205.

15. Ibid., p. 206.

16. Norman Mailer. An American Dream (New York: Dell Publishing Co., 1972), p. 46.

17. Saul Bellow. Mr. Sammler's Planet (Greenwich, Conn.: Fawcett Crest, 1971), p. 74.

18. Saul Bellow. Humboldt's Gift (New York: The Viking Press, 1975), p. 146.

19. Bullough, p. 287.

20. Haskell, pp. 363-64.

21. Leslie A. Fiedler. Love and Death in the American Novel (Cleveland, Ohio: A Meridian Book, 1962), p. 309.

22. Ibid., p. 310.

23. Ibid., p. 309.

24. Toni Cade, ed. The Black Woman: An Anthology (New York: The New American Library, 1970), p. 9.

25. Ibid., p. 17.

26. Ibid., p. 102.

27. Ibid., p. 83.

28. Joyce Maynard. New York Times Magazine, September 28, 1975.

29. Elizabeth Janeway. Man's World, Woman's Place ... (New York: William Morrow and Co., 1971).

30. Gerda Lerner. Black Women in White America (New York: Pantheon Books, 1972).

31. Tony Tanner. City of Words: American Fiction 1950-1970 (London: Jonathan Cape Ltd., 1971), p. 18.

Chapter 1

1. Joyce Carol Oates, ed. Scenes from American Life ... (New York: Random House, 1973), vii.

2. D. H. Lawrence. Studies in Classic American Literature (New York: Viking Press, 1966), p. 2.

3. Philip Roth. Portnoy's Complaint (New York: Bantam Books, 1970), p. 154.

Chapter 2

1. D. H. Lawrence. Lady Chatterley's Lover (New York: The New American Library, 1962), p. 208.

2. Thomas Hardy. The Return of the Native, ed. James Gindin (New York: W. W. Norton Co., 1969), p. 57.

3. Lady Chatterley's Lover, p. 228.

4. James Joyce. Ulysses (New York: The Modern Library, 1961), p. 34.

Chapter 3

1. Ralph Ellison. Invisible Man (New York: Signet Books, 1952), p. 20.

2. Ibid., p. 498.

3. Ibid.

4. The Diary of Anaïs Nin: 1934-39 (New York: Harcourt, Brace & World Inc., 1967), p. 209.

5. Margaret Atwood. Surfacing (New York: Popular Library, 1972), p. 222.

Chapter 4

1. Francine du Plessix Gray. Lovers and Tyrants (New York: Simon and Schuster, 1976), p. 206.

Chapter 6

1. "Maya Angelou: In Search of Self, " in Negro History Bulletin, Vol. 40, No. 3, May-June 1977, pp. 694-95.

2. Lorraine Hansberry. To Be Young, Gifted and Black (New York: Signet Books, The New American Library, 1970), Foreword, xviii.

3. Alexander Pope. Letters to Swift, December 5, 1732.

4. William Blake. The Marriage of Heaven and Hell.

5. Zora Neale Hurston. Their Eyes Were Watching God (New York: Negro Universities Press, 1969); originally published in 1937 by J. B. Lippincott Company.

Chapter 7

1. George R. Gissing. Charles Dickens: A Critical Study (Pa.: Folcroft Library Ed., 1974), rpt.

2. "Why the Novel Matters, " in D. H. Lawrence: Selected Literary Criticism, ed. Anthony Beal (New York: Viking Press, 1967), p. 105.

3. Lawrence, "Morality and the Novel, " in D. H. Lawrence: Selected Literary Criticism, p. 113.

4. As quoted in Gissing in Context by Adrian Poole (Totowa, N. J.: Rowman and Littlefield, 1975), p. 135.

INDEX*

---

*For an explanation of certain symbols (letter codes) used
in this index, see pages vii-x.